RAF BOYS

IN THE MIDDLE EAST

To all those thousands of men and women of the Royal Flying Corps and Royal Air Force, many of whom lost their lives, who served their country so far away from home

RAF BOYS IN THE MIDDLE EAST

True Stories of RAF Aircrew and
Groundcrew East of Suez 1918-1977

STEVE BOND

GRUB STREET • LONDON

Published by Grub Street
4 Rainham Close
London SW11 6SS

A CIP record for this title is available from the British Library

ISBN-13: 978-1-911714-39-2

Design by Myriam Bell Design UK

Printed and bound by Finidr, Czechia

CONTENTS

FOREWORD 6

INTRODUCTION AND ACKNOWLEDGMENTS 9

CHAPTER ONE
AIR CONTROL AND COLONIAL POLICING 14

CHAPTER TWO
WARTIME CHANGES AND OPERATIONS 25

CHAPTER THREE
KEEPING THE PEACE 48

CHAPTER FOUR
THE RAF'S LARGEST STATION – KHORMAKSAR 78

CHAPTER FIVE
TRANSPORTS – 'READY FOR ANYTHING' 123

CHAPTER SIX
FAR AWAY PLACES WITH STRANGE SOUNDING NAMES 165

CHAPTER SEVEN
THE OTHER SIDE OF LIFE 209

AFTERWORD
THE AIRFIELDS IN 2026 242

GLOSSARY 244

SELECT BIBLIOGRAPHY 248

INDEX 249

FOREWORD

AIR MARSHAL G A 'BLACK' ROBERTSON CBE BA FRAES FRSA

When Orville Wright took to the air for the first time at Kitty Hawk, North Carolina on 17 December 1903, he could surely never have conceived the exponential rate of progress that would follow. Less than 66 years later, on 20 July 1969 Neil Armstrong set foot on the moon.

By the time of World War I, armed biplanes were flying at more than 100 mph. Their wings, held in place by struts and tensioned by wire, were covered in Irish linen, doped to provide a smooth, taut surface. Some 50 years later the SR-71 was capable of speeds greater than Mach 3. While aircraft cannot yet be rendered invisible, technical advances mean that we can now minimise their chances of detection, this thanks to surfaces coated in radar absorbent materials and stealth design. At the same time the element of risk, the dangers associated with flying, have reduced immeasurably – albeit they remain ever present. Neither technical nor human failures can ever

G A 'Black' Robertson.

be eliminated totally.The nature and the pace of change, of progress in recent years – not just in the aviation world – have been little short of astonishing. Advances in other areas affecting everyday life may have been less rapid, but they have been no less profound. Letters mailed from the other side of the world that once took weeks to arrive have been superseded by electronic messages that appear on screens almost instantly – screens that facilitate real time face-to-face conversations. In a sense this represents a communications revolution.The stifling heat our forebears suffered in far-flung lands, in the outposts of empire, has been replaced by the comfort of temperature-controlled air conditioning. Mechanical processes that once took hours, and sometimes days, have been reduced to a matter of minutes by innovation and by the design and development of purpose-built equipment.One consequence of the rapidly changing world in which we now live is that people are forced to adapt to new realities. In that sense, the lives of today's RAF personnel are very different from those of their predecessors. Some things, however, remain unchanged. Foremost in this respect is the need for professional competence – a requirement that embodies inter alia knowledge, adaptability, ingenuity, empathy, resilience, a sense of humour and, perhaps most important, courage – moral as well as physical. Such qualities are as relevant now, as important in the modern day, as they ever were.The timeless nature of these human attributes provides a background to the various contributions Steve Bond has assembled in his latest book. The reader can only wonder at how these cheery individuals from a temperate climate coped with the searing heat of the tropics, let alone the Middle East. The serviceman's irrepressible and occasionally irreverent sense of humour, so often his salvation in a crisis, helped of course; but it was hardly an antidote. Lengthy separations from loved ones with whom it was often difficult to communicate, compounded by changes of location, often at short notice, was another burden that took its toll. Most people simply learned to cope, emphasising the importance of resilience and even courage.

Through the pages of this book other factors emerge that certainly helped. Of these, camaraderie, that special bond of friendship, is one of the most significant; it contributed much to the enjoyment of service life. As did the acceptance, mostly willing, of hardship and the almost matter-of-fact acknowledgement that fatalities could, and regularly did, occur. When, in his House of Commons speech of 20 August 1940, Prime Minister Winston Churchill dubbed the youngsters of Fighter Command 'the few', he was borrowing from Shakespeare. But Henry V's inspiring speech on the eve of the battle of Agincourt is about much more than a few individuals; it embraces the collective whole: 'We few, we happy few, we band of brothers.' It's this same corporate spirit that acts as a thread, linking so many of these recollections from the past 90 years or so – not because of any heroism, it must be said. Rather, the connection reflects the very best of the human spirit: the ability to cope with adversity, whatever form it takes, and a readiness to laugh in the face of danger. It would be all too easy to represent these reminiscences as pure nostalgia. But they are far more than that. The reader is privileged to hear the authentic voices of those who served, in most cases, more than half a century ago. The language, the terminology and phrasing – the aircraft, the bases, the locations, the experiences too – all help to define a different era. Such stories capture unmistakably the spirit of an air force developing into what was to become one of the world's most professional and effective. If those days are past, thanks to the contributors to this book, the voices of those ordinary people who helped forge the RAF's extraordinary reputation live on.

Black Robertson
Cheltenham
June 2026

Air Marshal Robertson earned his wings in 1966 after three years at Cranwell. With postings worldwide, he flew all the RAF's front-line fast jets and also qualified as a helicopter pilot. He had five staff tours in Whitehall, and counts his command of 92 Squadron and an appointment as ADC to Her Majesty Queen Elizabeth II, as the twin highlights of his 36-year career. He is the author of a number of aviation books, not least on the wartime experiences of his father 'Robbie' a decorated Spitfire ace.

INTRODUCTION AND ACKNOWLEDGEMENTS

The area of responsibility for the Royal Air Force (RAF) in the Middle East was vast, encompassing the whole of Arabia plus substantial parts of East Africa. The operational challenges were substantial not least the frequent need to operate into and out of remote and minimally prepared desert landing grounds, in areas sparsely populated by often less than friendly inhabitants. Add to the mix World War II, tribal uprisings and squabbles between neighbouring countries, and the RAF certainly had its work cut out. This book is not intended to be a detailed history of RAF operations in the region, although many are covered in the chapters that follow. Here there is a collection of stories from those air and groundcrew who were there, covering many locations, units and aircraft types.

The Royal Flying Corps (RFC) had a presence in the Middle East from 1915 with operational responsibility for Egypt, the Sudan and Kenya, and administrative responsibility for Palestine, Trans-Jordan, Iraq and Aden; tasks carried on by the RAF from 1918. The critical World War II campaigns in Egypt and Libya came under RAF Middle East, whilst in 1945 Middle East Command was absorbed into RAF Mediterranean and Middle East. Middle East Air Force (MEAF) was formed on 1 June 1949 at Nicosia in Cyprus.

Following the Suez Crisis of 1956, the command found itself split into two; one half to the north of Egypt, the other to the south-east. Later in the year, British Forces, Arabian Peninsula was formed at RAF Steamer Point in Aden with MEAF as the RAF element. The three service elements retained their individual structures. On 1 March 1961, the RAF, army and navy elements were combined to form Middle

The Middle East in 1914. [Unimaps.com]

East Command (MEC), the RAF element being renamed Air Forces, Middle East (AFME). From the same date, the Near East Air Force Command (NEAF) was formed in Cyprus. Following the Aden withdrawal on 29 November 1967 and redeployment of a number of squadrons to Muharraq and Sharjah, MEC was re-established as RAF Gulf Command (RAFPG).

This somewhat complicated and varying command structure means that, for the purposes of this book, the area included is primarily bounded by the Suez area of Egypt then east to Aden. It also includes stations in East Africa and Cyprus, both of which have been key factors in the wider area.

The ending of World War I brought about the collapse of the Ottoman Empire. Large areas of the Middle East were removed from Turkish rule and new states were established.

By that time the potential oil wealth in this part of the world had been recognised, although the new impoverished states were totally unorganised. The League of Nations devised a system whereby these countries would be placed under the mandatory power of Great Britain and France. France had Syria, whilst Britain was given control of Iraq (Mesopotamia), Palestine and Trans-Jordan.

These new states were not recognised by Turkey or Ibn Saud, the most powerful Arab ruler at the time, and there were many border clashes. This, coupled with almost total lawlessness within the states, placed the existing British policing forces under considerable strain. At the Cairo conference of 12 March 1921, Chief of the Air Staff Sir Hugh Trenchard proposed a system of "air control" whereby the RAF, including its armoured cars, and in conjunction with the civil authorities, would undertake the control of unrest.

The changed Middle East showing the principal RAF airfields. (Author's collection)

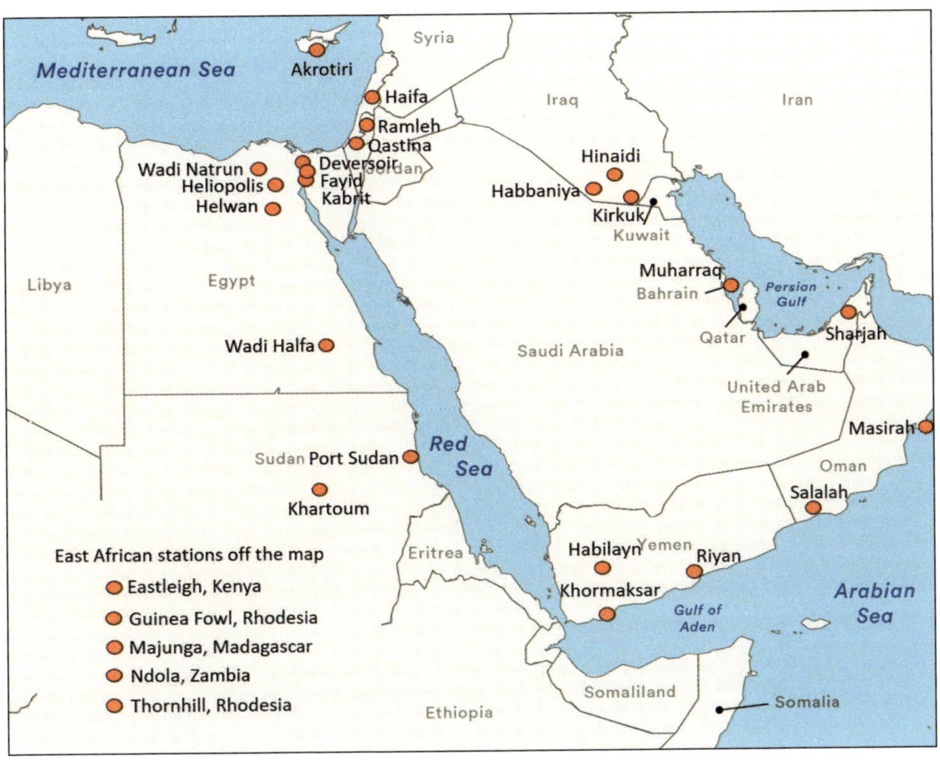

The foundation of this air control force was already underway. In 1920 Hugh Trenchard had successfully persuaded Winston Churchill to centre the RAF's overseas deployment on Egypt, Iraq and India, covering vital trade routes. By early that year more than half the RAF's front-line strength was based in the Middle East. In 1936 the Colonial Police Service was formed to cover the Crown Colonies, protectorates and Palestine.

World War II saw major increases in RAF strength throughout the Middle East, but once the war had ended Britain's military involvement waned as countries in the region gained their independence. For example, the Trucial States were a group of tribal confederations south of the Persian Gulf, whose leaders had signed protective treaties with the United Kingdom between 1802 and 1892. They remained a British protectorate until the treaties were revoked on 1 December 1971, six of the sheikhdoms forming the United Arab Emirates (UAE). To support the dwindling RAF presence in the region following the final withdrawal from Aden, HQ Air Forces Gulf at Muharraq Bahrain came into being in September 1967, disbanding on 15 December 1971. Thereafter only RAF Masirah remained until it too closed in March 1977.

In those 62 years of an established RFC/RAF presence, the geographical and political environment in the region had changed out of all recognition. Along the way there had been many challenges for the British forces to contend with, including widespread unrest, rebellion, political posturing and the emerging nations' attempts to throw off colonial influence. The RAF was constantly in demand from Cyprus south to Kenya and Rhodesia and much of the land between, and many of the first-hand responses to the challenge will be found in the pages that follow.

This book has only been possible with the help of the following people (many no longer with us) who have so enthusiastically contributed their memories and photographs, plus those who have passed on stories from relatives and friends: Brian Ashley, Alec Audley, F J Baldwin, Eric Barfoot, Ken Beere, Eric Bradley, Colin Butler, Ray Carran, Len Clayton, Chris Dance, Ray Deacon, Caroline Dennard, Harry Dennis, Norman Didwell, David Drinkwater, Bryan Elliott, Ray Evans, Roy Fensome, David Forsyth, Alan Foster, Guy Gibbons, Peter Goodwin, Paul H, Ron Hall, Stephen Hall, Pete Jackson, John James, Peter Kendall, John King, David Langley, Richard Lennard, Peter Lewis, Ian Macmillan, Dave McCandless, Mick Maidment, Jock Manson, Michael McRitchie, Chris Mead, Desmond Penrose, Jonathan Plumley, Jerry Pook, Bob Pountney, Dean Pringuer, Peter Proctor, David Richmond, the family of Charles Saunders, Brian Shadbolt, Guy Sharp, William

Slack, Mick Speake, Bill Tyack, Peter Verney, Nick Von Berg, Jack Wade, Crispin Williams, Norman Wilson, and those who wish to remain anonymous. I thank and salute you all.

Warrant Officer (WO) Jim Fenn served the RAF in a ground trade from 1918 to at least 1943. During his lengthy time in Iraq, he took and acquired many fascinating photographs, some of which appear in this book. When Jim's widow died in the 1990s all his photos went into a dustbin. It is only thanks to a neighbour who rescued them and subsequently passed them on to me that this man's long service can still be recognised. This highlights a serious issue that, as eras of aviation history pass from living memory, much of it is in danger of being lost – what does survive often only does so by chance.

All my research archives are retained in perpetuity by the outstanding charity West Raynham SHQ – Veterans Central, run by fellow author and ex-Canberra pilot Ken Delve. A thought for others to follow perhaps.

Once again, I express my gratitude to John Davies, Miya Libman and Debbie Marr at Grub Street, who have supported and encouraged my literary endeavours for a good many years now. Finally, and most especially, thanks and love go to my darling wife Heather who, as always, has been a driving force and great support throughout this project, feeding me ideas and advice and proof-reading my draft manuscripts. I have endeavoured to correctly credit the origins of all the photographs and other material I have used. In the internet age, the true origins and source of some material is not always possible to identify with certainty. If I have inadvertently omitted anyone, please accept my apologies and grateful thanks.

A final important point. The stories in the pages that follow are from the people who were there. These are their words, their memories, unedited other than for grammar and punctuation.

Dr Steve Bond
June 2026

CHAPTER ONE

AIR CONTROL AND COLONIAL POLICING

The Turkish Ottoman Empire entered World War I as a member of the so-called Central Powers (with Germany, Austria-Hungary, and Bulgaria). Turkish forces achieved initial victories against British forces in the first two years of their campaign in Mesopotamia. However, the 1916 Arab Revolt (of Lawrence of Arabia fame) turned the tide against Turkey.

The earliest days of British military aviation in the Middle East came in response to this, seeing a number of RFC squadrons moving in from 1915 to assist operations against Turkish forces. They flew a wide range of aircraft types mainly from the principal bases at Heliopolis and Ismailia. There were many detachments throughout the region, as the following examples show.

On 24 March 1915 a detached RFC Flight at Moascar, Egypt, was redesignated 30 Squadron. It was equipped with the Maurice Farman Longhorn and Shorthorn, also the BE.2c; later these were joined by the Caudron G.III and Martinsyde S.1. At the change from RFC to RAF in April 1918 the unit was flying from Baghdad with just the BE.2e.

On 23 November 1915 14 Squadron arrived at Ismailia with the BE.2c maintaining detachments at several locations including Heliopolis and Mersa Matruh. Bristol Scouts and Martinsyde G.100s arrived the following year, followed by the DH.2, FB.19 and RE.8 which remained with the changeover from RFC to RAF.

Martinsyde G.100 A3945 67 Squadron Heliopolis 1916. [Author's collection]

In December 1915, 17 Squadron arrived at Heliopolis with a mixed fleet of BE.2s, DH.2s, Bristol and Nieuport Scouts. The squadron moved to Salonika, Greece, in July 1916. September 1916 saw 67 Squadron also positioned at Heliopolis with Avro 504K, BE.2c and Martinsyde G.100.

Both 14 and 30 Squadrons remained in the Middle East until well into World War II, during which period they re-equipped several times; 14 Squadron switching over time to the Fairey IIIF, Fairey Gordon, Vickers Vincent, Vickers Wellesley and Bristol Blenheim, while 30 Squadron went over to SE.5a, RE.8, DH.9A, Westland Wapiti, Hawker Hardy and Blenheim.

Throughout the colonial policing period the RAF was called upon many times to assist the army in maintaining order and quelling dissent. For example, the 1921 riots in Palestine led to over 7,000 troops being stationed there. Winston Churchill, as Secretary of State for the Colonies, proposed replacing the troops with both local gendarmerie and the RAF. By 1925 most of the army garrison had been replaced by a company of RAF armoured cars, plus 14 Squadron with Bristol F2bs, DH.9As (known as the 'Ninak') and Fairey IIIFs.

Meanwhile in early 1922 Turkey had sought to regain her old province of Iraq. Initially this included a trade embargo, armed support to dissident tribes, political unrest, propaganda and occasional border penetration. The air forces available to the commander of British Forces in Iraq, Air Marshal (AM) Sir John Salmond, consisted of eight squadrons; four were equipped with DH.9As, one with F2bs, one with Sopwith Snipes, and two with the RAF's first large transport aircraft, the Vickers Vernon.

Vickers Vernon J6867 70 Squadron 1923. [Jim Fenn]

AIR TRANSPORT – BORN OF NECESSITY

The Vernon was a military derivative of the Vimy Commercial airliner, having a capacity of three crew and up to 13 passengers or four stretcher cases. It entered service in August 1921 with 45 Squadron at Hinaidi, followed by 70 Squadron at the same station. Their initial major operation came in 1923 when the Turks occupied the Rawandiz area in Kurdistan. British troops were sent overland to repel them, whilst the Vernons were used to good effect, flying in such items as 1,000 pairs of boots, 7,500 pairs of socks, 190 sets of horse and mule shoes and 400 lbs of waterproof dubbin. In addition, no fewer than 246 sick and injured were evacuated by air, saving a six-hour journey by donkey.

With vast areas of mostly undeveloped desert to be policed, it was clear that relying solely on ground forces could not be effective. An Iraq Command Report [1] written in about 1932, highlighted the growing use of aircraft for transportation.

"The first major airlift of troops came in February 1923 when the Kurds of northeastern Iraq, disenchanted with Arab attempts to rule them from Baghdad, decided to try and recover their lost territories. After distributing arms and ammunition amongst their own followers and hill Arabs, they advanced on the town of Kirkuk intending to oust the garrison there. It became obvious to the British commander that reinforcements were needed in a hurry! However, the nearest railhead was 75 miles away at Kingerban. The poor hill road between had suffered from recent torrential rain, giving a best journey time for lightly equipped troops of some five days - the only option was to fly troops in. The whole of 45 Squadron, plus about half of 70 Squadron, consisting in all of 13 or 14 Vernons, flew from Hinaidi to Kingerban on 21 February, where they found 480 officers and men of the 14th Sikhs awaiting them. The airlift began at once with the outward journey to Kirkuk taking, on average, 50 minutes. The return flight, due to a strong headwind, took about 70 minutes. The desired effect was achieved, with the rebel hordes melting away into the hills at the sight of the Sikhs – they had not expected reinforcements to be in Kirkuk for several more days.

"Later that same year a similar situation was resolved, without a shot being fired. Sikhs living in the Samawah region, which was not under anyone's direct control, decided to take it over. Immediately three aerodrome sites were selected, with troops and stores being flown in by the RAF. The Sikhs then accepted government control of their region.

"Perhaps the Vernons most rapid response came, again in Kirkuk, on 4 May 1924. On that day three men of the Assyrian Levies (a conscripted force) ran amok after an argument with a local trader. That same afternoon two platoons of British soldiers were flown in from Hinaidi, comprising 66 officers and men, with a section of armoured cars following by rail. By that evening order had been restored.

"In addition to their troop-carrying duties, the Vernons were locally modified as bombers. They were used as such on many occasions, including the bombing of the insurgent-held village of Diwaniya Liva by eight aircraft on 26 April 1924."

ESTABLISHING AN AIR ROUTE

Perhaps the role for which the Vernon squadrons were best known was the carrying of mail over the route from Cairo to Baghdad. This had been pioneered by Vimy and DH.10 aircraft.

"The Air Ministry had looked into the possibility of a routine aerial route from Egypt to Iraq in place of the slow voyage through the Red Sea and the Persian Gulf. It was decided to mark out a route across the southern part of the Syrian desert (which extends into Iraq) by a single ploughed track, dotted along the way with frequent landing grounds marked with either a letter or a Roman numeral. The crews were under strict instructions to report their position by wireless as they passed over each landing ground. In case of bad visibility, such as a sand or dust storm, the aircraft were forbidden to proceed by compass navigation, but must land as soon as possible at the nearest landing ground and wait for the weather to clear. Some of the landing grounds had hidden fuel stocks. 70 Squadron flew the route alone from September

1923 until September 1924, when 45 Squadron relieved them. In addition to their mail carrying duties the aircraft were also utilised as air ambulances, including the evacuation of disease-stricken troops from Northern Iraq to Baghdad.

"These units were joined on the mail route by 216 Squadron, also with Vernons. These were superseded by the Vickers Victoria in August 1926, with a troop-carrying capacity dramatically increased over that of the Vernon to 22. The Victoria was in turn supplanted by the further improved Vickers Valentia."

QUELLING ASSYRIAN DISSENT

"On 1 June 1932 a manifesto was issued by Assyrian officers in the Iraqi Levies that, as the British Government had failed to safeguard an Assyrian future after termination of the Mandate, all Assyrians would end military service on 1 July. Civil disturbance flared which threatened to postpone Iraq's entry into the League of Nations. Against 1,500 armed levies, a show of force was needed.

"On 18 June the Northamptonshire Battalion was ordered from Egypt, and the RAF commenced the move on the 22nd. A total of 560 officers and men were flown in 36 flights by 25 Victorias from 70 and 216 Squadrons operating in groups of nine aircraft. Permission was granted to carry 14 men with desert equipment in each aircraft fitted with W/T equipment, and 17 men in those aircraft not so equipped. The route flown was Ismailia – Romani – Ziza – Azrak – Rutbah – Ramadi – Hinaidi. Except at Ismailia and Hinaidi, refuelling was, with the passengers helping the crew, from four-gallon cans poured through chamois leather into funnels. Coolie labour and Iraq police

Valentia KR3163 N 216 Squadron Heliopolis 15 December 38. [Dave Underwood]

vans were also used. Each aircraft carried two days' rations per man, plus 20 gallons of water. Tea was provided at Ziza and Rutbah (*typically British*) and on arrival at Hinaidi, with each man being given cigarettes and two bottles of mineral water.

"Although originally planned to be completed in five days a dust storm on day five necessitated an extra day. The move was completed on the 27th. The return airlift commenced on 18 July. There had been eight engine failures – requiring a new engine each time, so the spare aircraft was continually employed ferrying replacement engines." [1]

STEPHEN HALL – WIRELESS OPERATOR/AIR GUNNER

"On 18 March 1939 I joined B Flight 216 (Bomber Transport) Squadron Heliopolis Egypt. I was allocated to Vickers Valentia KR2341, a twin-engine biplane with a part plywood, part fabric structure. The fore section, to approximately midships, being fabric-covered plywood, the rest was metal structure and fabric. It had seating for 20 troops and equipment, with the cockpit being open air. The crew consisted of first and second pilot, wireless operator plus an aircraft fitter and an aircraft rigger. The squadron was unique as each aircraft was self-supporting, only needing further technical assistance for major/minor inspection.

"Overseas station working; reveille 4:30 a.m. awoken by Abdul with a cup of char, (our boy had been with the squadron since way back and was old enough to be our father). First parade 5:00 a.m. slacks and tunic, march to the hangar, carry out usual maintenance, return for breakfast at 7 a.m. Second parade 8:30 a.m. shirt/shorts/topee (pith helmet), continue duties until lunch (Tiffin), then the rest of the time was yours; sleep, swim, go to Heliopolis or Cairo. The station food was good and was supplemented by an extra ration system costing ten ackers per person. Sunday breakfast consisted of grapefruit, egg, bacon and tomatoes; with lunch we had extra melon or whatever fruit was in season. An aircraft was always conveniently flying to Palestine near the weekend – for the sole purpose of obtaining fruit.

"The Gold Coast route was pioneered in much the same way that Imperial Airways had used earlier. Heliopolis to Wadi Halfa, and a dual stop near the 2nd cataract on the Nile where the Empire flying boats could land, plus an airstrip. There was also a transit hotel, which was later taken over by the RAF. The next stop was Khartoum, Sudan, where we had a small ground staff resident to give that extra technical assistance if and when needed. The route then followed El Obeid or El Fasher, Fort Laury French Equatorial Africa, Kano, Lagos and finally Takoradi. We gradually built up these stops with supplies of oil and fuel.

“My first early flying incident happened when we, that is Flying Officer (Fg Off) Chisholm skipper I/C, were leaving Khartoum. We were Takoradi bound and carrying on board in addition to supplies, some government chaps, along with three bottles of whiskey for our Flight Commander (Flt Cdr) P G Chichester. Take-off was okay and the flying uneventful, until we ran into a terrific electrical storm which forced our skipper to land. This was accomplished safely, our only problem was the sandy soil, meaning we were unable to taxi. We were fortuitous in having an Arabic speaking passenger who negotiated with the tribal chiefs to help in preparing a take-off run. By the means of wireless, an okay was given for the presentation of a cow, which seemed the protocol way of thanking for help.

“Meanwhile our water supply ran out, and we were forced to use the local water. This had to be boiled and quinine tablets added, and as a further safety precaution the end product laced with whiskey! Despite the hardships, it was not the most joyous of greetings when the flight commander had no whiskey. It is only now safe to say the life-saving liquid was thoroughly enjoyed at night around the campfire – ‘sorry, Sir’. I’m sure we are now forgiven.

“My troubles were not over. As I had injured my right elbow it necessitated my wearing a sling and being grounded for a week. Left on my own I decided to stroll across the airfield. Halfway across I was confronted by a full-grown giraffe towering over me and proceeding to lick my greasy topee. Those large teeth made me rack my brain as to whether these animals were carnivorous or vegetarian! Thankfully some natives came along and drove it off. Later I found out it had been befriended by Imperial Airways groundcrew for years.

“After a few more trips, plus Palestine and Trans-Jordan, Iraq, we returned to Helio for minor inspection. When I was in the hangar I was working on the wingtip with another rigger, when someone called, ‘tea up’. Passing our fitter working on the auxiliary engine in the nacelle, I said in passing, ‘tea up’, and he made some comment like, ‘I’ll have another go at starting this engine and be in’. I had just reached the annex door when there were shouts of ‘Fire!’ Looking round the flames were racing along the wing we had just vacated – panic! Still burning, our aircraft was pushed out together with the aircraft next to it, which in turn had caught fire. Thankfully two other aircraft in the hangar were OK.”

This fire occurred in May 1939, and with KR2341 being damaged beyond repair it was struck off charge on the 20th of that month.

"What had happened? The fitter had been having trouble starting the auxiliary engine. This was housed in the starboard nacelle and was used for pumping up the air bottles, which in turn started the main engines. With his persistence to get the thing started, the petrol fumes had built up to such an extent that it finally ignited. This was the only accident of its kind, so there was no redress for anyone, senior or junior.

"About this time the squadron was being re-equipped with Bristol Bombays. These were truly a vast improvement in speed, armament and payload. Our own crews brought them out; I believe one aircraft was lost, landed by night in Gibraltar harbour – without success!

"Another good thing about peacetime life were the weekend trips which, depending on the response, were occasionally organised. One or two aircraft were laid on, loaded with food and goodies, and away we went up the coast. Swim, relax and a generally carefree break, maybe near Mersa Matruh, returning in time for tea break on Monday morning."

Foremost amongst the major RAF stations in this period were Heliopolis and Ismailia in Egypt, with Habbaniyah and Hinaidi in Iraq. There was also a flying boat station at Basra, Iraq, the main occupant being 203 Squadron with, at various times, Fairey IIF floatplanes, Supermarine Southampton, Short Rangoon and later Short Singapore flying boats for maritime reconnaissance.

Singapore III K4577 203 Squadron Basrah, Iraq. [Chris Orme]

Fairey Gordons 6 Squadron Ismailia including JR6942, K2620, JR9806. [Author's collection]

Other operational squadrons in the 1920s and 30s flew a mixed bag of aircraft types. The ubiquitous DH.9A had been the backbone of the army co-operation force for many years before being joined, and ultimately replaced, by the Fairey Gordon, AWA Atlas and Westland Wapiti. With no opposing aircraft to deal with, fighter strength was limited, relying on the aforementioned F2b and later the Snipe and Nieuport Nighthawk. However, as the only opposition was small arms fire from the ground, the fighter squadrons were disbanded in 1926.

CHARLES SAUNDERS – PILOT

Charles Gordon Saunders found himself sent to Ramleh, Palestine, in early 1939 to join 6 Squadron. At that time the squadron was equipped with the Hawker Hardy, but later that same year they added Gauntlets and Lysanders. Although we have no first-hand accounts from Saunders, a recent study of his logbook and the Operations Record Book (ORB) provide a fascinating insight into the kind of work that he and the squadron were doing, very much dominated by Air Policing. With thanks to Caroline Dennard at Halls auctioneers for allowing the author to study Saunders's logbook.

His name first appears on 10 February 1939 when he flew in a Hardy, from a detachment at Haifa, to carry out escort duty to the convoy carrying the chief of the imperial general staff from Jenin to Tiberias via Nazareth. This task continued the following day. In March he again flew from Haifa to carry out an 'air cordon' of Nahf between Lower and Upper Galilee. In April he flew a reconnaissance in the Wadi Yabes area to locate an armed band.

In September, by which time he had been promoted to flying officer, Saunders was flying Gauntlets featuring in "pinning" actions (keeping their heads down) at Mazari an-Nubani north of Ramleh, and Beit Iksa. Later that month it was back to Hardys for a while, with operations including an air cordon of Tarshiha in K5292 with "action taken", and reconnaissance of the villages of Farkha, Zawiya and Rantis in K4311.

October brought more action with Gauntlet I K4085 in low-flying attacks in Wadi Nahr, plus further air cordons. November saw a reconnaissance in Gauntlet II K5292 of a Jewish village Tel Litwinsky, reporting "No sign of Jewish meeting as reported". On the 6th he flew an air cordon of Beit Lid village and "co-operated with rounding up gang with leaders. Browning gun action against determined cordon breakers and three casualties were inflicted." On the 16th it was back to escort duty, this time in Gauntlet II K7863 as part of a formation escorting the high commissioner of Syria from Nablus to Jerusalem.

Similar flying continued until 6 February 1940 when 6 Squadron "became an army co-operation squadron". By now Lysanders had arrived. On 6 April Saunders left Ramleh at 09:25 hours in Lysander L6887 to carry out a photographic reconnaissance of an area surrounding Kefar Yedidyah, for the use of Force Headquarters, Palestine and Trans-Jordan. The reconnaissance was successfully carried out, both vertical and oblique photographs being taken, the aircraft returning to Ramleh at 10:50 hours. At 13:30 hours Saunders again took off in the same Lysander to carry out a large-scale mosaic of an area surrounding Kefar Yedidyah for the use of Force Headquarters, Jerusalem.

The following day he again flew L6887 to take a large-scale mosaic of Australian defensive positions near Julis, for the use of the 6th Australian Division. This was followed on the 23rd by a flight to take both vertical and oblique photographs of an area surrounding Khirbet Beit Lie, for the use of the Middle East Staff College Haifa.

On 23 May there was a Force Headquarters exercise in an area covering the Jerusalem-Ramleh Road. Saunders and "nine other officers watched the scene from the air from 05:00 to 07:00 hours, in order to give pilots practice in spotting ground forces".

On 11 June 1940, the ORB records that "Signor Mussolini declared that a state of war existed between his country and the Allies. A system of stand-by pilots came into operation."

In April 1941 Saunders, along with other 6 Squadron personnel, was captured near Tobruk and spent the remainder of the war in various POW camps. Saunders was awarded the DFC in November 1941 for his services on 6 Squadron and went on to reach the rank of squadron leader.

Throughout the colonial policing period, the RAF was called upon many times to assist the army in maintaining order and quelling dissent. Squadrons based in the area during this inter-war period included:

- 1 Squadron Snipe and Nighthawk
- 6 Squadron F2b, Gordon, Demon, Hart, Hardy, Gauntlet, Lysander
- 8 Squadron DH.9A, IIIF, Vincent, Demon
- 14 Squadron F2b, DH.9A, IIIF, Gordon, Vincent, Wellesley
- 30 Squadron BE.2e, G.100, SE.5a, RE.8, DH.9A, Wapiti, Hardy, Blenheim
- 45 Squadron DH.9, Vimy, Vernon, DH.9A, IIIF, Hart, Vincent, Gordon, Wellesley, Blenheim
- 47 Squadron DH.9A, IIIF, Gordon, Vincent, Wellesley
- 55 Squadron DH.9/A, Wapiti, Vincent, Blenheim
- 70 Squadron O/400, Vimy, Vernon, Victoria, Valentia
- 84 Squadron DH.9A, Wapiti, Vincent, Blenheim
- 203 Squadron Southampton, IIIF, Rangoon, Singapore
- 216 Squadron O/400, DH.10, Vimy, Victoria, Valentia, Bombay

---

[1] Taken from AP1560 Iraq Command Report with amendments

CHAPTER TWO

WARTIME CHANGES AND OPERATIONS

By the start of World War II, on 3 September 1939, RAF units in the Middle East had already been changing. Habbaniyah's 55 Squadron had re-equipped with Blenheims, whilst 70 Squadron Valentias were moved to Helwan south of Cairo. Habbaniyah adopted an aircrew training role with the arrival of 4 Flying Training School (FTS); they had been moved east from Abu Sueir for safety. The unit was equipped with Ansons, Harts, Gordons and Oxfords. At Heliopolis 216 Squadron was briefly joined by 208 Squadron with Lysanders, and the station also became a major staging post for Blenheims passing through en-route to India.

Over in Aden, Khormaksar's resident 8 Squadron, with Blenheims and Vincents, continued its internal security role against dissident tribesmen. Sharjah had come into use by Imperial Airways in 1932, whilst the RAF operated a staging post there, mainly for 70 Squadron Victorias, from 1933. By 1939 it also hosted detachments, including 60 Squadron with Blenheims.

WAR AGAIN AND OPERATIONS

STEPHEN HALL – WIRELESS OPERATOR/AIR GUNNER

"Suddenly, on 10 June 1940, when Italy entered the war, for us peace turned into war. Frantic activity! Our 216 Squadron Bombays were put on operational duties. On the first raid aircrew carried webbing – 50 rounds a rifle, and pilot's revolvers.

Harts of 4 FTS Habbaniyah. [Dave Underwood]

Thankfully this order was countermanded within the week. Thinking back, it was so easy to distinguish each and every target long before we got there. Trying to land at Mersa Matruh after a raid, we had levelled out, and were about to touch down, when the airfield defences opened up on us (at that time New Zealanders). The skipper put the engines in overdrive, and a few words like 'I don't think we'll bother'.

"Tobruk never failed to fascinate me with its colourful display, plus the 'flaming onions'. These consisted of strings of seven or eight yellow fireballs, like large footballs, reaching a few thousand feet into the sky. Derna and Bomba had very light defences, but Benghazi – what a reception, amazing! I used to look back (I could do no other, I was in the rear turret) and I wondered how anyone could fly through it and get away with it. Our usual height was 10-12,000ft. This was until the arrival of a squadron leader with new tactics; fly out to sea and glide in over the target at 5,000-6,000ft. His theory was we'd be too low for the heavy ack-ack, and out of range of the small stuff. Despite the moans, Sir had spoken!

"On one memorable occasion we were already committed to our bombing run, and suddenly, just above us, one of C Flight dropped a flare. How we survived the resulting concentrated barrage one will never know. Just when we thought we were clear, *bang! wallop! crash!* I looked around! There were two gaping holes, my parachute harness was torn, a shell had blown the tailwheel in and gone out the rear end. Thankfully it hadn't exploded. My Guardian Angel had to work hard all through my wartime service. Next night we raided Benina low level and strafing when one solitary gun opened up with tracers which followed behind us just a few feet away. Had it opened up a few seconds earlier, it would have cut us in two.

"It must have been around this time when I had done three consecutive night raids, and on landing was ordered to the armoury to clean my gun in readiness for another raid. I refused, and refusal in wartime was a court martial offence. I was threatened with the cells, which I said I would willingly accept for a few hours' kip. After a short while, chiefy sent me back to the billet for a sleep.

"What caused this tantrum? Going on a raid meant crews were notified, then briefing, service aircraft, taxi to bomb-loading area. Then depending if fortunate or unfortunate, the armourers having been notified of the type of bombs, you load up, and then taxi back to the refuelling dump, top-up, leave the aircraft at dispersal point and have lunch. After lunch, take-off and fly to a desert airfield maybe two hours or so flying away. Land, top-up with petrol, have tea and await take-off time; this naturally will depend on if the raid is a short or long distance. Take-off, complete the raid, land, visit the intelligence tent, have a meal, refuel, return to base, where the whole system starts again.

"Well, after three continuous raids, one becomes very weary from lack of sleep. It was pure luck we never crashed on landing. Our skipper was taken to the sick bay and rested for a month! I was forgiven, and red and white tablets were introduced (*probably methamphetamine as a pick-me-up*); the red for the crew and the white for the pilot – to be taken when airborne. One night our crew aborted a raid through engine trouble after an hour's flying, and we spent the rest of the night counting stars. Another bit of strangeness was introduced, but it never took on. Our meal

Bombay 216 Squadron El Khanka at Kabrit in 1941, supporting the Long Range Desert Group. [Guy Sharp]

on landing was an egg or slice of bully beef and two white pills, which represented vegetables. Not very filling and thankfully it was not a success.

"Bomba was a seaplane base with little or no ground defence. On one particular raid, when strafing and using sticks of incendiary, I reported an underwater glow. This later clarified as a stick that had hit and sunk a submarine. Another lucky or unlucky incident, depending which side you were on. Any bomb 'hang-ups' were shaken off over the sea, and this happened to one of our aircraft over Tobruk. Anchored outside the harbour waiting for daylight was a cargo ship which received a direct hit."

FIGHTER OVER TOBRUK

"Another incident on a Tobruk raid, with a flight of three aircraft, we were the first over the target area. I reported the presence of an unfriendly guest. The skipper told me to hold my fire and dived for cloud cover. Mission completed we reported the fact to the Intelligence Officer, who was not a bit convinced. The number two aircraft lands with the same story, only this time a few holes to help convince the still doubting officer. Number three proved an unbelievable fiasco; they landed with a peppered and a scorched tail. They had been shot up, one engine caught fire, and the skipper called the 'bail out'. Jock, the rear gunner, was not quite sure of the message, and proceeded to midship. There, standing at the open door, was the midship gunner, parachute clipped on and in his left hand a 'mug and irons'. Jock, seeing this, about turned, raced back to the tail, where he tried to crash out through the Perspex dome without releasing the catches and dazed himself.

"Meanwhile, the wireless operator stopped the midship gunner from jumping, and Jock was quietly soothed back to normality. At the same time the night-fighter had formatted under the starboard wing. The second pilot, entangled with the two sandbags carried in the nose, was trying to get his revolver out in an attempt to shoot at the fighter. After a little while the fighter pilot gave a thumbs-up and peeled away. You may well imagine the 'dog's life' reception that crew got; unbelievable but very true.

"The reason for having two sandbags in the nose. Fg Off Chisholm was flying over the Trans-Jordan at 10,000ft and found his aircraft L5841, going into a loop. It took both him and his second pilot all their strength to eventually regain control. At around the same time we were watching another Bombay was coming into land after a major overhaul test flight. We saw the flaps coming down, and suddenly its tail came up, and it plunged into the ground killing everyone on board. Investigation revealed that as the fuel tanks emptied the centre of gravity moved, causing sudden diving and loops. Once the tanks had equalised the aircraft behaved itself.

> *Bombay L5822 crashed on approach to Heliopolis on 23 September 1941 after losing control. The accident report said it was "probably due to the crew moving aft". Those killed were: AC2 Kenneth Adamson, AC2 Thomas Berrill, LAC Cyril Jenkins, Flt Sgt Pete McCue, Plt Off Jeffrey Turner and AC1 Ronald Winslade.*

"Now poor old Chisholm seemed to be dogged with trouble with 'shaky do' L5841. After a few more self-inflicted aerobatics the aircraft was tested, re-tested, and tested again with the same report – certified airworthy. Everyone knew it was a jinx, yet it was certified airworthy, so it was stored and tied down in the standby aircraft area. During a sudden dust storm, a Sgt actually saw it lift up off the ground and smash on its back making it a write-off, yet the two other aircraft parked with it survived.

> *This almost certainly refers to a different Bombay, L5826, which had been moved from 216 Squadron to 117 Squadron at Khartoum where it was blown over in a storm on 21 August 1941 and written off as described.*

FERRYING PEOPLE AND GOODS

"In 1941, when the Italian army collapsed, we brought Marshal Graziani (the commander of Italian troops in North Africa) and staff back to Heliopolis – and what VIP treatment they got! It was also in 1941, in April, when Rashid Ali overthrew the Iraq Government and besieged RAF Habbaniyah. We transported troops there and evacuated women and children. Later we landed at Baghdad airport with General Staff to sign peace terms. Back up in the Maaten Bagush, in Egypt, the free French were surrounded at Bir Hakeim and needed supplies; three aircraft were put on. Captain Bolt of South Africa was my skipper, and promised a bottle of whiskey if the trip was a success. True to his word, when we landed he brought the promised whiskey. The French broke out with a little help from their 'friends'. Sadly, Captain Bolt was killed shortly after transferring to a South African squadron.

"We had taken stores to the Fleet Air Arm base at Alexandria and when we went ashore that night we met up with a sailor off HMS *Ladybird.* We were awoken early next morning to fly back to Helio, and on landing were immediately briefed to do a support raid with the navy. Racks were fitted in the cabin to carry 160 fragmentation bombs, the correct way using five bombs per rack. This is all right in practice but flying to and fro over the target would take hours, so an extra man was carried. Over the target area the pilot opened the front escape hatch, the extra man used the flare chute, the fitter/AG the main door, whilst the wireless operator was at his wireless and myself in the rear turret. Once over the target the skipper lit the green light – it was all clear to start unloading. Each of us picked out a bomb, pulled the pin, and either dropped it through the hatch, down the flare chute or out of the main door and – magic flashes on the ground! All very unconventional, not at all cricket. We would dearly have liked to say to the *Ladybird* crew, 'Hi, we were with you last night'.

"The operation of landing 250 miles inside enemy territory *(9 July 1942)* was a most 'cheeky' affair. The Fleet Air Arm had sighted a large convoy making for Tobruk, but as they hadn't the range, the surprise element was adopted. We were to land on a satellite airstrip near Sollum. Their Albacores *(826 Squadron Dhekelia)* were given a one-and-a-half-hour start, so we all landed together. I signed out a Thompson sub-machine gun. Peacock, my fitter, was a 'nutter'! His comforting words were could he have the gun if I was injured or killed. I told him if it was the latter he could willingly have it.

"Our aircraft carried members of a Scottish regiment who on landing fanned out and set up defence positions. The rest of the aircraft unloaded petrol and helped refuel the Fleet Air Arm aircraft, then at a predetermined time they took off for home. I must say even though we saw enemy aircraft landing on the main strip, they seemed unconcerned about our using the airstrip – code name 'Chocolate'.

"Doing ambulance duty from the forward field hospitals was, we were all agreed, the most unpleasant task – especially the tank crews with burns. The smell of human flesh lingered for months, we were all pleased when our stint was over."

GREECE

"We were the first aircraft to land in Greece *(May 1941).* We were the navigational aircraft for a squadron of Gladiators going to Crete. Then, talk about variety, our sort of rest period in Palestine was suddenly shattered one day. Orders came to clean up, start-up, and taxi over to where a Hudson was parked. Things were hastily unloaded from the Hudson and given to us – cases of wine. Then up drives a staff car flying flags and bearing people of very high rank. All aboard, with me sitting comfortably in my turret aft. We were on our way down the runway, hotly pursued by our wireless operator, who not like in films, never caught us.

"The people we were carrying were the Prince and Princess of Greece, together with the air officer commanding (AOC). Some two or three hours later we landed at Habbaniyah, where the station was in a panic owing to W/T silence. We did a flying tour for a week until the Hudson was repaired and took over. The skipper was told his crew were a disgrace, however when he explained the unusual circumstances we were thanked (NO knighthoods!).

"One morning started like any other. We marched to the hangar, and I went to my aircraft to find it had 'destroyed' written on it in chalk – 'mine's the same!', 'so is mine!'. Everyone was puzzled. The refuelling doors had the same, what twit had been mucking about? Back for breakfast, who are those blokes? Don't know, but by ten o'clock all hell was let loose. The commanding officer's office had been entered and those 'blokes' had just disappeared. The squadron was fallen in, and we were given a pep talk. All crews will sleep in the aircraft with rifles and fixed bayonets. What had happened? Major Stirling (the 'Phantom Major'), who pioneered the Special Air Service (SAS) in the Middle East, used our squadron for training, and later a drop. Using the Long-Range Desert Patrol, we picked up one chap as far afield as Fort Lamy in French Equatorial Africa. On another occasion we picked up a well-known figure Lieutenant Colonel (Lt Col) Keyes, at Corfa Oasis. I believe he was later killed in a raid.

"I left 216 Squadron in August 1942. I later had reason to correspond with the Chief of the Air Staff Sir David Craig, as I was unable to substantiate my flying hours, duties, raids, etc., having lost my logbook through enemy action at sea on 12 September 1942 aboard HMT *Laconia*. We were torpedoed; I applied to the RAF Escaping Society, but my application was turned down. My total flying hours were 1,100 in Vickers Valentia, Bristol Bombay, Hawker Hart, Lockheed Hudson, and Douglas Dakota III."

LAC Stephen Hall was awarded the Distinguished Flying Medal (DFM) on 4 December 1942 in recognition of his service on 216 Squadron. By 1943, 216 Squadron had joined the ranks of Dakota squadrons and was based at Cairo West with various detachments.

ERIC BARFOOT – PILOT

WO Eric Barfoot DFC enlisted in October 1940. He flew 37 operations in Wellingtons in the Mediterranean theatre, with 37 and 70 Squadrons. He then flew Dakotas with 216 and 267 Squadrons in Burma, either side of a Middle East tour.

Wellesley K7782 45 Squadron Ismailia 1939. [Author's collection]

"In early 1943, in between tours on Dakota squadrons, I arrived at Habbaniyah the second largest RAF station in the world at that time. There I reported to Sqn Ldr Lennon, the commanding officer of Communications Flight Persia and Iraq Forces, and I was detailed to B Flight where I found my old pal Harry. We shared an airy room equipped with a ceiling fan, beds of the tubular hospital kind and real mattresses. The camp was a small town in its own right. It had riding stables, shops, bazaars, its own cattle farm, hospital, and indoor and outdoor swimming pools. When not flying we played bridge. In the hot season, when temperatures hit 125°F in the shade, we worked from 6 a.m. until 1 p.m. and then rested.

"I think we had, as a communications flight, 14 aircraft; three venerable Valentias, two Oxfords, two Gladiators, an Audax, Hart, Wellesley, Fairchild, Bombay, Blenheim, Gipsy Moth and Rapide. The Gladiators were the survivors of those which had downed a couple of Me 110s trying to take off at Baghdad airport. We used them for meteorological climbs at 6 a.m. each day. At 6:30 a.m., at 24,000ft and with oxygen on, the world was one's oyster! The Wellesley and the Oxfords were used to carry staff VIPs; the Audax was used to tow targets for the army Bofors gun school. Flights were usually short, but few days went by without a trip somewhere in something.

"The Wellesley was very nerve-racking; a huge geodetic single-engine monoplane, with two enclosed cockpits and a huge flexing pair of wings – confidence was drained rather than bolstered. It seemed underpowered and needed to be pushed around the sky, whilst the control cables seemed made of elastic, and it had the uncanny knack of dropping its tail onto the runway first. One of our pilots, 'Soda' Whiskey, was to fly a wing commander to Cairo in it when an erring 'erk' accidentally pulled up the undercarriage and bent the prop. Soda had the aircraft lifted, and the prop removed.

He supervised the straightening of the prop between two large planks, using a motor roller. They made it to Cairo a day late. How did she fly? 'Just a leetle more shaking,' said Soda!"

HARRY DENNIS – PILOT

"I served in the Middle East with 267 Squadron during the period 1940 to 1942; we were flying Hudsons, Dakotas and Lodestars. At the time I was with them the squadron commanders were Wg Cdr Wynne-Eyton and Wg Cdr Smyth. Sadly I saw Smyth get killed in a Lodestar *(EW984)*, along with 12 passengers and crew, when they took off from Bilbeis, which was about 20 miles from Cairo on the Suez Road. After take-off he 'shot the 'drome up' which was a saying in those days (*a very low-level flypast*). He came down too low, and his wingtip caught the sergeants' mess tent, and that was the end of Wg Cdr Smyth DFC, plus the passengers who were going to Lydda, Palestine, on rest leave.

> *The Lodestar accident occurred on 22 October 1942, when it hit the sergeants' mess tent after flying over the officers' mess. The others killed were: Flt Lt Ernest Copsey, Plt Offs Corliss Hawkes, John Trench, David Walker, Fg Off Roy Harper, WOs Vern Irwin and Walter Plant, Flt Sgt Brian O'Connor, Sgts George McBryde and Arthur Mills, Cpls Reginald Benson and Gerald Grant.*

"One incident concerning Wynne-Eyton was after taking off on a test flight. One of his wheels came off, and having no wireless operator on board, so obviously they could not contact him. There were red Very lights all over the landing strip, so in the end all the available squadron staff lay on the ground and spelt 'WHEEL OFF'! This did the trick, and he made a perfect belly flop after getting rid of all his fuel. There was a captured Me 110 which he used to fly, and I took a shot of it at Heliopolis. I don't know what became of him as he left the squadron before me."

> *Wg Cdr Charles Sandford Wynne-Eyton AFC commanded 267 Squadron from August 1940 until July 1942, and again from October 1942 until February 1943. The "Me 110" referred to was actually a Bf 109F, flown by the unit between February and June 1942, following its capture in Cyrenaica during Operation Crusader. Wg Cdr John Patrick Stracey Smyth DFC commanded 267 Squadron from August to October 1942; he was awarded the DFC while flying Hudsons with 224 Squadron at Leuchars in 1940.*

JACK WADE – WIRELESS OPERATOR

Jack was on Transport Command from 1943 to 1945, mainly flying Wellingtons and Yorks.

"In the Middle East we were mostly ferrying Wellingtons, and occasionally a Warwick – not an awful lot of difference. The aircraft could be fairly new out from the UK, or a 'patched-up' fly-back to the 'knackers' yard' at a maintenance unit (MU). The first job my crew had was to take one of three has-been 'Wimpy' ICs from Heliopolis in Egypt, to Blida in North Africa. Pinching bits from the other two, the three wireless ops got one complete set in our Wimpy HX685. My job was to get the QDMs (magnetic bearings), and flash them by Aldis lamp to the other two wireless operators in their aircraft. We ran into a sandstorm south of Mersa Matruh and never heard anything from the other two aircraft again.

"Whilst climbing over the Atlas, prior to letting down into Blida we lost our port engine cowling and arrived looking like something from an Oxfam shop. I remember thinking at the time that if it was always going to be like this, I hope Mum keeps up the insurance payments! Thankfully, this sort of thing very rarely happened. Considering what they had to work with, and some of the conditions in which they did their job, I don't think anyone can give the 'erks' too much credit. The cynical flight sergeant with his standard remark 'It'll clear itself in the air sarge', or the other gem 'It was all right on air test yesterday", was more of a cartoon character than reality, although he did sometimes exist."

NORMAN WILSON – PILOT

Norman was apprenticed at Sir W G Armstrong Whitworth Aircraft Ltd in Coventry. On his 18th birthday he volunteered to join the RAF and was called forward on 10 August 1942.

"After training I eventually found myself at Kipevu, Mombasa, Kenya joining 209 Squadron as a second pilot on Catalinas. My first operational flight was an anti-submarine patrol between Mombasa and the Seychelles on 19 February 1945, returning on the 21st. In the month up to 24 March, a number of similar flights to such places as Madagascar, Pamanzi and Dar-es-Salaam were undertaken. During this time, we were told that we were to convert to Sunderlands before departing to the Far East to participate in the Japanese conflict.

“I joined the Sunderland crew of Flt Lt Off Gibson, initially as third pilot. During the work up to become operational there were many exercises in radar, bombing, gunnery etc. On 20 April whilst on a bombing practice (during which a smoke bomb marker was dropped into the sea and then bombed by other smoke bombs), we had our first emergency experience. The apparatus for dropping the smoke bombs was somewhat primitive, in that the bombs were individually loaded onto a small rack. This was attached to the sill of the drogue hatch in the downstairs galley and then swung out ready for the pilot to operate the electrical release. Unfortunately our navigator, ‘Willie’ Hubert, dropped one of the primed bombs inside the aircraft, which detonated, and filled the ’plane with dense smoke. I was second pilot in the cockpit, and we could not see the control column, let alone the instruments!

“The captain – I couldn’t even see him – shouted that we must be on fire and that he would try to land, although we were some 50 miles from land. In an effort to see outside I attempted to put my head out of the rear sliding window on my side of the cockpit, but to no avail. I then slid the window panels back to see if I could do so out of the front window. This changed the airflow over the cockpit window which miraculously sucked the smoke out of the plane in a second. We were by then straight and level at about five feet above the water, with calm waves but a large swell.

“The captain landed and all seemed well. That was until the starboard wingtip float hit the swell and was knocked rearwards and upwards. This lifted the starboard aileron, knocking the control wheel from the captain’s hands and dipping the starboard wingtip into the water. Looking out of the cockpit I could see the starboard outer prop was thrashing up spray. I instinctively grabbed the wheel and applied full power. Luckily the

209 Squadron Catalina. [Author’s collection]

aircraft responded taking to the air at an incredible nose-up wing-down angle. We were able to resume normal flight, less the starboard wing float, returned to Mombasa and landed. Whilst being towed to a mooring, myself and another crew member climbed onto the port wing to keep the starboard wing up. The aircraft was taken out of the water, and a new aileron and wing tip float fitted. There was no other damage.

"A short while later, on the night of 14 May, two crews – Flt Lt Gibson and Pilot Officer (Plt Off) Thomerson – were assigned to fly one aircraft on a night radar training exercise; the crews taking it in turn. When we all boarded the aircraft, we realised there were more than enough pilots to carry out the work. I said to 'Willie' Hubert, 'I don't feel like going tonight' to which he replied, 'Nor do I, let's ask the skipper if we can get off.' Both captains agreed, and although the crew boat had left the aircraft, we managed to shout to him to return and the two of us went ashore. Later that night, when the aircraft was due to land, a thunderstorm covered Mombasa. They were told to remain out at sea until it passed. The aircraft flew into a hill and although some survived there were many who did not.

"I was then assigned to the crew of Fg Off Eric Yeomans and aircraft number PP159 squadron letters – WQ Q. Having trained to operational standard, the squadron moved east to our new base at Koggala Lake near to the town of Galle in the south of Ceylon (Sri Lanka). Our route took us via the Seychelles and Diego Garcia, arriving on 14 July 1945."

The Sunderland lost on 14 May 1945 was a Mk.5 NJ260. Three crew members were killed: Flt Lt John Gibson, WO Percival Stone and Flt Sgt Royston Williams. All were buried in Mombasa (Mbaraki) Cemetery. By 1946, Norman was out in the Far East to continue his Sunderland flying.

Another major change to aircrew training was the use of training schools outside of the UK, but under the British Commonwealth Air Training Plan. In January 1940 the Rhodesian Air Training Group (RATG) was established and continued to provide aircrew training until March 1954. With Headquarters in Salisbury, the RATG airfields were located at Belvedere, Cranborne, Guinea Fowl, Heany, Induna, Kumalo, Moffat, Mount Hampden, Norton and Thornhill.

PETER 'PERCY' PROCTOR – PILOT

Peter was told his standard of education meant he could not be a pilot, but he could be a rear gunner. He decided to wait until he was called up. The call came in 1942 when he was accepted for flying training.

26 EFTS Tiger Moth DX595. [Author's collection]

"I went to 26 Elementary Flying Training School (EFTS), at a place called Guinea Fowl, to do my flying training on Tiger Moths. I did my first solo after ten hours; that was a marvellous sensation. I went out that morning to do some more circuits and bumps, and I did one circuit and landed. The instructor was in the front cockpit and, after I'd done the first landing, he said 'Right, taxy over to the corner of the field' (there were no runways, just a field), so I did just that. The instructor climbed out on to the wing saying, 'It's all yours!' On that first solo, you're singing away up there; it's marvellous. After that it's back to the instructor doing aerobatics. One of the scariest things was learning how to get out of a spin. If your aircraft stalled, it dropped one wing and went into a spin. Your automatic reaction, as you are going down, is to pull the stick back to get out of it – but you make it even worse – you already don't have enough flying speed. You then go into what they call a flat spin, and that's more difficult to get out of. I got up to about 3,000ft for my solo one, put it into a spin. I did the old stick-forward and full opposite rudder, and I was out of it in no time at all.

"Then we moved from Guinea Fowl to 22 Service Flying Training School (SFTS) Thornhill, and Harvards – I didn't like those. Big clumsy things, radial engine and all the rest of it. I had a problem, being so short. You've got to push your toes down to put the brakes on, but I couldn't reach them and had a right struggle to make them work. Once you've landed and started to slow down on the runway, you think you're OK and relax; straightaway it can go into a ground loop – so you've got to concentrate right to the end.

"With the Harvard you could learn instrument flying. We did some training on the Link Trainer and had some fun and games. It was like a stubby little aircraft, a fuselage with little stubby wings. You climbed in, and someone was controlling it. You'd be flying a certain course, and the instructor would say, 'Do a shallow turn to port'. So, you turned on to a new course, however your artificial horizon in the cockpit would show that you were still flying straight and level, but you'd swear that you were still turning. You had really got to rely on that artificial horizon because if you didn't you were in all sorts of trouble. In the Harvard you were in the front cockpit with the instructor in the rear. They'd cover the whole cockpit and the same thing happened. If you weren't careful, you'd swear you were turning and yet you were straight and level. You had to rely on your instruments.

"Getting our wings was right fun and games. We'd seen these American films where there's a band and a parade and all the rest of it, then someone comes along and pins a pair of silver wings on your tunic. On our parade there were about eight or ten of us and two officers came along, one carrying a little cardboard tray. One officer would take a pair of wings out of the tray, flat cotton ones which I've still got. He pinned them on your tunic with a safety pin – that was your wings parade. We never wore them; we bought the raised ones. I've kept them ever since, complete with safety pin.

"After we got our wings, we went back to Bulawayo. There we got the train up to southern Rhodesia, then up to the Zambezi. We went over the bridge into northern Rhodesia and then left hand down to the River Congo; on the train all the way. There was a big party of us, and we carried all our own rations with us. We had a couple of tea chests for all the food and stuff. We got a ferry across the Congo and were picked by road transport. We did about 200 miles by road to the southern end of Lake Tanganyika and then sailed its entire length in a tender behind a lake steamer; we took it in turns to steer the tender. When we got to the northern end of the lake we had another train journey to the southern end of Lake Victoria. Then we had the same routine up to Kisumu in Kenya. When I was there, I met my brother-in-law who was on Catalinas. They were based in Mombasa but had a detachment on the lake.

"Next, we flew up to Heliopolis in Egypt, calling at Khartoum on the way. We had about three weeks there in the Heliopolis Grand Hotel. Grand it was. With all these massive, curved staircases to get to the other floors – the luxury of it! There was a great big room with about ten mattresses on the floor, and that was all you got for you and your suitcase. One night an Entertainments National Service Association (ENSA) party came along to do a show for us. We'd been told we were going to be posted to Ismailia to do our operational training on Hurricanes. However, they had bubonic plague on the canal there so we had to have an enormous injection in our backsides! That night, after the concert, as we were going up this fancy staircase you could tell who'd been posted because they were limping all the way up.

"We went from Heliopolis up to Ismailia, just off the Sweetwater Canal and that's where the problem was with the plague. They were washing their donkeys, doing their washing and all sorts of other things in the canal. You had been given your pilot's handbook and a couple of lectures at Heliopolis, then when you got to Ismailia, there was your aircraft and off you went. Up until then you'd always had an instructor, but there's only one seat in a Hurricane – it seemed to work though. We didn't get very many hours; we were only there for a few weeks. I thought I would be coming back to the UK by then, but instead of that they sent me out to India.

"I started on 11 Squadron in 1945 at Imphal in Burma. When I went to see the commanding officer he asked my name, so I said Proctor. He said he knew all his pilots by their first name, so I told him it was Peter – he said he already had two! It then occurred to him that there was a light aircraft company that made Percival Proctors. From then on, I would be Percy, and I was never known by any other name."

After Hurricane and Spitfire flying in Burma and back in the UK, Peter left the RAF as a WO in 1946. He became a carter, doing deliveries for British Rail with his horse Clarence.

To speed up pilot type-conversion to help cope with the demands of both the Western Desert and Burma campaigns, ten operational training units (OTU) numbers 71-79 were established in the Middle East. These were mainly based at Aqir, Ein Shemer, Fayid, Gianaclis, Ismailia, Nicosia, Wadi Gazouza in Sudan, Aden, Abu Sueir, El Ballah plus Nakuru and Rongai in Kenya.

ROY 'MICK' MAIDMENT – PILOT

Flt Sgt Mick Maidment enlisted in 1942. He did his basic pilot training in the UK before arriving in Rhodesia to complete advanced training; then it was off to Egypt.

"I was posted on a course to 73 OTU at Fayid by the Suez Canal. Its main runway ran due west with most of the buildings on the south-east side, Spitfires were at one end, Kittyhawks at the other. The maintenance unit was at the most extreme western end. This was early February 1944, and it was so bloody cold! We had what were called 'chatties' outside; there were six rooms with four men to each room, and I finished up in a room with two. We had earthenware pots with the lids on and one morning they had collapsed because of the frost. The beds were very low, and we wrapped up in everything we could find – balaclavas, great coats, flying suits you name it. Absolutely incredibly cold.

"The ultimate experience on the last week of our six-week course was to fly on a couple of occasions a battle formation to give us confidence in air-to-air firing and air-to-ground firing. Two of us were airborne in Kittyhawks when an American B-17 came over. We made a practice attack on it, one behind the other, but did we trust the Americans who might have shot first and answered questions later? There were certain things that you had to do in a formation of three. Flying near the ground over the desert was a bit like flying over the sea – very difficult to judge your height. We did one exercise, using oxygen up to 22,000 or 23,000 feet, in a rather extended formation of six, in order to check spinning. Our instructions were that it could become uncontrolled, the snag with the Kittyhawk being it lost longitude stability.

Spitfire 5C EF704 73 OTU Fayid May 1945, Sgt J Crabb flying. [Mick Maidment]

"Towards the end of the course we flew a complete operation exercise with six aircraft, taking off in pairs. Pete Taylor lost a wheel, but luckily, he was the sixth one off. We climbed up to five or 6,000 feet and were given a specific target. I heard 'Bristol aircraft, go in port, go'. He turns in port, and I dive underneath. We had to do cross-over turns, and eventually he says, 'Bristol aircraft, approaching target'. We are opposing the other pairs. This went on until we got to a couple of thousand feet and the shout comes over, 'Pick your baby, pick your baby'. At around 1,500 feet we would have to open fire; this was where there were convoys that we were supposed to attack. Once you have passed over your target all hell was let loose; get down close to the ground – you never go back to the same target. We climb back up, returning to the formation, and then fly home – you only make the one attack. So, this was how we finished our exercises with the Kittyhawks, sweating like mad.

"Later, when you were in the mess there was laughter between the Spitfire pilots. One of us was persuaded to go to the flight commander and ask if, after five weeks of messing around with Kittyhawks, he could unofficially borrow a Spitfire (there was much rivalry between the Spitfire and Kittyhawk pilots). All the Spitfire pilots were wanted in India to help the fight against the Japanese. The only Kittyhawks were in Tunisia and Italy, so we would be the quicker ones to get home.

"But then four of us were posted to India. We got as far as Basra when there was a storm in the Gulf. We stayed overnight in a hotel; it was an absolutely gorgeous place. On that evening, I sat at one table with some friends, and on the adjacent table was Vera Lynn. She was on her way out to Burma and went out in a flying boat with us.

"The first time I landed in a flying boat I thought I was going to die. Huge flaps come down, and you fly down onto the water until you hear the tip of the hull 'tick tick tick'. The pilot pulls back and it goes 'bang!'; the water comes up and hits the wings, goes all over the fuselage, it runs down and you think you're in a submarine – for about 20 seconds your life has come to an end. The next thing you are aware of is the gentle bobbing up and down on the water – it is an incredible experience. The first time, it scares the living daylights out of you. But the second time it is so exciting!"

Late in the war Mick returned from India to RAF Wroughton where he completed his service.

RON HALL – WIRELESS OPERATOR

Following training in 1943, Ron was sent to 13 Air Gunnery School at El Ballah, before moving to 77 OTU.

"I was posted to 77 OTU Qastina, Palestine from October 1944 to January 1945. This OTU was totally reliant on Wellington bombers, many of which were old and ex-Middle East squadrons. The latest marks I flew in were Mk.3s, although I believe there were also a few Mk.1Cs there. We were forced to divert to Shallufa, whilst on cross-country exercises, three times through engine problems – exciting stuff for a new crew. It gave me some operating practice. One or two aircraft crashed mysteriously, and it was thought that a few Ju 88s on Crete were involved. I never did learn what exactly happened.

"Our worst experience was whilst doing a scheduled practice with the Royal Navy defences over Alexandria. We seemed to be the only aircraft over the city at that time, and just about every searchlight was trained on us. The briefing was 'fire off the colours of the day and they'll switch off'. They weren't going to let us off that easily; they were enjoying themselves. It took all three of my cartridges before they obliged.

"I could not leave Qastina without relating a tragedy; it served to remind me that flying in the RAF could be dangerous. We were returning from a daylight cross-country and about to join the circuit, when we were warned that an aircraft was on finals and we were to hold. We watched this aircraft as it approached and touched down; however, it did not slow down, running off the end of the runway and nose down into a ditch (which ran round the circumference of the peri-track). Within seconds it burst into flames."

This was almost certainly the accident on 29 October 1944 involving Wellington X LP363. The port engine caught fire whilst doing circuits, and a forced landing was made at Beit Darras; the aircraft was completely burnt out. The only crew member lost was the Air Bomber Sgt Kenneth Maxwell, who is buried in Ramleh War Cemetery. The pilot, Flt Sgt Reynolds, and the rest of the crew escaped with minor injuries.

After Qastina, Ron returned to the UK and completed a tour on 57 Squadron Lincolns at Waddington. In January 1949 he went to 228 Operational Conversion Unit (OCU) at Leeming to convert to the Bristol Brigand. We meet him again with 8 Squadron at Khormaksar – see chapter four.

THE GROUNDCREW

Not to be forgotten are the ever-faithful groundcrew, living and working in extremes of weather, especially heat and humidity, to ensure aircraft were always available.

GETTING OVERSEAS
ERIC BRADLEY – FITTER

"I left to go overseas in 1940. We started with a 24-hour train journey from Uxbridge to Gourock in Scotland – all sealed so people couldn't see. When we arrived, we got on a ferry and boarded the liner *Georgic* which was moored out in the harbour. It was a beautiful ship, but the poor old troops had to sleep in hammocks in the hold. After several attempts I managed to get in mine, but in the middle of the night I forgot where I was, tried to turn over and promptly fell out. After that I found myself a corner and slept on deck. The following morning the weather was very rough. When we went to the mess deck for breakfast, we found the tables were laden with bread and butter, eggs and all the nice things we couldn't get at home. Most of the 3,000 troops aboard were seasick, so we did our best to eat all of their breakfasts! What a feast we had that day.

"When our ship stopped at Freetown, Sierra Leone for 24 hours, I was told to guard a small doorway in the side of the ship that had a ladder going down to the water. I dozed off for a few minutes during the night. Waking up with a start I saw the biggest native I'd ever seen in my life. He was standing right in front of me, armed with a huge spear and a large knife; luckily for me his intentions were friendly. We stopped off at Cape Town and spent a couple of days there; sadly, I had no money in my pocket. It was very nice and they were very keen to build up the British population, and wanted British people to come to live out there after the war.

"On the first night there was no bedding for us – nothing! We slept on the floor of one of the huts, and when we woke up in the morning, we were covered with bug

Cpl Eric Bradley in the desert 1941. [Eric Bradley]

bites. It took weeks for me to get them out of my clothes; you could squeeze them between your fingers and blood would spurt out on you – your blood. It took ages to clear them. There was nowhere else to sleep.

"We then carried on up the east coast of Africa, past Madagascar, and eventually arrived in Egypt and docked at Port Said. Then after a long journey by road, rail and river boat we ended up in Sudan. What a hot place that was. During the journey I can vaguely remember being knocked over by a camel at Wadi Halfa. At first, we were billeted in Port Sudan, on the Red Sea. Even at Christmas the temperature was about 100 degrees at midday, and it was known as the white man's grave. The heat was absolutely appalling. In fact, at the hottest part of the day, we had to lie under our mosquito nets for a couple of hours or so. We couldn't do anything; even lifting your little finger led to buckets of sweat. One afternoon I wandered around on the salt flats. As I didn't have any tinted glasses it didn't do my eyesight any good – I've worn glasses ever since! There was no escaping the blinding light from the salt flats and the heat was absolute murder.

PORT SUDAN

"I was sitting in the guard room at the beginning of our camp in Port Sudan, and the hours were dragging by. It was hot and sticky and I was staring at the little path outside. There was a white stone on the path. In the next moment when I looked at it, it was in a different position. When I looked at it a bit more carefully it was a little creature moving along very slowly, and then I dozed off. The next thing I knew there was a hand shaking me. 'Wake up corporal, wake up, you're supposed to be on guard duty.' It was the adjutant who, luckily for me, was rather a middle-aged father figure. It didn't go any further, otherwise I would have had it.

"One of my jobs on the camp was to raise and lower the flag, morning and evening. As I was lowering one evening one of the stays came out of the sand, and the flagpole came crashing down – right across the commanding officer's car! There was a big dent in the roof – I wasn't his favourite person after that.

"The Italians used to come over trying to bomb us (that was before the Germans). They wouldn't come down below bombing height because they were frightened of being shot down by our fighters, so they kept as high as they possibly could and of course the bombs went absolutely everywhere. In the evenings there was always a line of taxi drivers ready to take us into Port Sudan. When the Italians came over you could see all these drivers stream off all over the desert in a terrible panic, until it was all over.

"It was rather strange really. When we first moved into the desert, we only had ground sheets to sleep on. In the middle of the night the heavens opened and we were almost washed away, however next morning, when the sun came up, it looked as if the desert hadn't had a drop of rain for a hundred years. Amazing, isn't it? Another job on 33 Squadron was to wake the Hurricane pilots up at dawn – so they could get off and do mischief to the enemy.

"Later we had plenty of Luftwaffe bombing. On one occasion, it was just as we were collecting our lunches at the cook house, I was walking back to my tent with my mug full of tea and a plate full of food, and then this bloody German came over and dropped a whole string of bombs. I flattened myself on the sand and I could see them coming towards me, a whole line of bombs bursting and getting nearer. The next one luckily went right over me and burst beyond me. I could see red-hot shrapnel which seemed to be moving so slowly – another lucky escape.

"I don't think anyone was killed on that particular raid; it was just a surprise sweep by one aircraft. For a lot of these raids, they didn't have a specific target or they couldn't get to that target so they just wandered about looking for something worth bombing or strafing. I fired my revolver at them but I don't think I ever hit them. On our unit we had a Czechoslovakian. He had an enormous machine gun, which had come out of an aircraft, and he had mounted it on something. Shouting at the Germans as they came over, they missed him by miles every time! But sadly, he was killed later on."

PALESTINE AND THE WESTERN DESERT

"We moved up to Palestine in July 1941 for a short period. After that we travelled in convoy in the desert, all the way to northern Iraq when they had the troubles there. When the convoy was driving through Baghdad the crowds were glaring at us, booing and throwing stones. I was quite tempted to get my revolver out and shoot at them, but I thought better of it. We stayed for a while, out on the plains about 60 miles from Mosul. There were loads of insects there. Centipedes were about 12 inches long and if they got on to you, God help you! Tarantulas – they were vicious, and scorpions – they didn't run away from you. There was one idiot who saw a tarantula and started to throw stones at it. He panicked, and instead of running away the tarantula started to attack him. Luckily, I was close by so I shot it.

"In September 1942 I went to Wadi Natrun and Gazala (Libya) to join 53 Repair and Salvage Unit (RSU). We went out and collected 'bashed' aircraft and put them

53 RSU on convoy. [Eric Bradley]

back together again. My main job was to protect them in the event of our being attacked. The specialists quickly went out to crashed aircraft because the Germans also wanted to get hold of them.

"We were getting ready for a long convoy one evening, just the four of us, in our 'blitz buggy' – a captured German vehicle. I think it was Ted Palmer, Richardson, and Taylor. Some Arabs came wandering in and we traded a whole load of Navy Army and Air Force Institute (NAAFI)-issue cigarettes, which to us of course were completely un-smokable, for 60 eggs; although Arab eggs are much smaller than the ones we were used to. We sat up half the night boiling them and set up a tray across the back of the 'blitz buggy', between the two rear passengers and the two front passengers. As we were driving along in convoy we were eating the eggs. We got through the whole lot, 15 eggs each in one day!

"We had to go to the crash site of a Kittyhawk. That was unfortunate as it had dived straight into the ground and buried itself. Although we didn't really have many casualties in 53 RSU, I nearly got killed in the desert. I was walking back to the camp and some bloody plane came in to land with all its lights on – I was in the middle of the blasted landing strip. It was coming down, lower and lower, and heading straight for me. It was going much too fast for me to run away, so I simply sat down on the ground and luckily it passed right over me and landed."

Eric's unit then moved to Italy. He eventually got home just in time for Christmas 1944 and was discharged in April 1946.

PULL UP A SANDBAG

A well-known invitation to gather round and share stories.

RON HALL

"On 57 Squadron we were so short of wireless operators that I was often told to go straight to another aircraft as soon as we landed as it was waiting for an operator to take-off immediately. At one stage we had just five wireless operators for 12 crews."

CHAPTER THREE

KEEPING THE PEACE

Following the end of World War II, in many respects, the RAF in the Middle East continued in its pre-war primary role. Forces were maintained in support of the UK Government's remit to protect British interests in overseas territories, and the global trade routes passing through them.

For the two and a half decades that followed, keeping the peace would not be an easy challenge, as events throughout the region were to prove. To name just a few there was the Mau Mau uprising in Kenya in the early 1950s, the Suez Crisis in 1956 and the 1961 Kuwait crisis when Iraq threatened to invade the newly independent country. These were followed by the Beira oil blockade following Rhodesia's unilateral declaration of independence in 1965 and the long-running violent unrest in Yemen and the Aden Protectorate.

The RAF played a major role in all of these events. To do so it required squadrons with appropriate first-line types, used largely for ground-attack sorties, reconnaissance both overland and maritime, all supported by an extensive air transport capability. Initially a good number of wartime-era aircraft were still in use, eking out their final days of service.

JACK WADE – WIRELESS OPERATOR

"I was lucky enough, with my crew, to land a job as personal crew to Air Vice-Marshal (AVM) Ernest Cuckney, Director of Maintenance and Supply Middle East and Central Mediterranean Forces. This brought a posting to Mediterranean Allied Air Forces Rear Command. We got the job because we were an experienced crew (at least this was what we fondly believed). In practice I expect, following normal service

Wellington X LP201 L 'Sister Anna' Middle East Comms Squadron. [Jack Wade]

procedure, the commanding officer no doubt decided that here was a way to get rid of three deadbeats.

"The aircraft, Wellington X LP201 *(of the Mediterranean and Middle East Communications Squadron)* was a standard aircraft converted for VIP use. The aft section of the bomb bay was sealed, leaving a small forward section for stowing luggage. The crew could enter as usual through the nose, but the air vice-marshal and staff made a more dignified arrival via a door let in on the starboard side. Turrets were removed and their spaces faired over providing crew space for the fitter and rigger who we carried as part of the crew. A third seat was used by the air vice-marshal's batman/driver. Aft of this area, via a door in another bulkhead, was the passenger compartment with about a dozen seats for the air vice-marshal and staff. A most useful feature for me as wireless operator was that the W/T call sign 'FALOK' was known to all ground wireless operators. When I was calling with position reports, air to ground messages, ETA revisions etc., any brash lad who attempted to break in was told smartly to 'belt up'. It made life very easy.

"The duties were straightforward, tours of inspections, conferences with other service personalities etc. Usually after a trip we would be given a date when the 'Old Man' would require us again, and we would use the aircraft for normal passenger work until two days before that date. Since the aircraft had to receive a service and be air tested between each trip with the air vice-marshal, even if we had flown within the last 24 hours, those two days were always busy.

"When not required and on normal passenger work, we came into our own. We eventually acquired the name of 'Cuckney's Private Airline', a fact which was not unknown to the boss; but thankfully he must have had a sense of humour. We nearly always managed to select our own passengers, female if possible, but that was very rare as the female of the species was a bit thin on the ground in our theatre. Alternatively, we opted for people not too high in rank (they would not be in a hurry to get to an important appointment), sociable types who would appreciate the red-carpet treatment that we laid on for them, and who would respond when it came to their turn at the bar. Occasionally we got the awkward customer who wanted some outlandish place like Sardinia or Naples, not very often though. We were pretty careful, and we had friends in the Air Booking Centre; 'Oh dear, I appear to be overweight in my luggage, would you mind if I left that bottle of gin behind?'

"It couldn't last of course and eventually AVM Cuckney went home to a new appointment in Bomber Command, leaving a sorrowing crew behind – he was a thoroughly good type. In order to stay with his crew Ken, the skipper had remained overseas past his repatriation time, he was up for permanent commission and went home to receive it. Arthur and I had only completed just under three years at the time, and weren't due for a home posting. The air vice-marshal had us posted back to flying units, thus avoiding redundancy and ground duties."

Returning to the UK Jack went on to Avro Yorks flying the UK-Singapore and UK-Nairobi routes carrying passengers and freight with 40, 51 and 59 Squadrons. He left the service in August 1950.

JOHN KING – FLIGHT ENGINEER

Enlisted in 1943 Flt Sgt John King completed his training with 1665 Heavy Conversion Unit (HCU) at Saltby, prior to arriving on his first Halifax squadron in 1944.

Halifax VII NA363 644 Squadron officer commanding's aircraft, Castel Benito, June 1946. [John King]

Halifax III 644 Squadron after terrorist attack in Qastina, 25 February 1946. [John King]

"At the end of the war in Europe, I was on 296 Squadron Earls Colne when all the Australian crews were repatriated, so we lost our skipper and wireless op. They didn't know what to do with us, so they sent us on leave and I went home to Luton. When I opened the front door there was a telegram on the mat addressed to me, which said, 'return at once'. So I had a cup of tea, left my dirty washing behind for my mother, went straight back and met up with the crew. The following day we were wheeled into the commanding officer's office and introduced to our new skipper, Wg Cdr Hubert Ingle DFC. He had taken command of 644 Squadron at Tarrant Rushton, and told us we were going off to the Far East. However, the Americans dropped the atom bombs, and that put an end to that. They decided to send us to the next hotbed – Palestine.

"So we were sent to Qastina, Palestine (644 Squadron arrived there on 1 December 1945, with Halifax A.VII*)*. During our time there we were attacked one night by terrorists who blew up 11 Halifaxes. They got on the airfield and put phosphor bombs on the wings, so of course the petrol caught fire and destroyed the aircraft. They lost one person, but happily there were no losses on our side."

The attack was by militants belonging to Irgun, the National Military Organization in the Land of Israel. It occurred on 25 February 1946 and the aircraft destroyed were; NA358, NA359, NA362, NA430, NA431, NA464, PN255, PN303, PN306, PN310, PN311.

Halifax VII 644 Squadron engine fire Khartoum 6 May 1946. [John King]

“They shunted us down to Bilbeis under canvas while they sorted out Qastina, and then we went back. We had to do a trip to Khartoum, called Exercise Gordon. We were to make an attack on Khartoum by taking troops. The idea was that three aircraft would tow gliders loaded with troops (from the 6th Airborne Division). After releasing the gliders from the aircraft those troops would take control of the airfield, so that other paratroopers could come in and drop.

“As he was the commanding officer, the skipper said ‘We’ll take the first glider’. We were the lead, we overnighted at Wadi Halfa, then carried on to Khartoum; it was bloody hot down there. As we were towing a glider behind us, it was too hot for the engines which were overheating. They had put extra fans on the engine cowlings but were still overheating. I said to the skipper ‘We’re overheating badly, we’ve got to get rid of this glider’. But he dropped it on the spot, on the airfield, and the other two dropped theirs. We landed at Khartoum, taxied in, shut the engines down, and the starboard inner burst into flames! The local fire brigade had never had so much fun; they’d never had a fire there. They came out and smothered the whole ’plane with foam. You couldn’t see the aircraft; it was completely lost in foam. Fortunately, they put it out.

“We went into a big marquee with drinks and food laid on in beautiful silver urns. I asked the chap behind the counter for a cold drink. He gave me lime juice. I put my hand around it and it was freezing, beautiful. We were there for two or three days because our aircraft was knackered. However, the skipper said, ‘I can’t sit here. We’ll take off with one of the other aircraft and take a glider back to Qastina. The other crew can sit here and wait for our engine to be repaired, and they can bring it back.’ So, we took off, and although the glider was light this time, we started overheating again.

“We got right up into the Nubian Desert, and the outboard engines weren’t too bad. However, the two inboard ones were absolutely red hot; the oil pressures had dropped, and the temperatures were up. I said to the skipper, ‘The starboard inner’s going to blow up any minute. We’ve got to get rid of this glider.’ Communications between us and the glider had been lost, because the wire in the tow rope had snapped. I fired a red Very flare off. The glider pilot knew that we were in trouble as he could see the smoke coming out of the engine, so he cast off and landed in the Nubian Desert. Fortunately there was a ground party who were not too far away and rescued them. They set fire to the glider so the Arabs couldn’t do anything with it.

“Although they were rescued, we were still in trouble with the really hot engines. The skipper thought for a moment that we were going to have to land too. The only way that we got back to Wadi Halfa was to shut one engine down and keep the other three going. When that one had cooled down a little bit, we started it up and shut the other one down. We alternated these two inboard engines, a quarter of an hour at a time, until we got back to Wadi Halfa, where they put in two new engines.

"The hotel at Wadi Halfa was absolutely fantastic. The flying boats on their way to India used to land on the Nile. People then transferred up to the hotel where the staff were all dressed in their whites with red hats, and there was a swimming pool. In the morning there was a knock on the door when they brought you breakfast on a silver tray – it was absolutely wonderful. We used to lie by the swimming pool watching the flying boats coming in. Sadly, after two or three days we had to get back, so the skipper sent for another aircraft and we returned to Qastina.

"After nine months they decided that 644 Squadron should be disbanded. In its place, 47 Squadron was resurrected, and we became 47 Squadron (1 September 1946). A month later we came back to Fairford, Gloucestershire, where we were demobbed. I said cheerio to the crew and never saw any of them again. I was sent up to Lytham St. Anne's and spent a week in Blackpool spending my demob money."

ROY FENSOME – WIRELESS OPERATOR

Flt Sgt Roy Fensome RAF, Wireless Operator, Dakota / Halifax / Lancaster 216 Squadron/Group Communications Flight Helwan, Anson Shaibah Station Flight, 1945-46.

"I left 4 Radio School at Madley on Dominies, passing out in November 1944, when I was immediately posted overseas. We landed at Port Said after a terribly rough journey by sea, fortunately I wasn't sick. After a few weeks' acclimatisation, in May 1945 we went to 13 Air Gunnery School at El Ballah. Here we used Ansons and I did a six-week air gunnery course. They always said: 'Sergeant, you shoot at the drogue, not at the aeroplane! We don't want all the paperwork.' I scored 69%, so not bad. There were about three or four of us in the Anson, and I thought to myself, 'Well how do they know who hits the target and who doesn't?' But each student had different-coloured bullet tips, mine were 300 red or 300 blue. So when the drogue was retrieved, they could see the coloured holes in it. The shoots were filmed, so afterwards when we watched, you could see how you had done – I passed.

"I was then posted to the Cairo airport, Helwan, where I was crewed up with a special unit that used converted Lancasters, Dakotas and Halifaxes. We were used to take VIPs, Special Forces, and engines and equipment, all over the Middle East. It was part of 216 Group Transport Command *(Probably Special Transport Flight, which*

Roy Fensome with 13 AGS Anson El Ballah. [Roy Fensome]

was absorbed into Mediterranean and Middle East Communication Squadron on 1 April 1946). I think in total I did 500 hours all over the Middle East in 1945-46, with no real action except engine failures and undercarriages that malfunctioned.

"We used Lancasters most of the time that I was there, and we went as far as Mauripur on the coast of India with Special Forces. We had two goes at that, because on the way out one of the engines packed up, and we lost a bit of height. We had to turn back, get the engine sorted out, and try again with no mishap this time. That was a memorable flight because the skipper told me to send out an SOS, which I did. Thankfully the engineer did a good job and managed to get some power out of the engine, so I cancelled the SOS. We always had a full crew as if we were going on an operational mission, but we didn't get attacked or anything like that. It was just a matter of getting from A to B, delivering the stuff, and coming back.

"My crew left because they were demobbed, their number had come up. I stayed out there until 1946. The signals officer sent me on leave to Cairo for seven days. When I came back, he said, 'I've got a nice little job for you'. The commanding officer, Gp Capt Lowe, at 46 Staging Post, at Shaibah in Iraq, wanted a wireless operator for his Anson which he used to fly all over Iraq for meetings. I went down there by Dakota, landing in the evening. Even though it was sweltering hot, the group captain was waiting for me. He welcomed me, and even showed me where the sleeping quarters were. After I had a meal, I asked him if I could work either in the W/T cabin or the control tower if there was no flying; I did both.

Dakota IV 575 Squadron Bari, Shaibah 1946. [Roy Fensome]

"While I was working in the W/T cabin I had a message in plain language, which was unusual. It was from Mauripur. They said they were dissatisfied with the length of time it was taking to demob people, and they were going to take strike action. They wanted me to put the word out, pass the message on. Well I knew that this was mutinous talk, so I didn't say anything to the other lads in the cabin. I saw the squadron leader signals officer, and we both went to see the commanding officer who told us not to mention it to anybody. I don't know what action was taken, nothing more was said about it.

"When I was demobbed, a Lancaster came down to pick up a crowd of us to take us back home. Sadly the wireless operator fell ill, and they had to take him to sick quarters. So the commanding officer came wandering over and I thought 'What the hell does he want?' He said: 'Roy, the skipper wants a wireless operator so he can get you all home.' I asked him where we were going to land. Well I got the briefing, the signals, the frequencies and so forth, and we landed at Marseilles. The rest of the way home from there was on the 'Médoc' route, travelling all the way across France in trains, stopping often until we reached the Channel and got across to Dover."

Roy left the service in 1947. The staging post he served at was one of several strategically placed to provide handling facilities for aircraft in transit. These increased in importance as many of the wartime airfields closed and there were fewer aircraft based in the region.

NORMAN DIDWELL – FLIGHT RIGGER

Cpl Norman Didwell joined 99 (Wellington) Squadron at Mildenhall in 1938, and then Newmarket in 1939. He later went to various Middle East staging posts from 1943 onwards.

"On the Middle East staging posts, we serviced 'Wimpies', Spitfires, Hurricanes, Liberators, Dakotas, Hudsons, Halifaxes, Corsairs, Barracudas, Flying Forts, Mitchells, Mossies, Blenheims, Beaufighters, Beauforts, Lancasters, Albacore, Fulmar, DH.86, Oxford, Anson, Kittyhawk and many more! When I was at 40 Staging Post, at Habbaniyah, we had as many as 40 aircraft in the same evening. As and we only had about 50 officers and men, it was all go.

"One afternoon at 44 Staging Post, Sharjah, a couple of Beaufighters arrived, and a couple of 'Wimpies' (Wellingtons). One Wimpy had lost a lot of fabric on the starboard wing, between the engine and the fuselage. A bloke named Joplyn and myself were doing this job on it, when all of a sudden, a Comm Flight Delhi Dakota *(Air Headquarters India Communications Flight)* came in with an emergency.

"Well the station commander at Sharjah was there with his Jeep to meet the Dakota, so there must be a 'big-wig' on it. It was Field Marshal Wavell and his entourage. To put these VIPs up they'd got the old Imperial Airways fort in Sharjah, which was a couple of miles away from the village; that was the only main building there. The second pilot was Flt Lt David Niven *(not the actor)*, whilst the pilot was Wg Cdr Withers *(possibly Wg Cdr Harold Robert Withers OBE)*, and the sergeant wireless operator said to me he's known as 'Googy', after Googy Withers the actress.

Liberator C.V BZ760 102 Squadron Bassingbourn, Shaibah 1945. [Roy Fensome]

“The field marshal had a squadron leader liaison officer in his entourage; I think they were flying up to Cairo for a conference. Anyway, both the aircraft’s engines were pouring out oil; somebody at Comm Flight Delhi had ‘boobed’. Both engines had done over their hours and were worn out, so it had to have a double engine change. Comm Flight sent a replacement aircraft from 216 Squadron at Cairo West to pick Wavell up the next day.

“As we had no Coles crane there, we had to take the engines out using shear-legs, and two new Pratt and Whitney engines had to be flown up from 317 MU at Karachi. The only place we could work at night was near the fort, with Leigh lights running on a generator. As we were working old Wavell came out with his RAF liaison officer and a couple of others, including a major.

“Ted Prouch and I had been there eight months, Sgt Grant had been there about 12 months. Wavell said, ‘Take these chaps, names and service numbers.’ We wondered what was going to happen! ‘You’re working hard, I won’t detain you any longer,’ he said, ‘rather primitive isn’t it, rather primitive.’ With that he marched off. Wg Cdr Withers and the flight lieutenant were there the next morning, they never went to Cairo. We had quite a long chat. We got the Wimpy sorted out, we replaced the fabric on the whole of the top inboard wing – away it went. Then the Dakota was ready for an air test. Wg Cdr Withers said, ‘Would you lads like to come up on an air test? You’d better get something to cover the seats.’ That only left three on the duty crew. However, we went up and down the Gulf for about an hour; so, I actually flew in Field Marshal Wavell’s aircraft.

“They said we’d got a new commanding officer coming, it was Wg Cdr Bartram who I served under on 99 Squadron. He saw me one day servicing a Liberator, we had a lot of those coming through. He said, ‘I know you, don’t I?’ I replied, ‘Yes sir, I remember you, B Flight.’ ‘Of course, yes, Didwell.’ All the boys thought, ‘Oh, you’re well in’. Whenever he saw me, he would come and say, ‘How are you doing Didwell?’ Every time a Wimpy came in with a snag, he would air test it if the crew had been sent on. I would service the aircraft, and do the ground check on it before test flight. ‘Do you want to come up Didwell?’ ‘Yes please sir.’ ‘Go and get yourself a parachute and harness then.’”

Eventually Norman returned home. He spent the remainder of his RAF service in Transport Command at Waterbeach and Gatow (during the Berlin Airlift). He was demobilised in 1952.

PETER VERNEY – NAVIGATOR

Sgt Peter Verney volunteered in 1950 when he was 18. After Initial Training School at Jurby, he went to 1 Air Navigation School at Hullavington to learn his trade.

MOSQUITO TWILIGHT

"In February 1952 I was sent out to Kabrit, Egypt to join 39 Squadron. They'd still got crappy old Mosquito night fighters which I was very disappointed about, but I'm now very proud that I had a year or so on them (in March 1953, we changed over to the Meteor NF.13). With the Mosquitos we did exercises when they put us up as bombers during the day. There were three or four Vampire squadrons in the Canal Zone as day fighter defence, and they would be put up to intercept us. We were doing the bomber stream bit, half a minute or a minute apart when these two lads came screaming down on our tail and ran into one another! They were really

Mosquito NF.36s of 39 Squadron over the Canal Delta. [Peter Verney]

unlucky; they went down in the desert about 40 miles off the Canal – virtually all our flying was done over the Sinai Desert because there was sod all out there. Nobody saw either aircraft go in, so they thought they had both had it. However, one of them had got out at very low level. His parachute had only just opened so he hit the ground very hard and broke his hip. It was about 11 o'clock in the morning and some Bedouin had seen him come down. They reached him some time in the early afternoon and put one of their tents over him, otherwise he would have died of sunstroke. They gave him some water and some dates and left him, coming back the next morning to leave him some more – that saved him. Our people didn't get to the site by Land Rover until two or three o'clock in the afternoon of the second day. He'd been lying there for over 24 hours – a very lucky man."

> *On 30 April 1952, 6 Squadron Vampire FB.9 WG892, flown by Sgt Alan Murrells (who was killed), collided with WL576 of the same unit, whose pilot (name unknown) survived as Peter has described. The aircraft had crashed about 17 miles west of Ismailia.*

"One fellow decided to demonstrate aerobatics to me in a Mosquito, strictly forbidden. He did a barrel roll, no problems at all, then he did a loop which was very sluggish over the top and then he said 'We'll try a roll off the top'. We got up to the top; you're on your back and he pushed the stick over to roll out of it. It didn't roll out it just fell out of the sky on its back and started spinning. They don't spin regularly, and you don't know up, down, where the bloody hell you are! However hard you strap yourself in, it's never hard enough. I was sitting beside him; he'd got his hand on the top of the stick stirring it about. Luckily, we'd started at a fair height and after several turns he got it back into the normal spin (which is the only way you recover from an inverted spin), and did about another three turns. It was recommended that if you spun a Mosquito inverted you got out!"

METEORS ARRIVE

"My pilot Joe Halkiew, was first-class. He was first on the squadron to obtain his Master Green instrument rating on the Mosquito. I did help him a little by acting as safety pilot on the T.3 while he practised. The set-up required the pilot to wear special-coloured goggles, and different-colour screens were put over the windscreen and side windows. Whilst I could see out, he could not; he could only see inside the cockpit. Turns had to be done in strict time by rate of turn and height maintained within certain limits. It was hard work for him, but I got my little turn in handling the controls. When we were upgraded to the Meteor, we got the occasional trip in the T.7. He was also an excellent aerobatic pilot, and vainly tried to teach me to do a neat barrel roll. He also let me take it round the landing circuit, but took over when I was lined up for touchdown. As we were night fighters, we had to do aerobatics at night. We did 13 barrel rolls on the trot and I remember one loop, when he had lost both artificial and natural horizons, and we finished in a very different direction from which we had started out. He would sometimes complete a practice interception by accelerating and diving under the target, pulling up in front of it in a barrel roll. Our commanding officer did not approve when Joe did it to him!

"Joe said we had to be the best crew on the squadron. The minimum range on an Air Interception (AI) Mk.10 radar was about 300 feet. He made me keep giving him headings until I said 'I've lost him off the screen Joe, we're too close', about 300 feet. Then he'd say, 'OK you can look up now Peter', and there's this f*****g great Lincoln! You were so used to seeing a Mosquito just across the screen.

"I am very proud that my squadron commander, Sqn Ldr Cogill, and I were I believe, the very last squadron crew to fly a Mosquito night fighter. We brought NF.36 RL141 home from the Middle East to Benson, arriving on 25 July 1953. He

Mosquito NF.36 RL141 at Benson 25 July 1953. Sqn Ldr John Cogill is on the left; Sgt Peter Verney is on the right. [Peter Verney]

was a good bloke, Cogill. I'd had a girlfriend before I went out there, I'd also had a rough time because I'd had dysentery quite badly; he didn't say anything, but I guess he took pity on me. They had about four or five Mossies left over in the MUs being repaired and the ferry pilots would bring out a Meteor and pick up a Mosquito. Crews were given a chance to have a leave at home by taking one back to the UK, so he took this last one and took me with him."

Sqn Ldr John Cogill was awarded the DSO and DFC flying Mosquitoes on 142 and 192 Squadrons.

"One of my little claims to fame is, I think, I'm one of the very few navs who have flown all four marks of the night fighter. We were the last crews flying these Mosquitos. They were falling to pieces at quite a rate of knots. The other squadron out there, 219, re-equipped with Meteor NF.11s. We were due to re-equip with NF.13s, which were actually a modified 11, but ours weren't ready by that time. When they sent out a batch of NF.11s for 219 Squadron, we were given a couple at odd times to play with.

"The Mossie was all vibration and noise. Three or four hours in a Mossie, and your head was solid, whereas I wouldn't say the Meteor was silent but it was a lot, lot quieter, a lot smoother. Of course it went a couple of hundred miles an hour quicker, and about 10,000 feet higher. I liked the Meteor; it was a good solid aeroplane. I've heard it described as a gentleman's aeroplane. It was very difficult for pilots to convert from a single seater to having some idiot in the back telling them what to

39 Squadron Meteor T.7 WL431 attempting take-off Kabrit, 13 May 1953. [Peter Verney]

do – they didn't trust him! A lot of pilots couldn't even trust the navs. If you imagine, on a black night, the idiot in the back is saying, 'We're at 600 feet, turn port hard', it must have been quite difficult for some of them to accept that they'd got to do what they were told – squadron leader or not!

"We were doing a formation of four take-off; a 'V' and one in the box. Joe Preston was leading with the T.7, which in retrospect was a stupid thing to have done with three NF.13s. I was quite a keen photographer in those days and wanted to take a picture of it getting airborne; of course, being a lot lighter, he raced away from us. I suddenly realised that we were then closing on him, so I took a picture. As I took the camera away from my eyes, I saw, out of the corner of my eye, he was going back relative to us. As I lost sight of him, his belly tank was touching the runway. He'd realised he'd run away from us and throttled back, then, realising that we were catching him, he opened up. Of course, on the old Derwent engines the throttle lag was tremendous and it just didn't happen. He went sailing on a couple of hundred yards off the end of the runway on his belly tank. That was hilarious!"

> *This happened on 13 May 1953 and, despite only suffering minimal damage, T.7 WL431 was not repaired.*

"The Meteor was a much more civilised aeroplane to fly in, with a refrigeration unit to keep us cool, a lamp to use at night to see charts etc., and a bit more room to spread out in. The big drawback was our remoteness from the pilot and his instrument panel. That separation took a lot of adapting to, and the closeness one felt to one's pilot was never the same. We had been told at Leeming OCU that being a member of a night-fighter crew was like a marriage. Eventually we were given an altimeter and airspeed indicator, which were essentials for navigation."

TROUBLES IN EGYPT

"In 1952 there had been a tense period with Egypt when the Egyptian army overthrew King Farouk and General Naguib became president. We sat about in the crew room with the aircraft fully armed waiting to take our appointed place in a plan to invade Egypt, but it all came to nothing. A rather similar situation occurred the next year when Colonel Nasser in turn ousted Naguib. I remember visiting the Egyptian camp barber who, while trimming my neck with a cutthroat razor, told me how the Russians were going to supply Nasser with MiGs and we would at last be driven out. Quite a number of servicemen lost their lives due to hostile acts by the Egyptians, mainly ambushing transport and sniping. These actions continued throughout the time we spent there. The airfield had an RAF Regiment Squadron of Bofors guns for defence which were normally lined up inside the wire perimeter close to the guardroom. In an incident early one morning there were a series of explosions when the Egyptians had crept through the wire and blew up several guns.

"We had a 'telescramble' system whereby the aircraft on standby, at the end of the runway, were connected to group by a telephone line plugged into the aircraft. These lines would be laid out from the control tower during the afternoon. On several occasions thieving Egyptians would remove large lengths before we took the aircraft out at sunset. It got so bad that the lines had to be permanently concreted in! One of the more arduous duties we non-commissioned officers (NCOs) had was that of guard commander. The whole camp, except for the actual airfield and the control tower, was enclosed by a barbed wire fence which was patrolled at night by armed guards. In addition, the unit was responsible for guarding a dredger when it was working on our section of the Sweetwater Canal. So, in total the guard comprised some 60 men who would be organised into the standard three shift system: two hours on and four off. The guard commander had to be awake all the time, and his orders stated that on no account must he leave the guardroom. However, the supplementary orders for guarding the dredger instructed him to visit the dredger guard every two hours. Most of the men comprising the guard were young, frightened National Service airmen with minimal weapons training."

AWAY DAYS

"It was usual practice to send us away for weekends to Malta, Cyprus, or Habbaniyah in Iraq. This was a navigation exercise and one or two crews would be told, 'Off you go to Malta' (or wherever). 'Friday afternoon, returning on Sunday afternoon or early Monday morning.' These weekends were great fun enabling us to get a good meal and a drunken night out, and some cheap booze and fags – the Meteor ammo tanks in the wings were a good store! I remember getting bottles of gin out covered in ice after the trip back from El Adem – they had cost 6/8d (33p). The cockpit was rather cramped and I used to fly with my travel bag upended between my legs. If I dropped a nav instrument on the floor the only way to retrieve it was to ask the pilot to invert the aircraft, then sort it out from the rubbish which collected in the top of the canopy. Navigation was quite tricky at times. We had to plot our tracks and courses on a small-scale chart. This was folded on a clip board together with a log, (a paper record), a Dalton computer, a ruler, protractors, and dividers all balanced on one's lap. It was essential to keep a supply of pencils and at night a small torch, although in the Meteor we had the luxury of a small lamp.

"Once on returning from Malta to El Adem we had a problem when the ventral fuel tank failed to feed. A hurried calculation showed we did not have enough fuel to make El Adem or return to Luqa. I made a rapid course alteration for Benina, which was roughly at right angles to our track. We made it there with no more course changes and before the tower was manned, landing with the gauges reading empty. When we subsequently landed at El Adem to refuel again we noticed a car waiting to cross the runway. The pilot, forgetting that we still had a full ventral tank and so were overweight for landing, dropped the aircraft quite heavily on to the runway. While we were having a meal the waiter came up to us and asked the pilot to come outside. There he was faced with the station commander who tore him off a strip for damaging his runway!"

DETACHMENTS AND EXERCISES

"In October 1953 the squadron went on a week's detachment to Habbaniyah in Iraq. This required us to divert around Israel, via Aqaba, landing at Mafraq in northern Jordan to refuel. Mafraq was an oiled sand strip and great plumes of dust were thrown up by aircraft, particularly on take-off. We were told that Habbaniyah was our 'war station' so we carried out sector recces around the north and east borders, having to find the three passes into Iran at Rawandiz, Penjwin and Khanaqin. The northern oilfield at Kirkuk had a very large flare where surplus gas was burnt off; this could be seen from a great distance, as could the gold-plated dome of the mosque at Samara. While at Habbaniyah we did some air-to-air firing for the benefit of the wing commander flying there. He was a very keen type and would press on in below the laid down 30° angle off, with the result that a shell ricocheted off the nylon target flag and passed through one of the tug's engines. As we only had one aircraft modified to tow targets that curtailed the fun! We also went down to Shaibah, near Basra and did a sector recce around Abadan and Kuwait. There was an oil derrick immediately beside the approach into Shaibah; it was a little unnerving flying past this red light at night.

"Another wonderful detachment, particularly for the navigators, was the annual Armament Practice School at Nicosia in Cyprus. We were not required to fly as it was all gunnery, although I enjoyed that and would always fly on the monthly gunnery sorties we did from Kabrit. This however meant we could enjoy the delights of Cyprus to the full. I can well remember experiencing a mild earthquake when I was washing one morning. I had put the room swaying about down to my elbow bending exertions of the previous night, until someone else urged me to get out quick. Three weeks of that was absolute bliss for us, as the night clubs treated us as honoured guests and the pilots were never slow to join in the parties.

"Between times we returned to the normal routine enlivened by exercises. During one of these we were vectored on to a Vampire on a nice moonlit night. He must have seen us as we were turning in behind him so he started some mild evasive action. I held on to him for a few minutes until he thought he had lost us, and then levelled up so that we were able to complete the interception. When we pulled up alongside him, he did not see our nav lights, however we could plainly see the dark shape of his head in the cockpit. Once more we had to tuck a wing in and give him a close-up flash. The dark shape went pale as he turned his face towards us. He must have had quite a shock when someone turned a light on about 15 feet away from him; I have never seen an aircraft break away so sharply. We also carried out a large radar calibration operation for the army who were installing an air defence system. This involved low flying over set routes with no low limit – most exhilarating. I flew six of these, three of them in one morning with three different pilots.

"Formation flying was all the rage and large formations would be flown for any occasion. We took part in the Coronation Flypast which went all around the Canal

"Gash formation" 39 Squadron NF.13s including WM310 and WM315. [Peter Verney]

Zone. I can remember particularly another large flypast which was led by another keen wingco flying who would keep too low. Joe had a position at the extreme left of a large formation of squadrons; this put us about five aircraft displaced laterally from the leader. The turns tended to be steep with the result that, when on the inside of a turn, we were in great danger of being flown into the ground. I had to remind Joe of this because it was a bumpy day and 100% of his attention was required to maintain formation; this resulted in his station keeping becoming a bit ragged at times. The leader could check this by watching the shadows of the formation on the ground, reprimanding Joe who gave an immediate curt response 'If you can do better come back here and do it yourself'. There was no answer, but at least he took the hint and took us up another 100 feet. A pilot in that situation really had to work hard with throttles and airbrakes, working overtime to maintain station. In 45 minutes, both he and 500 gallons of fuel were exhausted."

LIVING IN KABRIT

"Kabrit was a poor place with little in the way of amenities, conditions for the non-commissioned airmen were really bad. Ours were not much better, but at least we got our trips away. Water was obtained from the misnamed 'Sweetwater Canal', which had been built to provide water for the builders of the Suez Canal in the 1860's. It came via a tortuous route from the Nile and every Egyptian along the way had disposed of his dead animals, and done whatever else he needed to in it. To cope with this, we had a water purification plant which produced slightly sand-coloured water which curdled the milk in tea. Sanitation was of the bucket variety, and these were emptied periodically by a gang of Egyptians into an old dustcart – something to steer well clear of, the smell being indescribable. They spread it on their fields and sold us the resultant melons; the medics wondered why there were dysentery epidemics.

"As we were on the edge of the Great Bitter Lake we could go swimming from a jetty which had been built by German prisoners of war. There was also a winter theatre/cinema, where we had occasional ENSA shows, and an open-air cinema for the summer. This generally showed three films per week, although very popular films were sometimes only on for one night. One such was 'The Sound Barrier' which all the aircrew and the station commander wanted to see. Needless to say, that was a night-flying night! Whilst our commanding officer relented, 219's insisted on his night flying and was not popular. One of his pilots flew over the cinema at very low level and rolled as he climbed away. There were four aircraft airborne and they all kept their mouths shut so the culprit was never identified.

"I finished my tour (you did two-and-a-half year tours in those days) with Joe, and then we were posted home to RAF 'What-a-shame' (*Wattisham*) on 152 Squadron. This had only been formed about three or four months earlier with Meteor NF.12s and 14s". [1]

Peter's final posting was to Air Electronics School to teach V-bomber signallers. He completed his eight-year engagement there in 1958.

In the 1956 Suez Crisis, Operation Musketeer was the Anglo-French plan to invade the Suez Canal Zone and capture the canal. The operation made extensive use of both home and overseas-based RAF units, which mostly operated from Malta and Cyprus. Middle East-based units involved included: 6 and 8 Squadron Venoms, 13 Squadron Canberras and 249 Squadron Venoms all operating from Akrotiri; 37 Squadron Shackletons at Khormaksar; 39 Squadron Meteors, 70 Squadron Hastings, 84 and 114 Squadron Valettas at Nicosia and 208 Squadron Meteors at Ta Kali.

Around this time, although not directly involved with the Suez campaign, 541 Squadron in RAF Germany sent a pair of high-altitude photo-reconnaissance Meteor PR.10s to Kabrit, on exchange with 13 (Canberra) Squadron. Brian Ashley was one of the Meteor pilots.

BRIAN ASHLEY

"I was told I had been selected to go on the next squadron exchange to 13 Squadron at Kabrit in the Canal Zone of Egypt. This was one of the squadron's most sought-after tasks, and I could hardly believe I had been selected to go after only three weeks on the squadron.

"We were kept busy by 13 Squadron during the two weeks in Kabrit. A long low-level flight took me across barren desert to St Margaret's Monastery at the base of Mount Sinai. On the return flight I came across an Arab with his camel plodding steadily in a westerly direction. My curiosity was aroused, so I turned and set course in the direction he was following. Within about 20 miles I flew over a small oasis – I am still amazed that he could navigate so accurately. I frequently complained about having no navigation aids, but he did not even have a map and compass! On 28 April we left Kabrit for our return journey to Germany, giving them the customary low flypast. As I passed the control tower, I was pleasantly surprised to see that I was way below the wind sock."

Shackleton MR.2 S and C 38 Squadron Majunga 1966. [37Aden.co.uk via Dave McCandless]

On 11 November 1965 Rhodesian Prime Minister Ian Smith (a former Spitfire pilot with 237 [Rhodesia] Squadron), unilaterally declared the country to be independent from the United Kingdom, the first British colony to break free in such a way since the United States in 1776. The British Labour government, under Prime Minister Harold Wilson, elected to respond by imposing sanctions. These included a Royal Navy blockade of the oil supplies Rhodesia received via the Mozambique oil ports at Beira and Lourenço Marques. By far the longest RAF effort in support of the oil blockade was Operation Mizar. A detachment of Shackletons was sent to Majunga, on the island of Madagascar, to patrol the sea approaches to Beira seeking blockade-running tankers. The detachment continued until May 1972.

RAY EVANS – AIR ELECTRONICS OPERATOR

An English teacher's report at Ray's grammar school stated, "Evans prefers to twiddle with bits of wire, and whatever gadget he has in his pocket, rather than muse on the intricacies of English prose." His nickname as an apprentice at Halton was 'gadget man'. It never left him even through pilot training, and his life on the various other squadrons he flew as a pilot.

"Our 210 Squadron crew's name came up, and we set out to ferry an aircraft down to Majunga. The deployment was to be for four or six months. So, we collected our summer weight gear, loaded up the Shack and set off. First stop was Malta, 12 hours flying at the dizzy altitude of 8,000 feet. Next day we headed for another exotic place, Djibouti. It was over 35 degrees, and the accommodation was in a glorified Nissen hut with one rattling air conditioner in the end wall for all ten of us. Heading for the 'shower' and 'toilets' we found the Arabic definition of toilets was even more of a shock. A hole in the floor, no toilet paper, and a rusty dribble of water from an overhead tap, three between ten of us. The French air force, who were running the base, had not been expecting so many in the crew; however, they redeemed themselves somewhat by serving wine with every meal. The following day we launched off on the last leg to Majunga, again at 8,000 feet in the cooler air. We arrived after another 12 hours or so, having made it in three days – the next crew took ten. They broke down in various places en-route, finishing up in Nairobi, and then Mombasa whilst a spare engine was ferried out to them.

"Back at the accommodation there was a rush for the showers after flying. The overhead water tank was not very large, and it usually ran out before everyone had showered. The tank was supposed to be topped up automatically from a well in the grounds, but it seldom worked. We eventually discovered that the pump wiring was

Majunga crew tent. [37Aden.co.uk via Dave McCandless]

badly corroded, and the float switch was duff. Whilst we were waiting for spares for this, the local fire service, 'les pompiers', were called to top up the tank. This was fine until there was a fire in the area, so we lost this facility. Someone organised a local oil company to do the job! Much hilarity ensued as the logo on the side of the water tanker read, 'Rhodesian Oil Company'. One day after a sortie we arrived just as the rain was starting. We all rushed in, dumped our flying kit, and proceeded to shower in the rain. This was much to the amusement of the locals, and the non-amusement of a wing commander WRAF who turned up to inspect the accommodation!

"We manned the ground radio station callsign '6XA'. This was in a prefabricated metal shack with noisy air conditioning for the radios, not the operators. It was manned whilst an aircraft was airborne, passing weather to, and receiving information from, the aircraft in Morse code. To get to the shack, one passed a very large tree with bundles of cloth bags hanging in it. We were warned by the local 'number 1' boy in the mess, not to touch it as it was 'big ju ju'. One Sunday morning I was on duty in the radio shack when I heard lots of singing and music approaching. I poked my head out of the door and saw a crowd of locals, all dressed in white, dancing around a coffin on the ground. They opened it, cleaned and polished the bones, put them in a bag and hung it in the tree! After much querying of 'number 1' for an explanation, he said it was a spirit thing. They dug the body of their ancestor up after one year to release his spirit, and celebrate his freedom from earthly confines.

"Unusually, on one mail-dropping sortie to a Royal Navy blockade ship, we had two sets of Lindholme gear and were told which one to drop first. The procedure was to run past the frigate at about 150 feet and drop them close to the ship; a launch had been deployed some distance away to recover them. One of the navigators had rigged the first container full of rubbish – so when it hit the water it exploded open and scattered the contents over a wide area. The navy were not amused and requested us to 'stop messing about, and could we have our mail please?'

"On days off we sometimes had transport to go down to the refuelling mole at the harbour to go fishing. I had never been fishing before, and winding in slowly, as advised, it seemed as if it had stuck on a rock or something. As I heaved on the rod the line came free, along with a huge stingray attached to the end of it. 'Now what do I do?', I thought. A bunch of locals came rushing over and took charge. They steaked and cleaned it for us, and it made very good eating in the mess that night!

"With one week to go to the end of the detachment a trip was arranged to a crocodile farm. Some of the crew went along and brought back a baby crocodile. They kept it in one of the bathrooms, much to the distress of the maids! The croc

Javelin FAW.9 29 Squadron at Ndola airport, Zambia, 1966. [Ken Beere]

was christened 'Lightning', as it would sit quietly until someone poked it to see if it was real and got a shock as it whipped round and bit them. The big day arrived and a Belfast took us (and Lightning) to Akrotiri. There was a ladies guest night in the mess, and someone thought it would be a good idea to take Lightning along; it was placed on the bar. A lady came along, said, 'it can't be real', poked it with her finger and screamed as it bit her (tiny teeth, so it didn't break the skin). The chairman of the Mess Committee (CMC) promptly threw us out. No sense of humour. In the foyer there was a large fish tank which proved to be an irresistible place for Lightning. He was put in the tank and we left to find beer elsewhere. The following morning at breakfast all hell broke loose. The CMC was storming around threatening all kinds of mayhem on us, 'get that ******* thing out of my sight!' Lightning had an extremely full belly and a smug look on his face. He was removed from the tank and taken to Limassol Zoo – they were delighted." [2]

Ray then left the 'Kipper Fleet' and went to Lindholme, as an air electronics operator and signaller on Hastings and Varsities.

One unfortunate side effect of the oil blockade was the fact that Zambia received its oil supplies from Rhodesia, who turned off the tap. In December 1965, RAF Britannias commenced flying oil into Zambia, and were quickly followed by aircraft from other civil and military operators. To guard against any possible Rhodesian threat to the oil lift, 29 Squadron in Akrotiri was ordered down to Zambia to provide an air defence capability with its Javelins. They arrived on 3 December 1965, with Ndola as the headquarters and principal operating base, and a detachment at the capital, Lusaka.

KEN BEERE – AIRFRAME FITTER

"I joined in 1965 as a direct entrant, just before my 18th birthday. I went to Bicester 71 MU and applied for an overseas posting at the end of the year. I was posted to 29 Squadron and arrived at Akrotiri in December 1965. While I was there, we had a station alert; I had to do a night guard on a Canberra's A-bomb. It was odd sitting on an A-bomb's trolley, smoking a fag at 2 a.m., armed with a pickaxe handle!

"We went down to Zambia on 9 January 1966. The routing for us was via Muharraq (Bahrain), or El Adem – Nairobi – Ndola in a Hastings or a Britannia. The whole squadron went down apart from the two 'T-birds' (T.3s). We stayed down there for about a month at a time, before rotating back to Akrotiri for a couple of months. There were four Javelins at Lusaka (which became RAF Lusaka, BFPO 645) and the rest were at Ndola; there was talk at one time that Ndola would be made into a one-year overseas tour. The flying was quite restricted because of a fuel shortage, with 45-gallon drums of fuel being flown in by Britannias and Royal Canadian Air Force Hercules.

"The living quarters at Ndola were a bit rough. All the squadron personnel were in one huge shed, known as the Zambia Hall of Industry. It leaked when it rained and was very humid when it was hot. It was divided up into seven squares by hardboard sheeting, and all the beds had their head to the wall and feet towards the centre. We had no lockers, only one table in the middle of the room – there were clothes hanging from everywhere. There was a local gentleman named Isaac who did all our washing and ironing for five shillings a week, and swept the place out in the mornings.

"I was on first-line servicing, i.e. replenishment and a general check-over, but this also included a number of mainwheel changes and a hydraulic reservoir change (a six-hour job). I also had to do progressive servicing and modifications if necessary. At first, I was the only airframe chap on the line, so I had to do all this by myself and sign for it, so I was kept pretty busy. After eight straight days working, I finally had a day off. This was whilst we were changing wing pylons from the wet pylons to carry drop tanks, to the ones that were wired up for the Firestreak missiles. We also

Undercarriage retraction tests on a 29 Squadron Javelin FAW.9 at Ndola, Zambia, 1966. [Ken Beere]

had to remove the inboard pylons if an aircraft needed an undercarriage retraction test, in order allow clearance for the jacks. They sent two chaps up from Lusaka to Ndola to help me. They were both LACs but weren't Javelin 'trained' at all and had never worked on them before.

"The Firestreaks were kept in a small hangar. Although the RAF Regiment was there to protect us, we had to do guard duty sitting in a chair outside the hut all night, armed with a .303 rifle and five bullets to stop anyone from taking our missiles.

"We had a great spate of airframe snags and two of us changed four brake units in two weeks. Then we had an aircraft whose undercarriage wouldn't lower, so the pilot 'porpoised' the aircraft and they finally came down. After he landed, we did a retraction test and found that the uplock was misaligned. I had a hood seal change and a hydraulic pressure switch change, all in one day. Even though we still only had seven airframe chaps, I later went onto both first and second-line servicing.

"In June 1966 the airfield at Ndola was closed because the runway was cracking up, not for the first time, and there was no flying for about two weeks. I spent one session at Lusaka, which is where I had a start-up fire, a fairly common thing on Javs. The drop-down panel, with Dzus fasteners covered a big bay with all the hydraulics, avionics and stuff like that. After start-up, you had to duck underneath, stick your head up in this hole and check that nothing was on fire; obviously with an extinguisher standing by. So, they start engine one – you have a look, OK; start two – have a look, OK, and then you had to put the panel up, which meant you were enshrouded in aviation isopropyl nitrate (AVPIN) starter fumes. So, it was with a big breath and eyes streaming that you got under there and whacked the panel on as quickly as you could.

"One day at Lusaka they started number one, then number two. As number two started, a great sheet of flame came out of the avionics hole. Panic stations, 'Cut! Cut! Get out!' to the crew. We grabbed the fire extinguisher, stuck it in the hole, fired it off and we all legged it into the distance. The Zambian fire brigade came rocketing up and took over. What happened to the aeroplane, I can't remember.

"There was one FAW.9, XH764 coded C for Charlie, which did a wheels-up landing in May. It was sent to 103 MU at Akrotiri to have a mainplane change. The Javelin's brakes were not weak, but they had a propensity to overheat, and the wheels were made of magnesium alloy. The main undercarriage legs were prone to cracking. After the wing change this aircraft had to be ready to fly down to Ndola by 30 December. On the 28th we worked all day getting it ready, checked all the wire locking, put all the panels back on, connected all the supplies, checked the whole aircraft and then it went up for a test flight. I was in the starting party and we got it away safely. When it came back, the pilot said it was a lovely aircraft to fly. Again, we did the necessary and he went back up again for the long test flight. Two hours later it came down and went to the compass swing pan, prior to going down to Zambia. It hadn't been there more than five minutes when the starboard undercarriage leg and wheel caught fire. The nav and pilot got out and the fire brigade arrived to put the fire out. However, the airframe was Cat 3/unfit to fly as the mainplane and fuselage were badly warped and burnt. Charlie was once again in the MU for quite a long period as they had to reskin the burnt areas.

"I've no idea what caused the fire, maybe a hydraulic leak. In pre-in-flight refuelling days, the Javelins had been fitted with four long-range fuel tanks. The inboard tank was quite close to the undercarriage, and was full of fuel vapour, so we all kept a great distance from it."

> *Having been repaired again in 1966, this aircraft was fated. A year later it suffered a heavy landing at Manston, Kent while en-route to 27 MU Shawbury for storage and remained at Manston as a gate guard.*

"Because Zambia was a copper-mining country, copper dust used to get all over everything. We used to get lots of it piling up on the wings, so it was decided that we needed somebody to come and brush it all off. We had a couple of local labourer lads, and I was charged with taking one of them out to an aircraft to show him what to do. He didn't speak English, and when I got up onto the wing he wouldn't walk out onto it. I think he was just a bit frightened that it was going to snap off or something! So I had to walk out to the wingtip and bounce up and down a bit to prove that it was quite safe. I then gave him a brush and showed him what I wanted him to do, being very careful not to knock off the vortex generators that were sticking up all over the place. It was part of my pre-flight routine to walk out and check the vortex generators, the lights and the wingtips, and do a little bounce on the tip." [3]

Ken left 29 Squadron in 1967. He moved over to 56 Squadron who had arrived in Akrotiri with Lightnings. He left the RAF as a senior aircraftman (SAC) after five years, later working for 20+ years at British Airways.

BRYAN ELLIOTT – AIR RADAR

Bryan joined 29 Squadron in 1960; it was his first tour.

"When the Rhodesia crisis came about, I was very lucky to get detached from Cyprus to Zambia. The groundcrew were supposed to turn around every eight weeks or so but I was single, playing rugby for the local town (Ndola) and enjoying life. So, I volunteered to stay permanently, which suited the married guys in Cyprus who could stay at home. We had one incident when the undercarriage collapsed on one of the Javelins when landing. After I spent a few days stripping out all the radar gear from it the aircraft ended up in a children's playground in Ndola. It looked a sad sight."

Former 29 Squadron Javelin XH890 in Ndola Park. [Bryan Elliott]

> *This was XH890 M which came to grief as described on 2 June 1966. It was struck off charge as Cat 5(unrepairable) the next day and abandoned on site when the RAF detachment left for home. The remains of the aircraft were still in the children's playground well into the mid-1970s.*

"We heard there were questions being asked in the Zambian parliament about what the Javelins were doing, as nobody ever saw one flying (not surprising due to the height they were at). However, one of the aircrew took it into his head to show them and apparently went down Cairo Avenue (the main street in Lusaka) at fifth floor level. On another occasion someone stood up in the Zambian parliament and asked, why couldn't the visiting aircraft be used to aid the Zambian economy? Furthermore, he highlighted crop spraying as a possibility. Commander British Forces in Zambia (COMBRITZAM) in Lusaka then brought out a spoof modification leaflet regarding drilling holes in the rear of the ventral tanks and fitting spray nozzles!" [3]

> *Like Ken Beere, Bryan moved on to Lightnings went he left 29 Squadron.*

PULL UP A SANDBAG

NORMAN DIDWELL

"When I was attached to Amman landing strip, we had an old Arab foreman who remembered Lawrence of Arabia, and had fought with him in the Arab Revolt."

---

[1] *Meteor Boys* by Steve Bond
[2] *Shackleton Boys 1* by Steve Bond
[3] *Javelin Boys* by Steve Bond

CHAPTER FOUR

THE RAF'S LARGEST STATION – KHORMAKSAR

RAF Khormaksar (motto 'Into the Remote Places') came into existence in late 1917 when 31 Squadron detached there from India to form the Aden Flight, with a few Henry Farman F27s. They were joined the following year by 114 Squadron also with F27s, plus some BE.2es. Following a period of inactivity the station came back into use in 1927, and thereafter became increasingly busy with a variety of squadrons employed on colonial policing duties. Wartime use included convoy patrols and anti-submarine work by 203 Squadron using Blenheim Mk.4fs, 8 Squadron Vickers Vincents, and 621 Squadron with Wellingtons on Maritime Reconnaissance (MR) work.

After the war on-going operations against dissident tribes in the region ensured that Khormaksar had a major role to play, and it quickly became what was, in 1964, the largest station in the RAF. Three-quarters of Middle East Command aircraft were based at Khormaksar, with nine squadrons and three flights. It was a joint user airfield as it was also Aden's civil airport. In addition to squadrons of fighter, transport, maritime reconnaissance aircraft and helicopters, the RAF also provided airfield, navigational, meteorological and communications facilities to the civil airlines.

On 18 January 1963, against the wishes of North Yemen, the Colony of Aden was incorporated into the Federation of Arab Emirates of the South. The city became the State of Aden and the Federation was renamed the Federation of South Arabia (FSA).

RAF Khormaksar from the air. [37Aden.co.uk via Dave McCandless]

STRIKING THE TROUBLE SPOTS

8 Squadron continued to be a major player with Tempests, then Brigands, Vampires, Venoms and finally Hunters. The Bristol Brigand light bomber and ground-attack aircraft was not exactly Bristol's finest hour. It first arrived on 8 Squadron in June 1949. ***Ron Hall*** *had the misfortune to be a wireless operator on the type in the summer of that year.*

"I was on two weeks leave and when I came back, I'd been posted to 8 Squadron in Aden on Brigands. I went to Leeming to convert onto Buckmasters; that was more for the pilot really because my radios were still the same. They used to pull the aircraft out of the hangar an hour before take-off; it was so hot under that long canopy. The wings used to come off the Brigands and, not long after I had finished my tour, my pilot Fg Off Scott and his crew were killed when that happened. It wasn't one of Bristol's best.

"We were keeping watch on the Yemeni tribesmen. We used to attack their forts which were made out of camel dung – they just disintegrated. The Brigand was well armed; as well as rockets we had 20-mm cannon in the nose, and could carry bombs.

Brigand B.1 VS835 8 Squadron Khormaksar 1949. [via Richard Andrews]

It had air brakes (inflatable bags) under each wing; it was all right if both punctured, but if only one did, you'd probably had it!"

On 30 December 1949 Brigand B.1 VS839 went down without a trace off Perim Island, Aden during a night cross-country exercise. Those lost were: Fg Off Terence Scott, Nav III Peter Cross, Sig II Lionel Hayes and AC2 Dennis Mastin.

In December 1952 Vampire FB.9s began replacing the Brigands, with the last of the Brigands leaving two months later. In turn, the Vampires were replaced in 1955 by the much more capable Venoms which remained with the unit for five years.

COLIN BUTLER – PILOT

Sqn Ldr Colin Butler enlisted as a National Serviceman in September 1954. He trained on the Provost and Vampire at Ternhill and Oakington. He then went to 233 OCU Vampires at Pembrey before arriving on 8 Squadron.

FLYING THE VENOM

"As the Venom was only a single seater, I started my training on the two-seat Vampire. I converted to the Venom on the squadron. In order to do a tour after gaining my wings I transferred my commission from being a National Serviceman; this took me from two to four years' service.

Venom FB.4 8 Squadron Khormaksar, starting up at Sharjah. [Martin Stephens]

"Basically, the Venom wasn't very different from the Vampire, but it had more power and powered controls on the FB.4. We had about half FB.1s and half FB.4s. Sadly one pilot, when coming back from one of the out-stations after six months, forgot the difference between the Mk.1 and the Mk.4 and hit a hill top. That was the first casualty.

"In 1956 during the Suez Crisis, I joined 208 Squadron in Akrotiri during the Suez Crisis. I was posted to Khormaksar only to find, when I flew out from the UK, that they had all gone. Then I got a signal to come up to Cyprus. I spent a couple of days in Nicosia, waiting to be picked up by the squadron. Eventually they picked me up in a Vampire T.11. Back to Khormaksar by Christmas, and operational on the squadron by about February. That's when the real work started!

GROUND ATTACK

"Colonial policing was the generic term for what we and the Shackletons, and the Lincolns before them were doing – mostly flag waving. Routinely we flew in pairs, but occasionally as fours. We occasionally went as air liaison officers (ALO) or air contact teams. We were a single air contact team with the army when they needed airborne escorts.

"We carried various types of three-inch rockets, including a semi-armour-piercing one. However, the best one was the squash-head rocket, a great big balloon-shaped thing. Accuracy was a problem, so we spent a lot of time on the range – I got quite

Venom FB.4 8 Squadron at Sharjah armed with 'Squash Head' rockets. [Martin Stephens]

good at it. The army would call us in to attack one of the Yemeni forts, and we'd go and smash it. Bearing in mind the conditions in Aden, which were very sandy and mucky, the aeroplane had amazing reliability. However, our old-fashioned three-inch rockets were a bit hit-and-miss, whereas the two-inch ones on the Hunter were more accurate.

"In about the middle of 1957 I went up to Sharjah with another three pilots; it was my first time there. We had been sent to support the Sultan in his disagreement with Oman, and we were being used to attack forts. One or two we damaged quite badly; however, some were more solidly built and needed more effort. We were hitting them on a regular basis trying to make them listen to the Sultan's word. Izki was one fort we knocked out, but we did it in a very gentlemanly fashion and dropped them warning leaflets first. Nizwa was a difficult one and their occupants used to go into the hills to sit and watch us, coming home after we'd gone. The forts were next to mosques, which was very tricky because we had to miss the mosques! We also had to 'investigate' any vehicles seen around the area.

"Return small-arms fire in Sharjah was insignificant, we were seeing more from the Yemenis. From time to time I was hit by their 12.5-mm Russian machine guns. Fortunately, they didn't do much damage. The Venom was so simple, it was built around the engine which has a centrifugal compressor; this was much more robust and workmanlike than the later axial-flow engines. That was just as well because we were operating off sand runways at Sharjah. We were going off four aircraft at a time, and by the time we had all taken off we'd moved 20 tons or so of sand off the runway. The local workmen queued up behind us with 3-ton trucks full of sand to put it back as soon as we'd taken off so that it was fit for us to land on again. Those of us who went up to Sharjah hit the headlines in the local UK papers referring to the 'four-man war in Oman', and there was a photo of Duncan Sandys shaking our hands after a sortie. That caused great excitement in my family – my picture in the local paper.

CASUALTIES

"Whilst I was there, I think we had 16 casualties in two years (that was the squadron's established pilot strength, and obviously we got replacements). The worst loss was at the end of my tour when Flt Lt David Foster was doing a bit of 'colonial policing' near Dhala, a town inside the Aden Protectorate, and right on the border with Yemen. We think he either got hit by one of the Yemini guns or his engine failed, but either way he bailed out. His ejection seat worked perfectly but he came down in Yemen, where he was captured by Yemeni soldiers. They took him to Sanaa, the capital, where he was paraded in the streets; then they executed him.

"Most of the losses were basically pilot error or simple accidents, although some aircraft were shot down. One pilot was on the range when his engine suffered a flameout. As the range was close to the airfield, he was able to glide back and land – he had been hit. There were several occasions like that, where they were possibly picking up ricochets. Some flew into mountain tops, possibly caught out in FB.1s without the powered flying controls of the FB.4. As we were having too many losses,

Venom FB.4 WR550 8 Squadron belly-landed by Dave Foster after being hit by ricochets from his own ammunition, 22 August 1957. [Peter Goodwin]

I was the last first-tour pilot to be accepted by the squadron. Subsequently they all came in as second-tourists from Second Allied Tactical Air Force (ATAF), or from Hong Kong or Singapore.

"Fortunately, I didn't have any hairy moments, though I was hit a few times. You didn't realise you'd been hit until you landed, unless it went through you or your cockpit! There were holes through the wings and minor leaks, but we had very good self-sealing wing tanks that did their job pretty well, so long as the opposition weren't using exploding bullets.

OPERATIONS

"During an army-sponsored operation in the eastern Aden Protectorate, we were flying very low at about 100 feet (you could get away with it there) when my friend managed to knock the aerial off an armoured car. We were just screaming overhead, trying to impress the rebels. 'Do what you're told by the provincial governor or you get our attention!' A lot of target requests came from the army, but we often sent our own Meteor FR.9s to photograph the targets first. That way we knew exactly what we were aiming for, rather than trying to find it.

"Jebel Akhdar in Oman was an operation in support of the SAS who had moved into the area in support of the Sultan. We flew in to support the SAS who were climbing up to Jebel Akhdar to attack the rebels who were in a particularly well-guarded and fortified cave. With a 10,000ft mountain ahead of you, it was like flying into a brick wall effectively – and pretty steep at that. We came in at about 45 degrees to fire our rockets, then immediately turned and pulled hard otherwise we would slam into the rocks.

VENOM PERFORMANCE

"The Venom's performance in those temperatures could be a bit short of 'grunt'. I got used to it as I had nothing else to compare it with. It was a very simple aircraft, made of plywood and with this great big engine behind you. Fuel was a bit short, and for example we had to refuel twice on the way up to Sharjah from Khormaksar – we'd stop at Beihan and Masirah, though we did have underwing tanks which we sometimes took.

"Sadly, I lost the best friend I had out there, Brian Bachelor. He was killed in an accident on an air test at Sharjah when unfortunately, he didn't pull out of a dive and went straight into the shore by Sharjah village. There was nothing left, no recognisable bits of aircraft or anything. I had flown that same aircraft on the previous sortie and I could smell hydraulic fluid during a rocket attack. You had to 'bunt' slightly and I smelt it then, so I declared the aircraft u/s. They did some work on it, then Brian took it up on air test – he didn't come back. At the Board of Inquiry, they asked me whether the fluid smell was hot or cold, but I really couldn't remember as I was breathing through an oxygen mask. Brian was a good pilot, and we shared a room for a long time – I missed him a lot. Like me he was a flying officer, but he was just ahead of me having trained in Canada and was on an 8-12-year commission.

"In central Oman, not far from the port of Misra, there was a huge rock-built fort. It was so well built that it would have taken an atomic weapon to remove it. As it was just in the desert, we caught a few rebels out in the open – but only one had a gun. The Venom had four 20-mm cannons but, having just attacked the fort nearby, I'd almost run out of ammunition and I had only a few shells left and I missed him. I didn't half have him dancing around on the ground though!

"I thoroughly enjoyed my time on 8 Squadron. It was a wonderful tour and for a young man it was magic. The only thing was the lack of women in Aden – even the camels were looking attractive! It wasn't a good place for a social life, so I used to go into the mess bar after dinner and get 'pie-eyed'. I left the squadron in September 1958 to come back to the UK."

In September 1958 Colin moved over to Shackletons, on 42 and 205 Squadrons, followed by Nimrods with 203 Squadron at Luqa. He retired in January 1991.

NICK VON BERG – PILOT

"I was on 8 Squadron on Venom 4s and just prior to the Suez Crisis we were attached to Habbaniyah for armament practice. There was an Iraqi squadron equipped with Venom 1s also doing weapons training. The Mk.1 had spring ailerons, which arguably were more suited to accurate weapons tracking than our powered ailerons which gave us a higher rate of roll. Their crew room was adjacent to ours, and occasionally we got to meet them. Air-to-air gunnery was done with a 30-feet long flag towed by a Meteor. This was fired on by two separate pairs of Venoms with different-coloured shells. It was then dropped over the airfield, and the hits recorded before they were marked with red paint for re-use. However, we could not help noticing our neighbours were not bothering to mark the hits, so the next four would get the same score as the previous four even though they may have missed it. No doubt lots were drawn to fly the final details. Just then Nasser seized the Suez Canal. When we conjectured with our Iraqi neighbours, that we could be up against one another if a conflict arose, it produced an angry response. One pilot said, 'We will hack you out of the skies'. I thought to myself, 'not by cheating on your air-to-air scores you won't Abdullah!'

"I was detailed for low flying, which was done in the eastern part of Cyprus just prior to the Suez Crisis. There's a lighthouse on the south coast, and I thought I would do a 'split-arse' turn round it before going inland to the low-flying area. Unbeknown to me there was another Venom with the same plan coming the other way. We met (or nearly met) at a closing speed of about 1,000 mph. I yanked the stick, and we missed one another by what seemed like a coat of paint. The Venom 4 was equipped with a G meter (the maximum was supposed to be 6.5G) – I pulled 9G! Why the wings didn't fall off (as they did on the Mk.1), we did not know. Somewhat shaken, I flew a very low-key detail. On return to Akrotiri I snagged her for over-stress, and then repaired to the mess for a stiff one where another officer asked how I was. I explained that I had just missed another aircraft from a head-on collision, he replied 'How do you do, my name is Leckie-Thompson'. He was the other pilot, and was later to achieve fame for his exploits in the Harrier. Apropos the Venom I over-stressed; the groundcrew had a checklist to spot cracks in the wings, and the aircraft was cleared for service that day. The Mk.1 had a history of wings falling off, and De Havilland was particularly keen to see the same fate did not befall the Mk.4.

"Pete Goodwin, who was with me at Driffield, joined us on 8 Squadron after a spell on 32 in Malta. He got engaged to his girlfriend when she came through Aden on her way to India. When her liner sailed, Pete and his number two, 'Titch' Kennedy, caught up with it and beat it up! Titch was sure their numbers had been taken and reported it to HQ Aden. However, Dorothy, Pete's fiancée, charmed the captain who asked her to join his table whilst he overlooked the whole matter.

"I was flown into the Eastern Aden Protectorate as air liaison officer, with a wireless-equipped Land Rover, to join a force supporting a sheikh loyal to the Raj. He was being threatened by a neighbouring sheikh. The Levies were commanded by a colonel, assisted by a rather pompous subaltern from a cavalry regiment. I had brought a case of lager, and the colonel a bottle of whisky. Our pompous friend, stating that the East Aden Protectorate was dry, had nothing to share as a sundowner so I offered him some of my grog, which he took a taste to!

"On reaching our destination, camping on a tall building, we were visited by a pair from the squadron who enquired how things were going. I told them all was

OK, but that there was a 'pongo' drinking all my grog. The reply was to be expected, 'Tough Nick, we'll have a cold one on your account when we get back'. My reply was unprintable. As luck would have it the station commander was in the ops room when they were being debriefed. When asked if they had contacted me, they relayed what I had said. He then asked if there was a Shackleton going up that way the following day. Having been assured that there was, he said to tell the dispatcher to draw a case of beer on my account and have it dropped to me. The following day the sound of four Griffon engines announced the arrival of a member of the 'Kipper Fleet'. I retrieved my package and on opening it there was a note: 'Dear Nick please return the package and the parachute – you may drink the beer!' The subaltern said, 'Do you mean to say you chaps in the RAF just call up on the radio when you run out of grog?' 'Yes Old Boy, we are organised!'"

After he left the RAF Nick became a VC10 captain with East African Airways.

PETER GOODWIN – PILOT

A former RAF apprentice, Pete switched over to aircrew and, as Nick has said, first flew the Venom with 32 Squadron in Malta in 1955 prior to joining 8 Squadron.

Peter Goodwin 8 Squadron, Aden 1957. [Peter Goodwin]

"I was just about the most junior guy on 8 Squadron, and was with them on Suez in December 1956 – it was exciting. We were on ops all the time. I got shot up once, though nobody seemed to think much of it. I came back streaming fuel, with a hole in my wing and a fuel pipe hanging out of it, the engine cowlings were shot off and the rocket rails were gone.

"One thing, which was really awful, was when there were certain areas identified for our attacks; they gave us dreadful, khaki-coloured mosaic maps. These areas were identified because one of our informers said that a named village was responsible for an attack on a convoy going north. The day before we were to strike, Shackletons overflew the village and dropped leaflets telling them to get out. Our briefing was that anything that moved should be shot at. This even included camels! But if you saw a lady running across a field you had to use a bit of discretion – we were given *carte blanche.*

"I can't remember leading a formation but we used to say, 'Right, we'll come in from the west, go tactical formation starboard' and then you'd pull up, one after another, and go down and plaster the place. We had a competition once with Joe Blythe, an ex-career guy who'd been in Korea and had a DFC and Bar, and he always beat everyone: front guns, rockets and bombs – he was always on top. Initially on these raids up into the highlands, they didn't shoot back, but then they started to – which we thought was very unfair. Once we found there was a high velocity anti-aircraft gun in a cave on the side of a mountain. There were four of us, with the boss leading. After pulling up he said, 'Put 'em there' and proceeded to fire a rocket straight into the cave – I couldn't believe it. After a while those strikes became reasonably routine, but we did lose some people.

"Every so often we had to take turns being air liaison officer. We'd go out with the army, in a Land Rover with the radio on the back, to Riyadh or up-country from Aden. The army would attack somewhere, and then they'd call in the aircraft. I would put a cross down on the ground and then radio the pilots 'a mile and a half north of that – plaster it!' I would simply do what the army asked. However, one day one of our pilots was in the area and I asked him to do a fly-by. I was standing on a rock and he bloody nearly hit me! (*See centre photo spread*) We didn't always have an air liaison officer; sometimes we went out and did a strike without one, but it was so difficult navigating. All we had was distance-measuring equipment (DME), and mosaic maps with just contours on them.

"There was a good atmosphere on the squadron. I arrived in Aden in January 1957 and when I got off the aircraft, I said to the bloke who met me, 'Bloody hell,

Air liaison officer and his wireless-equipped Land Rover. [Peter Goodwin]

this weather's absolutely ridiculous'. He said, 'You wait 'til the summer!' You were soaked in perspiration all the time. They used to put a sun canopy over the Venom's cockpit, and we had air conditioned flying suits; but they didn't work until you were airborne."

Peter took advantage of the early release opportunity. This followed Duncan Sandys notorious Defence White Paper predicting the end of fighter aircraft. He joined the Fleet Requirements Unit down at Hurn, flying Sea Hawks and Sea Furies, but then re-joined the RAF to fly Javelins.

Effective though it was by the late 1950s the Venom was getting rather outdated. So in January 1960 the first Hunter FGA.9s arrived in Aden to re-equip 8 Squadron. With frequent detachments to Bahrain/Muharraq, Masirah and Sharjah, this set-up lasted until 21 December 1971 when the squadron was disbanded at Sharjah. Sharing the ground-attack task was the other half of the area's Hunter Wing, 208 Squadron, which also acquired Hunters to replace its Venoms at Eastleigh. Runway limitations at Eastleigh caused the squadron to move to Khormaksar in 1961 and Muharraq in 1964. On 10 September 1971 208 disbanded.

8 Squadron Hunter FGA.9 XE618 with Ray Byatt marshalling Bill Shepherd, Khormaksar 1964. [Ray Deacon]

THE GROUNDCREW

RAY DEACON – ELECTRONICS/AIR

After two years servicing Vampires at the Central Flying School (CFS), Junior Technician (J/T) Ray left Little Rissington and joined 30 fellow airmen for a voyage out to Aden aboard HMT Nevasa *on her last sailing as a troopship.*

SUN, SAND, HEAT AND FLIES

"On disembarkation at Steamer Point those destined for Khormaksar were taken by RAF transport to the airfield, where they were assigned transit accommodation to await unit allocations. I was assigned to 8 Squadron and moved into the aptly named Hunter block, one of three newly constructed blocks comprising four-man air conditioned rooms. With hindsight I need not have worried about the sun or the heat as, after an initial month or so of discomfort and gradual loss of my 'moonie' image, I got used to it. 'Don't forget to take your salt tablets' was the regular advice but, having discarded my lunch outside the mess, after the first couple of pills I gave them up as a bad job. Perhaps the most difficult aspects of getting used to life in South Arabia were the flies and being in a constant sweat; continually mopping one's face, arms and hands with the ever-present sweat-towel.

"My whole tour in Aden was spent on 8 Squadron at Khormaksar. Located at the eastern extremity of the airfield right next to the civilian airport, the squadron operated 14 Hunter FGA.9s for fighter/ground attack, four FR.10s for fighter/

photo-reconnaissance and a couple of two-seat T.7 trainers. The other end of the pan was allocated to a second Hunter squadron, 208, equipped with 12 FGA.9s and a solitary T.7. We were tasked with supporting the multifarious British and Arab army units policing, not only in the Aden Protectorate, but the whole Middle East Command area. This encompassed Kenya 1,000 miles to the south, to Bahrain Island some 1,300 miles to the north; this heavy responsibility was shared by the two Hunter units.

GULF CRISIS

"Tranquillity in the region was a rare phenomenon. At the time of my arrival in April 1962 there was relative calm in the command area; much of the flying activity being devoted to training and familiarisation of new pilots in the operational arena. However back in the previous July things could hardly have been more different. General Qasim of Iraq had aligned his forces along the borders of Kuwait in readiness for invasion and capture of the lucrative oilfields. The British Government ordered 8 Squadron to fly up to Kuwait and prepare to defend the tiny kingdom from Iraqi attack. The Hunters of 208 Squadron which was stationed some 250 miles from Kuwait at Eastleigh in Kenya, were ordered up to Bahrain to support 8 Squadron should an attack occur. A number of Canberra units were dispatched from Europe to bases on Cyprus and Sharjah, whilst a third Hunter squadron, 43, moved from Leuchars to Cyprus. This left the errant general in no doubt as to the British intent should he dare cross the border. In addition, troop numbers in the Gulf area were rapidly increased with deployments from Europe and other Middle East bases. In the event the general backed down, and the situation soon returned to normal – well as normal as normal is for the area.

"Concerned that a total withdrawal of British forces from the Gulf might tempt Iraq into making a quick strike, the decision was taken to maintain a squadron of Hunters at Bahrain on permanent standby, together with a pair of 13 Squadron photo-reconnaissance Canberra PR.9s from Cyprus. The former was achieved by rotating a detachment of 8 and 208 Squadron aircraft from Khormaksar to Bahrain on a two-monthly basis, and this was standard routine by the time I arrived. Every other month Hunters from one of the Squadrons would depart Khormaksar for its two-month stint in Bahrain. The groundcrews flying up in a Beverley, Argosy, or even a Britannia if one happened to be passing through, and passing the returning squadron on the way. Although 'blessed' with permanently sunny skies the climate in the Gulf was quite different from that in Aden. It was much hotter and humid in the summer, yet cool enough to warrant a change into standard working blue uniform in winter. During these eight-week detachments the opportunity was taken for the Squadrons to spend two weeks down at Sharjah, on the air-to-ground range at Jeb-a-Jib.

LIFE ON THE LINE

"Because of the intense heat of the afternoon the normal working day at Khormaksar was from 07:00 to 13:00, followed by lunch and a two-hour siesta. This routine could change at any moment, and often did so when Hunter support was called for from up-country army units. Assigned to the aircraft line I was one of a handful of air wireless mechanics. My job was to ensure that the radio equipment on each Hunter was in good working order before, between and after each sortie. Inspecting the aerials required a challenging technique in order to clamber onto the wing. However, it did not take a newcomer long to master it if blistering of the knees on a hot drop tank was to be avoided. The knack was to stand back some ten paces from the front of the wing, then running at it, bouncing one knee on the drop tank while hauling oneself up and onto the wing using one hand on the 'saw-tooth' leading edge. Everyone developed their own technique, and a mistimed leap made for good spectator sport as the body ended up in a crumpled painful heap. In a Bahraini summer the metal surfaces were so hot that it was possible to fry an egg on a Hunter wing; one intrepid pilot taking 20 minutes to prove the point.

"One of the hardest jobs as a radio mechanic was working out on the pan in the cramped space of the radio bay – temperatures could reach 140 °F. It was so small that you could not turn or twist your body once inside. However, changing one of the two 30-lb VHF sets was not so much of a problem as they could be lowered on your shoulder, as you lowered yourself down and out of the bay. It was a different story when these were superseded with a single, much larger, 56-lb Collins ARC52 UHF unit. Changing one of these was a real struggle, the sweat literally pouring down, but it no doubt contributed to our general fitness.

"The radio/radar guys may have had it somewhat easier than some trades; the armourers, engines and airframes guys in particular, as their jobs demanded spending much longer in physical contact with the aircraft than us. In particular the energy and enthusiasm of the armourers deserve a special mention. They changed gun-packs and loaded rockets with great gusto when under operational conditions and when on air-to-ground range practice. Working in teams each would try to beat the 'record' for changing a gun-pack which, if I recall correctly, was a little over eight minutes. I thought I would try and help once and found lowering the empty pack onto the trolley quite easy, but winching a fully armed pack back up to the locking points was a different ball game! Nearing the top, arms aching, I ran out of energy and received a volume of verbal stick for stopping, thus forcing the armourers to await my recovery.

FLIGHT SAFETY

"From the first day of training the importance of flight safety is drummed into every airman. On front-line squadrons, where aircraft were regularly armed with live weapons, additional precautions were necessary. The start-up procedure on a Hunter was straightforward, but an alert mind and an awareness of what was going on around you was essential. One airman was assigned to each Hunter. Whilst the pilot proceeded with his external pre-flight checks the airman would check the area around his aircraft for clearance of ground equipment, and that a ladder was attached to the aircraft. With the pilot seated in the cockpit the airman aligned the parachute and ejection seat straps over the pilot's shoulders and, when requested, handed him his helmet and bone-dome, before plugging the radio connector into its socket. Finally, and again upon request, the ejection seat safety pin was removed, shown to the pilot, and stowed in a pocket on the side of the seat. On climbing down the ladder was removed and positioned in a safe place on the pan. A short wait then ensued as the pilot carried out his internal pre-flight checks.

"Once ready to start the pilot gave a quick twirl of his forefinger and, having checked that everything was clear behind, the airman reciprocated. On the press of the start button the automated engine-start sequence began. The highly volatile AVPIN fuel, used to start the FGA.9 and FR.10, habitually ignited the acrid exhaust gases as they exited from a duct under the fuselage. This had been the cause of several starter-bay fires, and the starter-bay door was left open until the starting cycle finished and the AVPIN gases had dispersed. An asbestos glove would be used by the airman to pat out any flames issuing from the duct. The starter-bay door was then closed, and the airman stood ready to remove the nosewheel chock before walking to a suitable point to marshal the aircraft out.

A 'PHANTOM' ON THE TRIGGER

"Sometime during the early period of Hunter operations in Aden the cannon on an armed Hunter, parked on the pan, fired off several rounds across the Khormaksar runway. The shells hit the wall of the barracks on the opposite side of the airfield.

Fortunately, there were no aircraft taking off or landing at the time and no one was hurt in the barracks, but the outcome could have had more serious implications. Reality soon dawned that no-one was working on or near the aircraft at the time. A hasty investigation discovered that the excessive temperatures had caused a short break in the gun-firing circuit. A microswitch, located in the port undercarriage bay, broke the circuit between the invertors supplying power to the gun-firing circuit when the undercarriage was down, so the guns should not have been able to fire! As double insurance a modification was introduced whereby a safety plug was inserted into the same gun-firing circuit; it was known as the master armament safety break (MASB). Access to the plug was via a small panel under the port wing, directly behind the engine air intake. It became the responsibility of an assigned armourer to stand by the peri-track and disconnect MASBs on aircraft as they taxied in, and connect them again on the peri-track as they taxied out. An order was also issued that armed Hunters must be identified by placing a red-painted ammunition box in front of the nose, which was attached via a rope to the top of the nosewheel door. Personnel were prohibited from walking in front of armed aircraft.

"Despite all the precautions accidents still occurred. On one occasion a Sgt armourer, who was walking behind the line of Hunters deep in thought, stepped directly into the jet blast of an aircraft about to taxi out. The force flung him across the pan, which in itself did not cause injury, but the side of his face quickly reddened and blistered. He was rushed to sick quarters for treatment, and on return to work a few days later the 'toasted' half of his face was jet black! This earned him the nickname of 'black and white minstrel' after the popular TV programme of the time.

TIME TO RELAX

"After an afternoon's kip, and with the heat of the day relenting, it was off to Steamer Point to haggle with shopkeepers in The Crescent. We would also take a dip in the pool or one of the shark-net protected beaches, or a game of tennis, football or rugby for the more energetic. Afterwards we wound down with a can or more of 'Slops' (Allsopps lager) in the Camel Club.

"All that changed in September 1962 when, following repeated strafing attacks on villages close to the Yemen border by Yemeni air force Mig 15s, the decision was taken for the Hunter squadrons to fly dawn to dusk patrols along the border as a deterrent. With the quieter times confined to history and with one of the two Hunter squadrons up in Bahrain, it was left to the squadron at Khormaksar to maintain the border vigil. Pilots and groundcrews were split into shifts, one shift starting at 06:00

and finishing at 13:00 with the second overlapping from 12:00 to 19:00. With the new routine two Hunters took off at dawn and flew north-east up the coast towards the Yemen then turning west to begin their lengthy patrol along the mountainous and indistinct border before returning to Khormaksar from the north-west. Further pairs would take off at hourly intervals, thus ensuring that there was at least one pair in the vicinity of the border at all times. Fully armed, and equipped with long-range 230-gallon underwing fuel tanks, a round trip would take approximately 1½ hours. Additional Hunters were maintained on armed standby, ready for dispatch at a moment's notice to support army units operating up-country. Needless to say, there was no time to get bored!

"During this period the pressure on both air and groundcrews was intense, with the high workload taking its toll on both man and machine. With only half the number of pilots and airmen on site at any one time, aircraft unserviceability became critical for a while. Relief arrived with a detachment of eight Hunters from the UK, 1 Squadron arriving at Khormaksar in late October 1962. A new work pattern evolved whereby 8 Squadron started work at midday, continuing through to dusk on day 1, and from 06:00 the following morning until 13:00. 1 Squadron started work at midday on day two and became the operational squadron for the next 24 hours. And thus it continued, alternating day by day. The system worked very well, but after a month in the desert, and its crews' tans suitably honed, 1 Squadron departed for home. This left 8 Squadron to revert to the split-shift system. In January 1963, 54 Squadron brought its Hunters out to Aden for a month's detachment; bringing short term relief for 208 Squadron, whilst 8 Squadron moved up to Bahrain on its two-month detachment. It was not until March that a solution was found – the permanent transfer of 43 Squadron's Hunters from Nicosia, Cyprus, to Khormaksar. Once the squadron had settled in detachments to Bahrain occurred every four months instead of every two.

HEAD FOR HEIGHTS

"Up in Bahrain the NAAFI was the hub of an airman's social life, and many an evening was spent sipping canned Tiger beer. On one particular detachment, in December 1963, the Khormaksar (8 Squadron) and Cyprus (13 Squadron) contingents held a joint Christmas Eve party – by the end everyone was 'two-sheets-to-the-wind'! Having decided to awaken the sleeping camp we staggered round the billeted area giving our rendition of raunchy songs and carols. On reaching the station's 50-foot-high water tower one bright spark suggested we climb it to continue our serenade from the top. So off we went one by one up the ladder. Within a few minutes a couple of 'snoops' (military policemen) appeared below demanding we come down, or face the consequences. A few choice words had the desired effect, and they soon disappeared out of sight. Walking past the tower a day or so later, it dawned on us how lucky we were that no one had fallen off the three-foot-wide ledge encircling it – there were no safety rails!

A QUICK DASH AROUND THE PROTECTORATE

"In February 1964, with only two months of my two-year tour remaining, I achieved my dream of flying in a Hunter T.7. During my time in Aden not a single airman had experienced a flight in one. So SAC 'Taff' John and I took advantage of a unit 'bash' to ask our squadron commander, Sqn Ldr Tam Syme, if it would be possible for airmen to experience a trip in a T.7. He saw no reason why not, and that he would bear it in mind. Not long afterwards a policy of offering airmen a flight in the right-hand seat, two months before their tourex, was implemented – thank you Tam, we very much appreciated it.

"In January 1964, 'Taff' became the first 8 Squadron airman to savour the delights of a trip in a Hunter, and my turn came early the following month. With Fg Off Sid Bottom at the controls, and me in the right-hand seat, XL613 Z took to the clear blue skies in the late afternoon of 14 February. Wheels up and keeping low we flew north-east along the sandy coast for a while. We passed a customs post and village on the way before climbing to 10,000ft or so for some aerobatics. Sid showed me how to loop and barrel roll before letting me loose. I'd been taught how to

Ray Deacon going flying in a Hunter T.7 Khormaksar, 14 February 1964. [Ray Deacon]

do both on Vampire T.11s by instructors while based with CFS, so I had some idea of what was required. My efforts were not as successful as those in the Vampire, but nevertheless it was fun and I enjoyed having a go.

"Sid then suggested we do some 'wadi-bashing', which sounded exciting, and so off we headed for the mountainous region towards the north of the protectorate. I found it surprising that some of the peaks here rose to more than 7,000 feet. My 'driver' clearly knew the region like the back of his hand. We hugged the sandy valley floors, flying at around 500 knots, the steeply sloping escarpments rising high above on either side. The roar of the Avon engine must have echoed long after we had gone. I had been quietly hoping for a more sedate ride so as to take photographs. On enquiring as to why we were flying so fast, exciting as it was, Sid calmly elucidated that it was to avoid being shot at! A plausible riposte and I settled back to watch in awe as we weaved in and out of the high-sided wadis. One startling sight that sticks in my mind was a narrow u-shaped rock formation jutting out from the walled sides; it narrowed the gap through which we had to fly. Once through, the valley floor dropped away a thousand feet or more. Down we went to continue our thrilling high-speed ride through the mountains. Suddenly we were out in the open, flying low and fast over a flat landscape endowed with a generous covering of green vegetation, and so we headed south and home to Khormaksar. On nearing Khormaksar I asked Sid if we could climb up, and fly around the volcano in order to take some shots of Aden and Shamsan; this he kindly did. After one of the most exhilarating experiences of my life we touched down, and I flopped forward in my harness as the brake parachute deployed and the wheel brakes were applied. Thank you Sid.

THE ATTACK ON FORT HARIB – MY SMALL PART

"Shortly before the end of my tour Yemeni MiGs flew a number of raids across the border. In one of them a frontier guard post and a village near Beihan, were attacked with rockets and bombs by an armed helicopter and two MiGs. Immediate retaliation was ordered and, at 03:30 on the morning of 28 March 1964, we were rudely awoken by the dulcet tones of the duty sergeant ordering us to report to squadron HQ immediately; no shaving, no washing, just get dressed and board the transport waiting outside. Fortunately the rare sobriety of the previous evening meant that hangovers were few, and apart from lack of sleep most of us had clear heads. As we were driven away the realisation soon dawned on us that we had never been called out in the middle of the night before, so something special was happening.

"On arrival at the pan several pilots could be seen talking to each other as they moved between the various offices. No explanation was given to us however until 'Chiefy' called us together. He told us to prepare seven FGA.9s, two in reserve, and two 1417 Flight FR.10s, one in reserve, for an important operation. 43 Squadron personnel had also been called in to prepare five FGA.9s, one in reserve, for a joint operation. With pre-flight checks completed those of us that were free assisted the riggers and armourers with the removal of the outer drop-tank pylons, and fitting of additional rocket rails. This was a lengthy and fiddly task on the poorly lit pan. An hour or so later the rocket trolleys were towed along the back of the line and, while some helped with the mounting and connection of these high-explosive projectiles, others stuffed warning leaflets in the wing flaps of the Mk.10s and two Mk.9s.

"The plan was that two Hunters would depart some 15 minutes ahead of the main force and, while flying fast and low over the target, lower their flaps to release warning leaflets onto the target. The lead aircraft of the pair, usually an FGA.9, would be closely pursued by an FR.10 taking photographs of the leaflets being released as evidence of a warning. By the time the inhabitants below had read the instructions they would have 13 or so minutes to vacate the area, or face certain

Rocket practice. 8 Squadron's Larry Forster (left) and Fred Rawson (right) on their last day, Khormaksar 1963. [Ray Deacon]

oblivion. The main force, usually comprising four to eight FGA.9s, would then carry out the attack with 30-mm HE (high explosive) cannon and rocket fire, while the leaflet-carrying aircraft maintained top cover. Once the attack was over the FR.10 would make a final sweep to photograph the damage inflicted on the target.

"As dawn broke the first two pilots, Flt Lt Peter Lewis in an FR.10 and Fg Off Sid Bottom in an FGA.9, walked out to the line hut and signed the F700s for their particular aircraft, both fitted with gun-packs but no rockets. Once strapped in they started up, and taxied out for take-off. I was assigned to start one of the eight main force FGA.9s which was being flown by a young-looking Flt Lt Martin Johnson. He was very excited and eager to complete his pre-flight checks, almost running up the ladder and jumping into the cockpit. I handed him his parachute and seat straps, waited until he was safely belted in, removed the ejection seat safety pin and stowed it away before removing the ladder. At a given signal from Wg Cdr John Jennings, in the lead aircraft, eight pilots hit their starting 'tits'. However, only seven AVPIN starters burst into life; the Avons lighting up within a few seconds. Why only seven? Sods law; if something can go wrong it will, and it did. The starter on my aircraft failed. Having applied a couple of hefty thumps on the starter panel relay boxes with the handle of my screwdriver, in the vane hope it might fire at the second attempt, I gave the signal to try once more – but it failed again!

"In an instant the straps were flying over Martin's shoulders, and he was standing on the seat ready for the ladder to be re-attached. He climbed out and sped to a spare aircraft, with me in hot pursuit. As he clambered in the other Hunters began to taxi out, and between the two of us he was belted-up in record time. Safety pin out, ladder away, a twirl of the forefinger and a welcoming blast from the AVPIN starter, closely followed by the healthy roar of the Avon. It could hardly have reached idling speed before he throttled-up and raced out onto the taxiway. By this time the others were accelerating down the runway on their take-off runs, while he must have reached a similar speed on his way to the threshold. Round the corner and onto the runway with the Avon seemingly at full power throughout, then off he went in pursuit of the rest who were disappearing into the distant haze.

"Did he catch them? Of course he did, and the attack was executed precisely as planned. Photographs taken by the FR.10 before and after the raid revealed that the stone-built fort was virtually destroyed, as were an anti-aircraft gun and a number of vehicles. So good were the photographs that the warning leaflets could be clearly seen lying in and around the fort. The attack had the desired effect, incursions by Yemeni aircraft ceased thereafter – at least for the time being.

TOUREX

"All-in-all with ten months in Bahrain, three weeks in Kenya to cover a rebellion by the country's army and a month home on leave, my two-year tour flew by. Come April 1964 my time was up. The camaraderie and family spirit on the squadron had made it a much more bearable experience than anticipated and, having survived the sun, heat, sand and flies, I could now look forward to the sanity of life in the UK. So I thought. After two years in a faraway land where the locals spoke foreign, the beer was tolerable and the climate unbearable, my posting came through – Valley, on Anglesey – where the locals spoke foreign, there was no beer on Sundays and the climate was 'iffy'. What had I done wrong?!"

FIGHTER RECONNAISSANCE

From early 1951 the fighter reconnaissance role in the region was filled by 208 Squadron with Meteor FR.9s based at Abu Sueir. In March 1956 the squadron moved to Akrotiri with a detachment at Khormaksar. It returned to Cyprus in March 1958 and re-equipped with Hunters. Thereafter the fighter reconnaissance role at Khormaksar was fulfilled by a handful of Meteor FR.9s, operated by the Aden Protectorate Reconnaissance Flight, also referred to as simply the FR Flight. These were replaced by the Hunter FR.10. As Ray mentioned, 8 Squadron had a mixture of FGA.9 and FR.10 Hunters until the latter were formed into a separate fighter/reconnaissance unit, 1417 Flight.

PETER LEWIS – PILOT

Flt Lt Peter Lewis was posted to 8 Squadron on 17 June 1962 from Aberdeen University Air Squadron at Dyce.

"Some time around the end of March 1963 Wg Cdr John Jennings (JJ), (OC Tactical Wing Khormaksar), sent for me and announced that the Hunter FR.10s were to be hived off 8 Squadron to form 1417 Flight, and that I was to command it. I would be given the five Hunters, the four other recce-trained pilots, and some dozen groundcrew drawn from the three fighter/ground-attack squadrons (8, 43 and 208).

"The pilots were Johnny Morris, a veteran from flying Mustangs in the South African Air Force in the Korean War; Jim Dymond, a pilot attack instructor; Tony Rimmer, a past member of the Aden Protectorate Recce Flight (APRF) which had flown Meteor FR.9s in the late 1950s, and Geoff Timms, a solid, quiet, ex-Halton

1417 Flight pilots Roger Pyrah, Johnny Morris, Peter Lewis, Jim Dymond, and Geoff Timms, Khormaksar 1964. [Pete Lewis]

apprentice. We were all over six feet; all 30 or over; all married with children; and all were 2nd or 3rd tour pilots. All the groundcrew were very experienced on the Hunter, and were those that the squadrons didn't want because they were difficult to manage!

"So we had it all; a qualified flying instructor/instrument rating examiner (QFI/IRE) – me, a pilot attack instructor, someone who knew a lot about aircraft maintenance, and most importantly, someone who had seen real combat and knew a bit about recce against opposition. We also had a set of highly competent groundcrew – who liked to work as individuals – co-ordinated by an extremely wise warrant officer who was a Fitter 1 in his time.

"The first task was to get the FR.10s back into shape. The FR.10 was undoubtedly the most beautiful of the Hunters. It weighed less than the FGA.9s, which had to carry ballast to keep their centre of gravity in the right place when carrying a load of external weaponry, and its mark of Avon engine gave a little more thrust than the FGA.9 engine – it was a thoroughbred. 8 Squadron had used these lovely aircraft as 'hacks', scorning them because they were not equipped to fire rockets or drop bombs, they had no DME, and worst of all had a funny instrument layout – the compass was where the artificial horizon should be and vice versa. The radio compasses didn't work and the 230-gallon drop tanks, (the contents of which could be incorporated into the internal fuel gauges), were rarely fitted as they incurred minor flight limitations which clashed with ground-attack manoeuvres. The cameras were a mess as many were polluted with sand which scratched the negatives, and some of the nose camera lenses had been sand blasted because their protective 'eyelids' had not been serviced regularly. Last, (but by no means least), the harmonisation of the guns was way out on most of the aircraft, and the switches which allowed two or all four guns to fire were 'iffy'. So there was a lot of work for the groundcrew. The warrant officer said it would take at least a fortnight's damned hard work to get those lovely jets back to the thoroughbred status they deserved. Which was a blessing in disguise as we reckoned that we needed at least that time to get the rest of the flight into shape. We were allocated a drop tank store as our accommodation. With a lot of help from the station 'works and bricks' we did DIY and set to building partitions to give us a groundcrew room, a pilot's crew room, an office for the engineering warrant officer, a little store, and somewhat against my wishes an office for the commanding officer – 'we don't want him breathing down our necks all the time'. I got the nickname 'Prussian Pete', and some months later two little notices appeared on the door to that office; one read 'Be reasonable, do it his way', and the other 'Diplomacy Department. He says and does the nastiest things in the nicest way!'

"To facilitate all this, there was some distribution of duties. Geoff Timms kept a close eye on how the preparation of the FR.10s was coming along; Jim Dymond, who was a very good artist and photographer as well as a photo instructor, was put in charge of harmonising the guns and getting the cameras running properly. He and the groundcrew came up with the idea of keeping the cameras in plastic bags in an old fridge – a primitive but effective 'dust free environmental control'!

"I annexed one of the wing's Hunter T.7s whenever possible and flew with each pilot on a 'QFI/IRE' check ride. A bit laughable really as they were all damned good flyers, but it did demonstrate that we could follow as well as read the dreaded 'Air Staff Instructions'. Johnny Morris meanwhile gave us all a very hard time on visual recce techniques, and had some masochistic variations on 'Jim's Game' with which he sought to tune our ability to remember and reproduce on paper what we had seen. One of his favourites was to stand each of us on a chair whilst he sprinkled mapping pins on the floor behind us. Then it was 'turn round' and you had 15 seconds (about the time taken to run past a target) to count the pins and memorise the pattern they had formed. It was amazing how good we all got at instinctively working the difference between looking and seeing. We designed cardboard 'prayer wheels' which we could use for fuel calculations in the air, and for speed adjustments to ensure a correct time on target. Johnny taught us the importance of planning a good initial point (IP), which would give the best photographic run past the target whilst maintaining whatever element of surprise was going to ensure a clean getaway; the desert is a very quiet place, and the Hunter will have been heard long before it appeared!

"I met one of the 'Arabists' (a nationalist sympathiser) who normally worked in the Lebanon, and was lucky enough to be able to convince him to spend a day with us talking about the Arab culture; the way they approach life and death, the honour of the Bedouin, and a mass of little things which came out in discussion in the flight and later in the bar on the general theme of 'know your enemy'. Something which was particularly interesting was his view that the 'goolie chit' and the gold coins (*a monetary reward offered to anyone who gave a downed airman safe passage*) were useless to the point of being an incentive to do away with their carrier. In his view, if we came down in the desert, food and water were much more important, and to offer them as a sign of friendship and submission would be more likely to succeed. If the Arab accepted the food and water then you were 'on his face', and he would see you back to your own tribe. If not . . .

"Our final flourish was to design a distinctive mark for all our Hunters; everyone had an input. We eventually went for a sort of arrowhead, with a crinkly front end to

Hunter FR.10 XE614 GC 1417 Flight, Khormaksar 1964. Code is for Flt Lt George Cole. [via Jeff Peck]

represent camera bellows; the colours were those of Aden Protectorate (yellow, green and black). The station commander agreed that we could use the Khormaksar crest as a centrepiece – so as not to annoy any of those chaps in the College of Heralds who have weird names. Last of all we decided that as there were five of us, and five FR.10s, we would not have fin letters we'd use our initials. All this make-over was plotted to happen overnight; the groundcrew were up for surprising the FGA squadrons. So the morning when five shiny FR.10s called PL, JM, JD, GT, and AR, resplendent in their new insignia, were wheeled out onto the pan caused quite a stir all round. Quite right too.

TRAINING

"Johnny Morris devised some testing training sorties for us involving finding and photographing unlikely 'targets' like watering wells way out in the desert, derelict buildings in the bottom of steep-sided wadis, watch towers, desert landing strips, and the most difficult of all, complexes of caves recognisable only by the black holes in the sides of hills. He also seemed to have a secret line to the army, and whenever there was a convoy going up to Dahla he'd want photos, and a vehicle count which had to include the various vehicle types. The 'operational' test was to get a picture of a target at a predetermined time with Johnny sitting somewhere over it, without getting bounced by him. One frame of gyro gun sight (GGS) camera cine film with you in the frame represented a 'fail'. We got a bit cocky about this ability, and challenged the FGA boys to the same game. As far as I remember, none of them got the vital frame of cine, but Chris Golds of 43 Squadron did see the 1417 Hunter on one occasion.

"The secret we had worked out was to fly low over the flattest terrain we could find on the run in to the target. Nine times out of ten it is not the aircraft that the defenders saw, but its shadow 'bouncing' along uneven terrain. Flying so that the shadow doesn't 'bounce' involves going down to 25-30 feet which, at 420 knots, is very low indeed. Every so often one pilot would fly chase to the other sitting out at four or eight o'clock and judging the height of his buddy. Interestingly, getting down to that height is hard work as the tendency is always to creep up to around 40-50 feet. These buddy checks were needed about once a fortnight to keep our eyes in. Another ruse was to fly over where the waves were breaking on the shore. The motion of the water under the aircraft, at roughly 90 degrees to the line of flight, is sufficiently distracting to put off all but the cutest.

"Because our role was to get the information and bring it back, we would do all we could to avoid shooting or being shot at. So Jim Dymond and Johnny Morris dreamed up an interesting air-to-ground shooting sortie for whenever one of the FGA squadrons was on the range. We would ask for a 'slot' and whatever we were offered, we'd take. But we only allowed ourselves one pass, and that had to be made on time after a navigation/recce training sortie lasting at least 45 minutes. We were not allowed to go above 250 feet on the run in to the targets. This was realistic, but meant that the gyro gunsight was unreliable as turbulence affected the gyroscope in the sight; but Jim had worked out a way of using the 'fixed cross' (the spot where the guns were actually pointing) to good effect, and provided we used his method we usually picked up a decent score. The flight average on air to ground was around 60%, a fact of which we were proud, but quiet – there was enough banter about 'the Kodak Kids' without our trespassing on the expertise of the FGA boys!

"We had a nice 'party piece' for visiting VIPs taking a march past, or a salute. With a little connivance from the control tower, as 'General Salute' was called, an FR.10 would make a low photo pass and land. By the time the VIP had inspected the parade and was back on his dais, say ten minutes, the film would have been developed and printed by the Mobile Field Photography Unit (MFPU) and, as he left the parade ground he would be presented with his picture. By the end of April, I was able to tell the wing leader that we were ready for ops.

OPERATIONS

"Until the campaign in Radfan really warmed up 1417's main task was Operation Ranji. This involved a sweep of the coast from Riyan to the straits of Bab el Mandeb, looking for 'gun runners' landing weaponry for the insurgents inland. We found a few, but not many. However Ranji was also a catch-all for other recce ops, and three were especially memorable.

"At this time the Russians were sending warships out to Indonesia, and the Shackleton squadron would patrol the south end of the Red Sea watching for them. On one occasion they spotted a Skory class submarine chaser which had hidden amongst the little islands off the east coast of Ethiopia whilst it refuelled. The Russians did not have a 're-supply at sea' system, as the Royal Navy have, and they transferred re-supply whilst stationary. The Shackleton spotted the submarine chaser on its radar going like hell out into the Indian Ocean. As they were low on fuel (having been up all night) they could not catch it to take a picture – could 1417 help? We'd try. The Shackleton climbed to keep the Russian on its radar for as long as it could and gave us its course and speed (about 32 knots). I plotted an intercept some 180 miles out to sea and scrambled. Some accurate flying was required, and when I estimated that I was some 40 miles (six minutes) away I let down to as low as was sensible. The Skory appeared on the horizon, roughly where it should have been, and I lined up for a pass down its port side for happy snaps, piece of cake! The photos were developed. They produced a nasty surprise: every gun on the port side was leading me, and the covers were still on the guns on the starboard side! If that had been for real . . . They'd seen me coming from way out.

THE HUNTER'S CEILING

"A similar sortie involved looking for a suspected Russian warship off Hodeidah. The weather on this trip was unusually poor, with a lot of cumuli about. I was about to throw the game away when I spotted a ship about ten miles away under a very black cloud. I turned towards it, and was delighted when the cloud base started to lift. The ship turned out to be an innocent cargo ship, but I simultaneously noticed that suddenly there was no horizon. Big cumuli bases are like an inverted saucer, so grey sea, grey cloud, no horizon: time to climb. Up I went, and for about the first 5,000 feet it was a bit bumpy (to be expected). But then everything went mad! There were flashes of blue and yellow light, and the aircraft began pitching and rolling all on its own. I reduced to 'penetration' speed, clamped my feet on the rudder pedals, and gripped the stick in both hands supported by both knees, whilst the accelerometer was 'off the clock' in both directions (minus four to plus 12) and the artificial horizon had toppled. The G4 compass was rotating gently – like a roulette wheel slowing down I thought at the time. The radio compass was swinging wildly from one bearing to another, sometimes going through all 360 degrees, the airspeed indicator was fluctuating plus or minus 30 knots, and the climb/descent indicator was bumping against the 'up' stop. The only stable instruments were the turn and slip indicator (and even it was having its moments), and the altimeter which was climbing at an alarming rate.

"I've no idea how long all this lasted, except that it seemed to be a long time; but it all stopped as suddenly as it had started and I was in blue sky with that towering white mountain behind me. None of the instruments looked trustworthy, and I could not see any land so I just turned towards the sun (home was in that rough direction) and concentrated on level flight to relax and think. I then noticed that I was at 56,000 feet so began a descent to something more sensible. Eventually the compass and the radio compass came back, the artificial horizon (now I didn't need it) re-erected itself, and I headed for home. A very gentle straight-in approach and landing, and the aircraft went straight into the hangar for a stress check. The fatigue meter showed that it had been a very rough ride indeed, but apart from that, the thoroughbred was just fine.

"Ranji was also used for surveillance of the port at Hodeida. The intelligence men on the hill were very interested in what was being landed there, particularly some large crates that they had heard of; one of them came down to the wing. In John Jennings' office it was suggested that some photos would be a great help. Not that they were telling us to go of course, that might cause an international incident, but it would be nice. JJ agreed that it would be nice, but quite out of the question, but he had an idea. So, I took off without signing for anything, telling the tower it was an air test – or something – and off to Hodeida. I 'sussed' the area from about 10,000 feet and 10-15 miles out, taking a couple of shots with the starboard camera (just in case we had to do this again sometime) and decided on the photo run direction; north to south at about 500 feet looked good with a long burst of port and nose cameras. Let down, gentle turn to starboard and line up – no problem. But then I saw an airfield a couple of miles inland which no one told me about. As I got abeam the port, snapping away happily, I saw a pair of MiGs turning onto the runway. The photo shoot was all but over, so nose down and out to the coast, low over where those waves are breaking over the shore, flat out. I didn't see the MiGs again, and I guess they didn't see me again either. Back to base to some very sideways glances from both ground and aircrew – what on earth is the boss doing buggering off without signing up?

"The port and nose films are developed and printed – no title strips – and delivered to JJ's office; I didn't even see them. But the starboard facers came back to me and I think they were useful to others on a couple of occasions. We never discussed these missions with anyone, not even the other pilots, but there was an interesting aftermath. One afternoon, on the beach, one of the air traffic controllers (a Polish man, who had been a World War II night-fighter ace) confronted me, and in a very loud voice asks what the hell 1417 is doing breaking air traffic rules – their radar is telling them that we are not doing what we'd said we would. I tell him to shut up, and eventually pull rank in a very grotty manner until, by the look on his face, the penny drops.

TO KENYA FOR INDEPENDENCE DAY

"In December 1963 12 FGA.9s and an FR.10 were sent down to Nairobi, ostensibly to provide a flypast for the independence celebrations – 'Uhuru' (*named after the president*). The Hunters were based on the small military complex on the dual civil/military airport, but on the far side of the airfield there was a Beverley transport

Hunter FGA.9 208 Squadron Eastleigh during Kenya Independence celebrations. [Peter Sawyer]

full of weaponry – just in case. All the Hunters flew with full 30-mm gun packs on every sortie. Two days before Uhuru I was ordered to carry out a sweep, following the railway from Nairobi to Mombasa to photograph and note any gatherings that might be the least bit hostile looking. Nairobi airport is some 7,000 feet above sea level, and the recce was to be at midday; this would be an interesting take-off! And so it proved. At maximum all-up weight, I went right to the very end of Nairobi's enormous runway. Resolving to put down ten degrees of flap once I was rolling (we never really needed to do that in Aden, even at midday), I ran up to full power before letting off the brakes. Poor PL began a gentle crawl down the runway and rolled, and rolled, and rolled, with the airspeed increasing very slowly. Dropping the flaps at the last possible moment I just got airborne at the very end of the runway. Despite a very rapid undercarriage clean up, I was in a more or less stable flight condition – raise the flaps and I'd sink into the ground, raise the nose and I'd stall. But the rift valley came to my rescue; the ground drops away dramatically a couple of miles from the end of the runway, and I was able to put the nose down, get some airspeed, clean up the flaps and begin to fly normally.

"Exercise 'Biltong' was, on the face of it, a communication exercise mounted out of Bahrain. In fact, it was a thorough recce of an area to the east of a line running south from Abu Dhabi down to Masirah. I think it was something to do with illicit oil prospecting, but provided Johnny Morris and I with some interesting navigation problems. There were no maps of the area at all, so we'd cross in over Abu Dhabi and fly an accurate speed and heading to trace out a very elongated and narrow rectangle. If we saw something we'd note the time, and then create a sort of plot of its bearing and distance from Abu Dhabi after the flight. The other pilot would then fly that bearing and distance and, if he found the same something, we'd say, 'that's where it is'.

"On one of these sorties, Johnny found something well to the south, and there was just enough light left to check it out. He'd found an unusual encampment with what looked like some technical vehicles, which were duly photographed. The low sun would have given the photographic interpreters (PIs) some good shadows to work off, and one very low pass would probably have given them mug shots of the people on the ground – most of whom looked surprisingly oriental. I finished the 'sweep', by which time the sun was setting, and as fuel was getting a bit tight (all that showing off for happy snaps) I started a climb out to return to base at high level. As I climbed, I followed the setting sun, with all the marvellous colours that come with sunset over the desert. Beneath was the dark, and gradually in what had seemed in daylight like an empty wilderness, little pinpricks of light began to appear. The Bedouins, I supposed, cooking their evening meals. At 40,000ft with the sun all but gone the sky was turning purple. The pinpricks of lights of humanity below, the stars not quite out yet and with a light frost forming on the canopy, there came a strange sensation. It was as if a little voice was asking 'who the hell are you, and what are you doing here?' Some have labelled moments like this a 'nearness to God'. I would not argue with them, and some lines from the Rubaiyat came to me: 'One moment in annihilation's waste, one moment at the well of life to taste . . .'

"At the end of 'Biltong' Johnny Morris came up with a ruse – why didn't I fly back across the Rub' al Khali alone? We'd take off as a pair, he'd have radio failure, and I'd carry on. So that's what we did. I used the cruise climb technique allowing the Hunter to drift up to some 50,000ft as the fuel burned off. When I eventually switched to the Khormaksar frequency there was obviously anxiety about my fuel state. When I told them that I may have to burn off before landing they were relieved, but disbelieving. In fact, the big 230-gallon underwing tanks emptied on the descent, and I landed with damn near full internal fuel. Two hours 35 minutes, and I could have gone on for another 45 minutes (at altitude). The first crossing of the 'Empty Quarter' in a single-engine jet I like to think. The next morning XE614/PL which had brought me back the day before, refused to start. There were sand blockages in some of the transfer valves apparently; the thoroughbred had showed her mettle again.

HARIB

"The strike on Harib fort began as an RAF classic. The wing had a stand down for two days, apart from one recce Hunter and four FGAs at two hours standby. So there was one hell of a party at someone's house which went on a bit. At around 4:00 am there was a beating on the door, and there was Roy Bowie, the wing ops officer, saying 'get down to flights, we're going to start some nastiness'. The wing leader, JJ, had laid on a mass of toast and coffee, but as the briefing started the adrenalin took over; I'm convinced that it is the best hangover cure there is. The fort was to be leafleted 15 minutes before eight Hunters led by JJ struck. Sid Bottom (8 Squadron) and I were to carry the leaflets in our raised flaps and I was to photo Sid's leaflets going down on the fort. We were then to pull up to 30,000 feet and keep an eye open for any opposition which might choose to join the party. Once the strike was over, I was to photograph the fort again.

"It all went smoothly until, whilst filming Sid's leaflets, I saw at least one and probably three AA guns on the ground just to the south of the fort. There followed an agonising 15 minutes; break radio silence and warn the strike boys, or keep quiet? As the strike was going in from 20,000ft the gunners would have to be pretty good to get a result, and they probably weren't that good, so shut up and sit tight. I need not have worried. JJ led the eight Hunters down and his salvo was a 'pickle barrel' shot. I guess he must have hit a magazine or something as there was a huge yellow flash and a 'mini mushroom' of dirty brown/black smoke. I reckon that the other seven could only fire into the smoke and hope for the best, but there were no more big explosions. I told Sid to join the others and go home as it was going to take some time for the smoke to clear and allow a decent photograph. The smoke cleared after about half an hour, and I made the second pass. The fort was an awful mess, and there were several bodies lying around where the guns were. The thought occurred that JJ's salvo had probably blown bits of the southern end of the fort all over them. I reckoned that I hadn't exposed too much film (a short length of film gives the MFPU a chance for a really quick turnaround), and that I'd got the line about right on the second run. So now it was go home and just wait and see. The MFPU did a smashing job, and the film was on the light bench by the time I'd walked in and signed up. The photos were good; I marked the two I wanted printed and went into the debriefing with them. I handed them to JJ, and his face lit up with a smile which was a mixture of pride and relief. All he said was, 'Thank you 1417'. That was enough and in the eyes of the FGA boys, we'd arrived!

FINDING OUR WAY

"The Radfan campaign was to strengthen the links between FGA and Recce considerably. The root of this was the lack of maps. By and large the only large-scale maps we had were the 'white maps', which were originally surveyed by Philby in the late 1940s. These were supplemented by 'chocolate maps', so called because they were mainly brown. They were just reproductions of the aerial photographs taken by PR Canberras, overlaid with minimal information of place names, roads, tracks and wadi beds. There was the odd spot height, but no contours, so we all had to learn to translate the shading on these maps into what a hill, plateau or wadi would actually look like when we got there. But the most crucial factor was place names and their locations. Often the place name had not changed, but the location had. The locals had just moved the whole place anything up to 15 miles from where it last was – perhaps in Philby's time. The army or the SAS would call for a strike and name the place (no grid references, they didn't have our maps). Unless there was a forward air controller (FAC), the FGA boys could not find the target. Even when there was FAC control, they often had to be talked in from positions many miles away.

"So 1417 often went looking for the missing village. We'd make some assumptions about where it might be, and then just fly from where it was supposed to be to where we thought it might be with bursts (to make the film last) from all three cameras. If we found the village we'd give the FGA boys the key pictures, and a briefing to supplement the chocolate maps on what to look for. This raised the success rate considerably, but didn't work every time. Early in the campaign attempts at 'proscription' were made. This involved dropping leaflets on specific areas warning the inhabitants that they were in an area which was, or was about to become, a war zone. This device had worked successfully in Iraq and India in the days of Empire, as it denied insurgents sustenance.

"One morning I was ordered to leaflet a plateau in Radfan. Intelligence had reported a massing of potentially active insurgents, and it was due to be struck by the FGA later that day. If I was fired on, which was considered unlikely, then I was to fire back. I approached the area at low level (below the height of the plateau) by way of a wadi which led to it. As I climbed to make my run across the area, I saw a crowd of people and as I got closer I saw that they formed a rough circle. In the middle of the circle were three tripod-mounted 18-mm machine guns – a very effective anti-aircraft weapon. These were surrounded by some 20-30 civilians, including women and children. Outside them were nine or ten others with Kalashnikov assault rifles all pointing inwards! The concept of 'human shields' existed in 1964, long before the first Gulf War. Then the 18 mms opened up on me; subsequent events are best forgotten.

"As the war heated up, the SAS would often find caves where the opposition was hiding out. As the FGA boys used to tip in from 15-20,000 feet for these strikes, they hadn't got much time to acquire the targets, which were little more than black holes on a hillside. So 1417 went and found them first, and using the telephoto nose camera produced a 'gunsight' picture which was given to every pilot on the strike. This helped them a lot, if only because it relieved them of working out the best IP and attack direction. Quite what the effect of a strike on a cave was, I never asked.

"There was a visit to Aden by a party of MPs, and on the day they came to Strike Wing things were pretty busy 'up-country'. The FGA boys were going at it hammer and tongs, and 1417 was supporting them with pre and post-strike photographs. Returning from one of these missions I saw a civilian hanging about 1417's flight line. Now 1417 had an Arab 'sweeper' – a lovely little man who kept the offices immaculate, made coffee for everyone, including the groundcrew – and was a general 'go-for'. As the groundcrew got to know him, they would let him help on turnarounds, nothing technical – pushing trolleys, unreeling the heavy refuelling hoses, passing tools and so on. To him, this was a real treat.

"On this sortie I had fired the guns, at what I can't remember, so when the armourers saw the smoke on the gun ports they geared up to change the 'gun-pack'. The Hunter was designed for fast turnarounds, so a magazine full of ammunition replaced the used one which was then taken away for reloading. The sweeper delighted in helping with this activity whenever he could, and so it was on this day. The MP ignored me as I got out of the aircraft, and walked up to the 'sweeper' to ask him if he was not ashamed of himself helping the RAF to fight his people. He got a surprise, the sweeper glared at him fiercely and said, 'No! Boss Pete is fighting the enemies of my tribe!' Collapse of stout party – labour/pacifist perhaps. The next day we found the sweeper out on the line polishing the nose camera 'eyelids'. He was a little hurt when we told him that they might reflect the sun from a long way away, and that was not good. Sometime later there was a timid knock on my door, and the sweeper appeared with a roll of newspaper in which there was a khanjar – the traditional Arab knife of the area. It differed from the better known jambiya as its scabbard is curved, not hooked. The knife was fairly primitive in appearance but had a lovely horn handle. The scabbard was made from silver – almost certainly smelted Maria Theresa dollars. The knife, he informed me, was a gift from his tribe but I must pay for the scabbard – 500 shillings – that was the custom. Later on he asked me why I did not wear it when flying, but time and a lot of patient explaining eventually soothed him. I wish I could remember his name and I wonder what happened to him.

"The army soon wised up to the benefits of having photographs of the terrain they were to fight over, and became regular customers. On one occasion they asked for complete cover of a wadi some nine miles long, which involved using all three cameras at about 200 feet. As our cameras only had 50 seconds of film in them this meant that, even at maximum speed we would not get the whole of the wadi, although the nose camera with its telephoto lens would give something at the end of the run. Because the wadi bed was about 1,000 feet below the plateau the sortie had to be flown between 1 and 2 pm, when the shadows would be at a minimum. At that time of day, the air became very turbulent, so it was going to be a bumpy ride at 540 knots. The final piece of grief was that at 0.9 Mach the Hunter undergoes a nose down trim change which at a sensible altitude is not a problem as you just switched in the flying tail. This effectively turned the tailplane into a slab which could cope perfectly well with transonic aerodynamics. Too well in fact, as it made the aircraft very frisky in pitch, and it was madness to use it much below 500 feet. So the prospect was one of riding this trim change on a bumpy day, making an interesting trip – and so it turned out. Some 20 seconds into the run the accelerometer was off the clock (again!) in both directions; so back in the hangar for a stress check. Once again, the thoroughbred XE614 PL was fine, apart from a hole in the fin where someone had taken umbrage at being photographed.

"Occasionally, when there was a rumour of a meeting of the opposition, or the collection of weaponry, we were sent out into the open desert. On these occasions we were told that, if fired on we should fire back, provided it would not interfere with the mission which was a picture of the event. On one such mission I was certain that a group of four Land Rovers, and a fair few camels, had opened up on me as I went past – guns pointing in my direction and little yellow flashes. So rather than just go home I turned through 180 degrees and gave them the benefit of all four Aden guns, firing alternate HE/Ball for about three seconds – probably around 150-160 rounds. Unless the airspeed is 300 knots or less it is unlikely that you see your rounds strike, and at 480 knots you most certainly do not, so what effect I'd had I'll never know. The vibration of all four guns is quite noticeable, and they knock the speed back a bit. As I opened the throttle and pulled up, horror of horrors – the fire-warning light came on. The drill for this is basically eject as there is a fuel tank sitting around the jet pipe. But there was no way I was going to join the crowd I'd just visited as there was every probability that they were a bit angry.

"So, no smoke in the rear vision mirror and normal jet pipe temperature (JPT), a gentle turn and still no smoke in the mirror. Then an inspiration: I felt back to where the fire-warning test switch was to find that the desert survival pack had come loose from its mounting with the vibration from the guns, and had fallen on the switch. Lift it off, and the fire went out. Thereafter these packs were taken out of all the FR.10s. If you'd ejected they'd be nowhere near you, and no one in his right mind was going to crash land in the sort of terrain we were flying over. We recommended that the FGA boys did the same thing. Quite often these missions involved taking off just before dawn. I loved those flights, flying low over the desert into a rising sun is a truly beautiful experience, and again the Rubaiyat had the words:

'Awake, for Morning in the Bowl of Night
Has flung the Stone that put the Stars to Flight:
And Lo! The Hunter of the East has caught
The Sultan's Turret in a Noose of Light.'

SUPPORTING THE SAS

"The SAS were very active in the Radfan and did a lot of surveillance of the enemy re-supply routes. One morning there was a message that a camel train had been spotted the previous night, and was resting up near the Yemen border. I was sent up for a look-see, but despite being pretty sure I was in the right place, saw nothing. Then a voice on the radiotelephony operational frequency said 'they're there'; that's all. So I looked more carefully. There was a sort of a track which followed the dried-up bed of a stream, and which went through the odd pool of water which had not dried up. I noticed that the colour of the track above these pools was different from that below them and remembered some of Johnny Morris' training – the camels' wet feet had probably washed the sand off the path below the pools. Then suddenly what had appeared to be just rough boulders turned out to be couched camels; but no sight of any humans – time to help the army. I turned round, and gave the camels no more than a two-second burst of four guns, then turned again to photograph what I'd done. There was that brown/black smoke (as at Harib) all over where the camels had been, and no hope of any pictures. On return to base, I asked Johnny Morris to go back up there and do some pictures, but he came back without any. He said that there were so many vultures in the air and on the ground, there was no way he was risking a bird strike just for my photo album!

"Not all missions were 100% in their execution, notwithstanding the fact that they were successful; luck sometimes intervened. One such mission involved getting some nose camera shots of some caves in the end of a wadi, the bed of which was some 1,500 feet below the Radfan plateau. I knew the wadi well having been there several times, and in the usual good Aden weather, the mission would have been purely routine. But this was February, when there is often a layer of cloud sitting over Radfan and the surrounding hills; only about 1,500 feet thick, but covering the plateau. When I got there, I saw that I would be flying into a wadi, the tops of which were in cloud through which I would have to pull up once the photos were done. I decided to fly at 300 rather than 420 knots as the camera would need to be slowed right down to make the most of the poor light, and in I went. The run was only about half complete, perhaps three miles out from the target, when self-preservation took over and I pulled up through the cloud thinking 'abort'. But then pride took over, so I went out to the edge of the cloud, let down to low level again, and made another run. This time, I got a bit closer, but once again, 'chickened out'; and set off for home. But half way home, pride cut in again: I just had to go back for one more try. This time I would fly at 320 knots with 10 degrees of flap to give me the sharpest rotation into a climb that the Hunter would do. I got my photos and rotated up through the cloud and back to base. But the photos were under exposed (although the best achievable) and not much good for the customer.

"The next day the cloud had gone, so I went back again and got some decent shots. But in getting them I realised that the day before my pull up through the cloud had taken me through a V-shaped depression in the wadi end, and that had I been 20 yards left or right I would have flown into the wadi wall. I then came to know what 'fear in retrospect' really means.

"What would probably have been the most interesting op of all was as bizarre in its conception as it would have been challenging in its execution. There was some trouble in or around Zanzibar, and there was to be a pacification exercise involving landing marines to secure the airfield, followed by the army who wanted their close-support Hunters with them. The problem was that no one knew if the airfield was operational, or if the runway had been obstructed. So, 1417 would take off about an hour before the show was due to start, and go and have a look at the airfield. If it was OK the marines would secure it, and the FGA boys who were airborne, but not up to their point-of-no-return, would keep on coming. The 1417 Hunter would hang about making its fuel last as long as possible, and then land on the newly acquired airfield and await the arrival of everyone else. If the airfield was not serviceable, then it was fly to Nairobi if there was enough fuel – which was unlikely – or find one of Her Majesty's nice warships and eject beside it. The latter option also applied if the marines could not secure the airfield in time, but it never happened.

"The beginnings of this episode involved my being knocked up at some ungodly hour, and told to pack some kit as I'd be away from home for a bit. This I did and when my wife Liz drowsily asked when I'd be back, all I could say was, 'I don't know'. She asked, 'Have you got enough handkerchiefs?' We were kept on the base at Khormaksar, incommunicado, for three days before the whole thing was called off and we could go home again. At the time I don't remember ever thinking about what Liz – and the other wives – went through at times like those. It must have been miserable for them, miles from home and beset by uncertainties. But go through it they did, never complaining about that side of their lives. Late back with the shopping or from the bar – that was a very different matter!

"It was odd, to say the least, to get up at 4 a.m., fly four or five missions some of which involved shooting and probably killing people, and then sit down with a wife and three children for a late lunch. The 'switch off' from violence had to be complete – until tomorrow. I now firmly believe that wives and families have no place in war zones. In all, I flew 112 operations in Aden, most of them routine and uneventful, but some quite character forming. The flight had been tasked for 601 operations, 600 of which had been successful; the one which was a failure was when the last sortie of the day had to be abandoned when the aircraft refused to start. Towards the end of the tour, I realised that something strange was happening: when it came to having completed an op, I couldn't remember walking out to the aircraft, transiting to the target, or coming home. But from the IP through to the breakout, I could give a faultless frame-by-frame debrief of everything. It was as if I'd been converted into an automaton programmed for perfection. A bit spooky really." [1]

THE HEAVYWEIGHT – AVRO SHACKLETON

The Venom, later Hunter, Wing was the most obvious proponent at Khormaksar of offensive operations. Alongside them, Shackletons from UK-based squadrons were detached there from time to time, but then a permanent presence was established in August 1957 when 37 Squadron and its MR.2s moved in from Malta. A significant shift in operating philosophy for their venerable aircraft saw them extend beyond their traditional maritime reconnaissance and air-sea-rescue roles to encompass colonial policing.

Shackleton MR.2 A 37 Squadron Khormaksar. [37Aden.co.uk via Dave McCandless]

BILL TYACK – NAVIGATOR

Bill got the flying bug when his father took him, aged about four, to watch Sunderlands taking off and landing at the Short Brothers factory on Belfast Lough. Seventeen years later he was flying Shackletons.

"Colonial policing came to be one of our major roles. Bomber Command Lincolns were available to support ground forces in the Arabian Peninsula up until 1956, but that year the task was passed to Coastal Command. After working up in the new role, 42 Squadron sent a detachment to Khormaksar, where they flew their first operational mission on 13 January 1957. From then on there was a permanent Shackleton presence in the area until 1971. 37 Squadron was based there from August 1957 until September 1967. Other squadrons sent detachments to the region throughout the period, operating at various times out of Bahrain, Masirah and Salalah in Oman, and Sharjah in the Trucial States. The tasks were many and various: photo reconnaissance, communications relay, air observation, vehicle convoy escort, supply dropping, leaflet raids, and coastal reconnaissance to interdict gun running. However, the aircraft were ultimately there to provide a 'big stick' in the form of more offensive tasks, such as bombing and strafing with the 20-mm nose guns. Some aircraft also carried a Bren gun in the starboard beam lookout position. Fifteen 1,000-lb bombs or 52 20-lb bombs (or an equivalent mixed load) could be carried at a time.

"By September 1957, the Shackletons had dropped over 530 1,000-lb bombs, and the focus of attention shifted from Aden to the Oman. Operations were centred on the Jebel Akhdar; routine targets were the dams and water systems needed to irrigate the tribesmen's crops, but specific attacks were also made under the direction of forward air controllers. This campaign lasted from August 1957 until February 1959. During this period Shackletons flew 429 sorties dropping 1,500 tons of bombs and firing 700,000 rounds of 20-mm ammunition. There were further short-term bombing operations in 1960, 1961 and 1962. During 1964 operations became focused on the Radfan with Shackletons mainly undertaking harassing night operations by dropping small bombs and flares. Things were relatively quiet after this and 37 Squadron was disbanded in 1967. However, a permanent detachment, mainly sustained by the MR.3 squadrons from Kinloss and St Mawgan, was based in Sharjah until late 1971. From there the crews flew anti-gun-running patrols, and practised medium level bombing with 1,000-lb bombs. The coastal patrols (Operation Bronze) flew from the Strait of Hormuz south along the Omani coast at 100 feet above the beach and back again, conducting a visual search for signs of suspicious activity. This would then be radioed to the Trucial Oman Scouts. I clocked up many hours in the nose gunner's seat, which was the ideal lookout position, and a sighting by my crew resulted in a capture by the Trucial Oman Scouts." [2]

Bill converted to the Nimrod MR.1 and joined the Nimrod Evaluation Unit at Boscombe Down. His subsequent tours of duty in operational requirements and policy staffs had a strong maritime flavour.

CHRIS DANCE – ENGINES

Chris left the jet world in December 1965. In their wisdom, the posters decided he was better off going on to piston aircraft with 37 Squadron on Shackletons, probably because of his previous experience with the Hastings in Nicosia – and they were short of manpower.

"The 37 Squadron pilots had to do mandatory flying to keep their hours up, and the squadron was also involved in preventing gun running; an aircraft being based at Sharjah most of the time. The squadron also carried out operations in the Radfan, which included bombing runs in support of the army. During those operations the Shack was very vulnerable to any tribesmen's ground fire. Squadron armourers were kept very busy loading 2,000-lb bombs and guns. The Shack was vulnerable because it was so slow and low flying, and I distinctly remember one aircraft coming back with bullet holes near the navigator's position. Those tribesmen with their 'blunderbusses' were pretty accurate. Hunters were a lot faster of course, so much harder to hit.

"The squadron was mortared at Khormaksar, and the 'enemy' said all the Shackletons had been grounded. To prove this statement wrong fabric patches were put over the shrapnel holes, and searches made to recover pieces of shrapnel from inside the fuselage. The aircraft flew over Aden the following morning.

"The Shack was not very reliable. When aircraft landed the flight engineer would fill pages of the F700 with snags, and the majority were airframes and engines. The engine snags were mainly magneto drops, oil leaks and problems with the props. One aircraft flown by Flt Lt Nichols (a very good captain) had an engine fire going into Nairobi. He didn't dive the aircraft but stalled it, thus starving the fire of oxygen and saving the aircraft. The No.1 engine had broken up, and the crankshaft had come through the side of the engine casing – a major disaster. The engine was changed and a new bulkhead was fitted. Manpower was a problem, and more tradesmen were sent from Khormaksar to Nairobi. The aircraft needed a full primary inspection, which involved all trades. Following this work a compass swing was required. Nairobi civil airport authority did not want a dirty Shackleton on display! They didn't mind shiny

Chris Dance, 37 Squadron, Khormaksar. [Chris Dance]

Britannias, but they didn't want this old Shack anywhere to be seen. In the end the aircraft was flight tested, and the compass calibrated in the air.

"After the air test it was time to return to Aden. On the return flight the aircraft started to lose oil pressure on No.1 engine, which was the one that had been changed. The captain said that if the oil pressure fell any lower, he would have to shut it down. This was done, and the prop feathered. Shortly after that oil was sighted leaking back from No.3 engine propeller – the captain shut down that engine as well. It was now flying on two engines; this situation necessitated getting flight clearance to fly over Ethiopia. However, the flight clearance never came and the captain said, 'look out for flak'. On the approach to Khormaksar fire engines and ambulances were alerted – fortunately the aircraft landed without further incident. The investigation found the fault for No.1 engine low oil pressure was an instrument fault. The oil pressure pipeline connector to the rear bulkhead had been wire locked but not tightened. It was a technical error by the instrument fitters loaned from another unit. The oil leak from No.3 engine propeller was found to be the inter-shaft seal coming completely adrift.

"In Khormaksar one aircraft had a fuel tank leak. This necessitated getting the aircraft into what was called the 'overseas hangar', for a fuel tank change. We asked why we couldn't get in the hangar before a stated time. We were told it was because the sea tide affected opening the hangar doors. The land it stood on was reclaimed from the sea, so when the tide was out the hangar doors could be opened, but when the tide came in the doors were jammed.

"We had lots of incidents. One was in Khormaksar when the captain was taxying in and there was a brake chute from a Hunter lying on the runway, so he told air traffic. They said the chute was not in his way and there was plenty of room for him to taxi past, so he did. As he went by the chute was picked up by No.1 prop and thrown into No.2 prop, and then all down the bomb bay, which split the fuselage skin open. When the aircraft came in it had bits of parachute and wire rope hanging from it. I think No.1 engine was changed plus the two props and a new bomb-bay door had to be sent out from the UK.

"The skill and dedication of the aircrew on 37 Squadron could not be faulted. Groundcrews worked hard, often in trying circumstances. What did not help was the 24-hour guard duty every three days. In order to escape this those groundcrew on an unaccompanied one-year tour volunteered for permanent detachments. Married personnel on two-year tours living off the camp had the worry of leaving their families in the Ma'alla housing area when they went on detachments. The situation got so bad that in March 1967 all families were sent back to the UK." [2]

Chris moved to Leeming looking after Chipmunks, then went to Halton as an instructor followed by Ministry of Defence London. After 25 years of service, he left the RAF in October 1979.

DAVE MCCANDLESS – ENGINES

Dave was on 37 Squadron and also remembers the mortar attack referred to by Chris Dance.

"It was a quiet Sunday morning. The duty crew went out onto the pan to do whatever they had to do. I was left in charge of the squadron office (probably the first time I had been in there) with the red telephone to ops up at Strike Wing HQ. I heard a bang, followed by a dull thump. 'What the f…?' My imprecation was stopped nano seconds later by a loud (much louder bang) followed by a thunderous thump, accompanied by the sound as if all the cats in Khormaksar were doing a clog dance on the hangar roof.

"I ran out of the office and through the hangar to the entrance, which led out onto the pan. I only just avoided death by Land Rover as the squadron vehicle came hurtling into the hangar. The ashen-faced duty crew were clinging on like limpets. We all piled into the office where the crew talked excitedly, and loudly, about being shelled/bombed etc., whilst all the time puffing nervously on their fags (even the non-smokers). Just then the Tannoy came to life and a voice told us the camp was under attack, and that all personnel should take cover.

"I showed my leadership qualities by promptly diving under the office table. About ten minutes later the red phone rang. By this time the lads had calmed down a bit (although I was still under the table). I gingerly reached up and brought the handset down to my ear. 'Hello,' I squeaked nervously, expecting an Arab voice to call on me to surrender (I already had a rather grubby white hankie ready). A voice on the other end, which I recognised as the squadron commanding officer, asked, 'Is there damage to any of our aircraft? Are they airworthy, if not how long to get them ready to fly?' 'Err, I don't know, I haven't been to look yet,' was my brave retort.

"There was an icy silence for a second or two, I realised I had not given the proper reply. Damn it! I thought, there goes my British Empire Medal. 'Why haven't you checked the aircraft for damage?' he demanded. Quick as a flash I had my answer. 'We were ordered to take cover Sir; we haven't been given the all clear.' A master stroke, I think you will agree under the circumstances – who says that engineers are slow witted? A longer, icier, silence, finally broken by a 'humph', then the phone put down, none too gently. Cowardice in the face of the enemy, dereliction of duty, lack of moral fibre, conduct to the detriment of good order and discipline – such was the sub-text of that 'humph'. For weeks afterwards I checked my mail for any attached white feathers.

"Some five minutes after this conversation the door of the office opened and in strolled the skipper (a Kiwi flight lieutenant) of the only aircraft due to fly. He was probably surprised to see all the duty crew in the office, with the non-commissioned officer in charge cowering under the table, but being an officer and a gentleman, he didn't comment. It transpired that he had no knowledge of the attack. He had driven in from his quarters and hadn't heard the explosions or the Tannoy. 'I thought it was a bit quiet this morning' he remarked! He then asked if any of the duty crew had been wounded during the attack, which is more than the squadron commander ever did.

"The whole station turned out to patch the holes in the Shacks with fabric and dope (after sniffing for petrol). We then loaded the bomb bay with 1,000-lb bombs to go on a mission in the Yemen. We wished to demonstrate that the terrorists' mortar mission to destroy the dreaded Shacks – that was being declared on the Yemen radio as a resounding success – had failed."

PULL UP A SANDBAG

DESMOND PENROSE – PILOT

"Peter Greensmith's 208 Squadron Meteor was being chased by a Venom over the Sinai Desert. He pulled through, and his tail came off. The Venom pilot saw no ejection – we thought Pete had gone in, but couldn't find him or the wreck. The RAF Regiment arranged a funeral. They rehearsed with a coffin filled with sand on a gun carriage, and it all looked very smart. However, on the day of the funeral Pete turned up! He'd ejected miles from anywhere and was rescued by Bedouins. One of the first people he met when he walked into the guardroom was the regiment officer, who said 'You bastard! After all the work I've done, couldn't you have waited a day?!'"

---

[1] via Ray Deacon and unedited
[2] *Shackleton Boys 2* by Steve Bond

CHAPTER FIVE

TRANSPORTS – 'READY FOR ANYTHING'*

** The motto of 24 Squadron, arguably the RAF's longest serving transport squadron. The sentiment is highly appropriate given the challenging demands faced by the Middle East squadrons.*

As outlined in chapter one, an early requirement for RAF forces in the Middle East was the provision of transport aircraft, and this need continued to increase throughout the wartime and postwar periods. The operational squadrons became increasingly

105 Squadron Argosy and 84 Squadron Beverley lines with a BOAC VC10 climbing out, Khormaksar 1965. [John James]

involved in detachments away from their home bases, and the essential support for army units continued to grow. Transportation was required between both the established stations and the various remote, typically very basic, desert landing strips.

The scale of the transport force to match the task was quite impressive. For example, the squadrons based at Khormaksar from the 1950s through to closure included: 21 Squadron Twin Pioneer; 26 Squadron Belvedere; 78 Squadron Pioneer, Pembroke, Twin Pioneer, Wessex; 84 Squadron Valetta, Sycamore, Pembroke, Beverley, Andover; 105 Squadron Argosy; 114 Squadron Valetta, 233 and 683 Squadrons all Valetta. There were also the Aden Protectorate Communication and Support Flight with Valetta, Auster AOP.6, Meteor, Pembroke and Sycamore; plus the Middle East Communication Flight/Squadron with Valetta, Pembroke, Devon, Meteor, Prentice, Anson, Dakota, Hastings and Andover. Muharraq had the Gulf Communications Flight with Pembroke and Andover. In addition. 152 Squadron operated the Twin Pioneer and Pembroke from Bahrain/Muharraq, with 21 Squadron Twin Pioneers and 30 Squadron flew Beverleys at Eastleigh.

DAKOTA

The venerable Dakota soldiered on for a few years after the war before being supplanted by newer types, mainly the Valetta. Two Dakota C.4s were based at Khormaksar in the 1960s, until one was blown up by a terrorist bomb in 1965, leaving the survivor to soldier on until 1967. They were mainly used to fly high-ranking officers and civilian dignitaries to up-country airstrips.

Middle East Communication Flight, Dakota C.4 'up-country'. [Len Clayton]

PETE JACKSON – PILOT

Pete's transport flying began at 240 OCU North Luffenham, followed by 1333 Transport Support Training Unit at Netheravon in January 1950.

"In February 1950 I was posted to 78 Squadron at Kabrit in the Canal Zone. There were six squadrons of Dakota 3s (70, 78, 114, 204, 216 and the Middle East Air Force Communications Squadron). At that time all the other ranks were being kept busy scraping off camouflage paint and then polishing the aircraft. In February we were detached to airlift Aden Levies from Italian Somaliland back to Aden, then fly in Italian carabinieri and equipment. Our points of landing included Bender Qassim and Abile. At Bender Qassim we slept on camp beds under the aircraft, and during the first night one Italian sentry had his throat cut. The Italians were not wanted back.

"We moved on to Mogadishu, where 8 and 84 Squadron Brigands *(from Khormaksar and Habbaniyah respectively)* dropped leaflets with a warning to clear troublesome villages, then followed up with a few rockets. We enjoyed campfire sing songs with the Italians and exchanged bottles of gin (30 pence a bottle) for small cases of vino. Three Mustangs in crates were airfreighted in and assembled by Italian fitters. One crashed on take-off for its air test, and the remaining two did not last very long.

"During March we moved to Nairobi. As Aden was duty free, the odd trip there and back allowed a little smuggling, mainly of cigarettes. The journey time was six hours 30 minutes out, and seven hours 15 minutes back. I eventually left Nairobi on 14 April 1950 and returned to Fayid, via Julia, Khartoum and Wadi Halfa, arriving the next day. The following month we started conversion to the Valetta."

VALETTA

The Valetta was a military derivative of the Vickers Viking airliner. Known throughout the RAF as the 'Pig', it entered service in 1948 and was finally replaced in the transport role in 1965.

Len Clayton was a navigator on both 233 Squadron Valettas and 84 Squadron Beverleys from 1962 to 1965. He describes what some of those desert landing strips were like to operate from.

233 Squadron Valetta C.1 VW149 refuelling at Masirah. [Len Clayton]

LEN CLAYTON – NAVIGATOR

"The navigator's position in the Valetta was immediately behind the pilot, facing left, but was rotated and locked to face forward for approach and landing. The approach to land a Valetta at Dhala (before Habilayn was completed) was always towards the jebel. The strip was barely long enough at 750 yards and required a really careful preparation by the crew. The check list for doing a go-around was: full power, gear and flaps up, pray that both Hercules keep going – squeaky bum time.

Dhala go-around. [Len Clayton]

"I took this photo from the locked seat, although at the time I wondered if it might be the last family snap I would ever take. The captain having his hands full of throttle and control yoke, the role of the co-pilot/wireless operator was to raise the gear and flaps, and then pray. On the photo his gloved hand is seen gripping the coaming – the prayer worked. We cleared the jebel saddle with about 100 feet to spare, although the actual ridge was hidden beneath a bit of cloud. Our safe landing was made the second time around."

PETE JACKSON

Pete (now flying the Valetta) continues with his story having moved to 204 Squadron at Kabrit, then to Fayid.

"Aircraft of all squadrons were involved in exercises, mainly supply dropping with the army. On route flying, the aircraft were positioned at Fayid to collect freight, and/or passengers. Routes included Aqaba, Mafraq, Habbaniyah, Karachi, Malta, Lagos, Asmara via Khartoum, El Adem via Benina and Castel Benito, Nicosia, Nairobi via Wadi Halfa, Khartoum, Juba and Malakal. When flying to the small military mission at Taif in Saudi Arabia, we would first land at Jeddah and pick up a guide. He was an Arab, dressed in turban and galabeya, and sat in the second pilot's seat. On take-off he set the course, and thereafter made alterations to the compass, thus ensuring we flew a circular track out of visual distance of Mecca.

"In October 1950 the squadrons moved to Fayid, and the following month, Sqn Ldr A H Piper took over as commanding officer of 78 Squadron. He brought with him an Austin Healey Sports with an alloy body and he wanted it painted underneath the chassis. He told an 'erk' to paint it; who decided to use black dope. The commanding officer took it on a fast run to Suez and half-way back the car burst into flames! He stopped and got out okay and was not pleased when he found that dope had been used. Whether he knew that the whole exhaust system had been painted as well, I don't know.

"In February 1951 I was transferred to 204 Squadron. In May, I took part in Exercise Leap Year 1 and 2, dropping paratroops over Jordan. This was followed by Exercise Charing Cross the following month, followed by a brief return to the UK in July. Two Valetta aircraft leaving Kabrit to position at Fayid were piloted by Sgts Docherty and Arrandale. I was in the aircraft with Ray Arrandale, formatting on Doc's aircraft. Tucking his starboard wing between Doc's mainplane and tailplane (port), they decided to beat up Kabrit. Diving down from 5,000 feet, Ray's wingtip struck the underside of Doc's port elevator, causing Doc's stick to hit him in the midriff. His aircraft climbed rapidly from about 250 feet, and Ray followed suit – spectacular! A station football final was being played and being watched by most of the camp, including the station commander. Both aircraft and crews were grounded at Fayid, one with a smashed wing lamp and the other with a crumpled elevator. Both pilots were reprimanded.

"There was an extract from station routine orders warning pilots not to beat up dhows on the Bitter Lakes. The method used was to fly low over the victim, haul back on the stick, and let the slipstream flatten the sails.

"During minor troubles in the area, the Lancashire Fusiliers were conspicuous. Paras were moved in when Egypt pressed for the evacuation of the Canal Zone, and one unit was flown to Nicosia. Their reply to an excess taxi fare was to lift the car and wedge it, bumper to wall, in one of the very narrow streets.

"An aircraft was lost in May 1951 when, during a demonstration supply drop, a parachute opened prematurely and wrapped itself around the port tailplane. Helpless in a shallow dive, it crashed and caught fire. As well as the three crew, four army dispatchers and an engineering officer died."

> *On 2 May 1951, VW156 was carrying out the supply drop Pete mentioned. When the parachute of one container was seen to pass over the tailplane it began to deploy, with the container hanging below it. After a few seconds the pilot said, "I can't hold it!" and the aircraft dived into the ground two miles from the airfield exploding on impact. Those lost were the pilot Fg Off Basil Ashton, Sgt John Beard, Sgt Ian Ross, Flt Lt Raymond Yandell and from 21 Royal Army Service Corps Cpl Frederick Bruton, Cpl John Nicholls, Driver Charles Battrick and Driver Nicholas Hall.*

"On 9 September 1951 I was at Abadan, in Iran, flying troops into Kuwait. Our orders were to overfly Israel during darkness on the outward leg, but nobody said to return the long way round over Jordan. We were buzzed by Israeli fighters on the way home.

"Eight days later, on the 16th, pilot Sgt Ray Arrandale and signaller Flt Sgt Derek Allen were en-route with a replacement engine, when the aircraft was struck by lightning between Wadi Halfa and Khartoum. On landing the aircraft had a superficial check. On the 17th when they were returning to Fayid, a wing fell off and the wreck burst into flames. From then on wing bolts were regularly checked."

Above: Cpl Jim Fenn with AWA Atlas I J9960 of 208 Squadron Heliopolis at Ismailia 1931 (Jim Fenn).

Below: Nieuport Nighthawk JR6925 8 Squadron over Hinaidi airfield (Jim Fenn).

Khormaksar dispersal 1958 with SAR Flight Sycamores (John James).

Below: Meteor FR.9 WH546 of Aden Protectorate Reconnaissance Flight Khormaksar 1960 (via Ray Deacon).

Above: 233 Squadron aircrew assembling for dinghy drill practice with Marine Craft Unit Khormaksar c.1962–63 (Dean Pringuer).

Below: 233 Squadron Valetta C.1 VW195 at Beihan supporting British Army and Aden Protectorate Levies c.1962. Beihan's Wadi was a source of water all year (Dean Pringuer).

Above: Pioneer CC.1 XL554 78 Squadron at Dhala Aden on 9 May 1958 (John Black via Adrian Balch).

Below: 233 Squadron Valetta C.1 VW821 over Little Aden returning from a supply drop (Dean Pringuer).

Above: 543 Squadron Valiant B(PR)K.1s WZ394 and WZ397 at Khormaksar (via James Thomas).

Below: Aden Protectorate Levies fortress, shared with the RAF, at Beihan 130 miles north of Aden c.1962 (Dean Pringuer).

Above: Crater in 1963 from a 233 Squadron Valetta (Dean Pringuer).

Below: Shackleton MR.2 37 Squadron taking off from Khormaksar in 1966 (37Aden.co.uk via Dave McCandless).

Above: 'Three Little Piggies' 233 Squadron Valettas set against Mt Shamsan, Aden, with Khormaksar in the background (Dean Pringuer).

Below: View towards Crater from Khormaksar officers' mess non air-conditioned accommodation (Dean Pringuer).

Above: Water vendor in the Crater district of Aden town in 1961. Safe to roam there before the 1964 emergency (Dean Pringuer).

Below: Wessex HC.2 XR522 78 Squadron airlifting from HMS *Albion* off Aden March-April 1965 (via Adrian Balch).

Above: 78 Squadron Twin Pioneer getting airborne in Yemen 1959-60 (Richard Lennard).

Below: 8 Squadron Venom FB.4 at very-low level as requested by the ALO, Riyan, Yemen (Peter Goodwin).

Above: 84 Squadron Beverley up-country, possibly at Ataq, 1959-60, David Richmond on the right (David Richmond).

Below: Beverley C.1 XH121 84 Squadron at Riyan or Salalah (Ian Macmillan).

Above: RAF Regiment gun pit at Mukeiras, looking north across the airstrip, 1963 (Len Clayton).

Above: Air Movements Masirah with a Beverley on approach 1967 (Bob Pountney).

Below: Hunter FGA.9 XE611 in dual 8 and 43 Squadron markings, Masirah 1967 (Bob Pountney).

Above: Large Arab fort in the mountains of Oman from a 208 Squadron Hunter 24 August 1971 (Jerry Pook).

Left: Twin Pioneer XM291 arriving at Awaifa Oman 22 February 1960 (John James).

Below: Belvederes of 26 Squadron airlifting from HMS *Victorious* in 1963 (Bob Woolley via Adrian Balch).

Above: Hunter FGA.9 XF435 G 208 Squadron taxiing out. Muharraq, 1969-70 (Adrian Balch Collection).

Below: Hunter FGA.9 XK137 F 208 Squadron loading bombs Muharraq 1969-70 (Adrian Balch Collection).

Above: Kamaran Island – Land of two moons (Dean Pringuer and Peter Morris).

Below left to right: Signaller name unknown, Fg Off Frank Easterbrook and Flt Lt Ron Wright 84 Squadron sheltering from the sun in the lee of the jebel at Dhala (Len Clayton).

Above: Shackleton MR.2 with Nos.1 and 2 props feathered for a beat up of Majunga beach (37Aden.co.uk via Dave McCandless).

Below: Singapore III K4577 and K6907 of 203 Squadron at Basrah, Iraq (Chris Orme).

Above: Hunter FGA.9 of 208 Squadron Eastleigh during Kenyan Independence celebrations 1963 (Peter Sawyer).

Below: Retirement nose art on 84 Squadron Beverley XM103 at Bicester 27 January 1968 (Adrian Balch).

The accident on 17 September 1951 involved Valetta C.1 VW813, when the aircraft dived into the ground near Loka in Sudan. It was thought to have broken up in turbulence. In addition to Arrandale and Allen, Sgts John McHarg and Richard Murphy were lost.

PEMBROKE

The Hunting Percival Pembroke was a widely used light transport and communications type. It entered service in 1953, and the last examples were retired in 1988. It served with the Middle East Communications Squadron.

JOHN JAMES – PILOT

"I met the old Sultan Said ibn Taimur, when I flew five Muscat bigwigs to Salalah in a Pembroke. We landed shortly after the first pair of Sultan of Oman's Air Force (SOAF) Beavers arrived from Aden. The Sultan was there to inspect his new toys, and when he was invited to take a short flight in one of the brand spanking new Beavers, he declined the offer as it only had one engine. He added, but if he ever went to Muscat, he was prepared to travel in a Pembroke. What he didn't know was that the biggest and wealthiest building contractor in the country (Indian Sub Continental) had spent most of the flight from Muscat locked in the toilet, courtesy of a stiff sliding door with a flimsy handle that came off in his hand!"

Pembroke C.1 WV700, 152 Squadron Muharraq, 1965. [John James]

Twin Pioneer CC.1 XM963, 21 Squadron Khormaksar. [Author's collection]

TWIN PIONEER

Scottish Aviation's Twin Pioneer was renowned for its short take-off and landing (STOL) capabilities, making it ideally suited to operate in and out of desert landing strips. 78 Squadron was the first at Khormaksar to receive 'Twin Pins', operating them from October 1958 to June 1965. They were followed by 21 Squadron at Eastleigh in May 1959, which moved to Khormaksar in 1965 and continued to fly them until September 1967.

JOHN JAMES

"During my Twin Pioneer conversion, with 78 Squadron in August 1959, we lost an engine on the way into Kamaran and had to night stop. Her Majesty's representative was a real Peter Sellers type who put us up in a disused bungalow next to the beach. Dimitri the Greek owner of the only shop on the island kept us supplied with copious amounts of beer – so a good night was had by all. We were rescued the next day, and the engine change was completed the following week.

"It was not until August 1959 that I first saw the remains of Valetta VW817 which crashed on landing at Firq, Oman, on 14 January that year; a witness to the accident told me it ran over a land mine. This was a common occurrence in those days, not only on the Firq strips, but also along the road to the Northern Frontier camp at Nizwa. If we were forced to night stop at the bottom of the jebel, being a coward who valued his crown jewels, I always flew the Twin Pin to the 300-yard strip inside the camp at the end of the day. Saiq was a much nicer option, although officially we were not allowed to shut down engines up there in case they failed to start again. The Northern Frontier Regiment major in charge was a very hospitable ex-SAS veteran called John Cooper. He had been David Stirling's driver in North Africa during World War II. I will always remember the cold beer and wild strawberries, and the tales of daring do in the deserts of North Africa and the jungles of Malaya.

"Like Khormaksar, Sharjah was not officially an 'air conditioned' station, which was why I spent so much time there with a Twin Pioneer. For a high proportion of my two-year tour, I was the only unmarried pilot on 152 Squadron, therefore I did most of the Twin Pin flying out of Sharjah. This was because my living out allowance (LOA) only dropped from three shillings to one and sixpence, whereas married crew members dropped from seven pounds fifteen shillings to one and sixpence. They and their families were entitled to a much higher LOA due to air conditioning costs, but only when they were present in Bahrain."

'TLITEB' – NAVIGATOR

"21 Squadron had a daily Twin Pin service to Habilayn and beyond. This was usually on to Dhala and across to Musamir, also to other destinations as required. The role was general re-supply and recovery. The standard way into Dhala was approach and land towards the mountain, turn around and depart the way you came. Standard operating procedure (SOP) was to land, keep engines running, unload/take on board any kit/personnel returning and fly out again.

"Landing there one morning we stopped and, engines idling, I went back to check the load going off, and see what was coming back on, when I noticed the pilot waving his arms frantically. At first, I thought this was not too unusual, until I noticed he had his .38 Smith and Wesson in his hand! At this point I thought I had better go and see if he had flipped altogether, but the problem turned out to be a donkey that was wandering slowly towards the arc of the port prop. The pilot decided the best course was to deter the donkey with a warning winging bullet. First pull nothing, as the SOP was to load five with the first chamber empty, but two and three nothing either. At this point the donkey sniffs the prop area and departs slowly stage left. Pilot settles down and we depart normally…

"The crew room rumour was that the armoury thought that aircrew shouldn't be issued with dangerous weapons, hence duff ammo, and that in an emergency the handgun could be thrown at an assailant! However this couldn't have been the case as shortly after this, when going up-country, we were issued with Sterling submachine guns – these were really dangerous toys.

78 Squadron Twin Pioneer with a Sycamore at Lawdar, Yemen. [Len Clayton]

"Up country improvisations were often required on 21 Squadron (and the 84 Squadron Beverleys too I believe). I remember the inevitable 'bump start' on a Twin Pin Leonides engine when, despite the normal nudge with the fire axe, the starter cartridge rotation mechanism packed in. The answer to the problem was a rope around the prop boss, with the other end attached to a vehicle's tow ball. Prime the engine, mag switches on, vehicle departs quickly – engine fires.

"The best improvisation was a ground engineering fix. At the larger up-country strips where the larger aircraft went in, for example Habilayn/Ataq, there was a fire truck manned by a crew of RAF sergeant and his senior aircraftman mate. We took off from one of these strips and got a fire warning in the starboard engine. This was handled, as per check list, and we went back in. Inspection showed no fire but a stub exhaust on the collection ring had blown a threaded stub plate, and hot exhaust gases were directed on to the fire-warning sensor wiring, hence the warning. Much scratching of heads. However, the RAF sergeant disappeared into his truck, and came back with 'bits' that would screw back into the vacant stub. Ran the engine and tested. Took the empty aircraft back to Khormaksar. Not SOP, but it was not the best procedure to leave an aircraft overnight in up-country locations at that time."

BEVERLEY

Blackburn's extraordinary Beverley was the first real heavy-lifter to enter RAF service, doing so in March 1956. They arrived in Aden in May 1958 with 84 Squadron, and were joined by 30 Squadron at Eastleigh in November 1959. Despite being the butt of many jokes ('easy to navigate on the return trip, just

Beverley C.1 XH119 30 Squadron, Muharraq, May 1966. [Peter Russell-Smith]

follow the oil slick') it was very good at carrying heavy loads out of minimal airfields. 30 Squadron moved to Muharraq in October 1964, disbanding there in September 1967. 84 Squadron moved to Sharjah in August 1967, the Beverleys being replaced by the far more modern, but considerably smaller, Andover.

DAVID RICHMOND – AIR SIGNALLER

"The first requirement, on arriving on 84 Squadron in 1959, was that I get enough flying hours to qualify me for a 'C' (passenger) category. For route flying I was crewed with an experienced screen signaller, but I was authorised to fly solo on the air support and re-supply sorties to the remote garrisons in the protectorate. These formed a major part of the squadron's tasking, and the Beverley, with its high-wing configuration and tricycle undercarriage, was the perfect aircraft to carry them out. Its wide-opening clamshell rear doors gave access at a convenient height to the 40ft x 10ft x 10ft unencumbered freight bay, with a level floor throughout. The 45,000-lbs payload meant that several armoured vehicles could be carried with their crews accommodated in the tail boom, which had a seating capacity of 32 personnel in the passenger configuration.

"The Centaurus engine was the Beverley's Achilles' heel; its overhaul life was 600 hours. On 84 Squadron, so few managed to reach that point that we actually held an all-ranks beer call to celebrate when we finally got an engine to achieve it. The higher power settings needed to maintain cruising speed in the high temperatures in Aden obliged us to use power settings of 2,200 rpm and +2 psi, with the inevitable deleterious effect on engine life and in-service reliability. Delays to route trips due to technical issues with the engines were so commonplace as to be almost expected. The Centaurus provided sufficient reserves of power that it was possible to undertake a three-engine take-off in an empty aircraft and return to base to get the problem resolved.

"One component particularly prone to failure was the starter motor. The unorthodox trick that our crews developed, when up-country, was a 'jump start' where they started the three sound engines, taxied to the take-off point and lined up on the runway. With everything else working correctly, the propeller pitch on the defective engine was coarsened off and the aircraft started down the strip at full three-engined power. As about 70 knots IAS was reached, the propeller was windmilling the engine with sufficient speed to start it when the ignition was switched on. As soon as that occurred the two symmetrical engines were selected to full reverse, maximum wheel braking was applied, and the other two engines were set to idle. The aircraft came to a stop, usually in a cloud of dust, with all four engines turning. Once temperatures, pressures and mag drop checks had been satisfactorily completed, the aircraft was turned round and returned to the take-off point. Departing in the usual way, we took the starter fault home to be rectified at base. On some of the softer surfaced strips where this technique was used the undercarriage could leave ruts up to six inches deep, notwithstanding being fitted with low pressure tyres.

"The Beverley had neither pressurisation nor cabin air conditioning. So the crews on the squadron devised their own method of regulating the temperature on the flight deck to provide acceptable conditions for low-level flying, such as up-country sorties or the hours of circuit bashing for pilot continuation training. We removed, and stowed, one of the escape hatches from the rear compartment of the upper deck. Once we were airborne the reduced pressure over the wing ensured that we had a steady and welcome flow of air right through the flight deck. This made working conditions more acceptable, although we rear crew members had to ensure there were no loose items of paper which we needed, as they would be quickly whisked away and lost.

"Our usual destinations on detachments to the east were Sharjah, and on to Bahrain to supply the garrisons and rotate personnel. One of our crews had an unexpected experience when they were flying a company of locally recruited Trucial Oman Scouts (TOS). As the aircraft was reaching cruising altitude, the captain was surprised to see a beaming TOS sergeant appear on the flight deck with a tray of steaming hot drinks; 'Chai (tea), captain?' he offered. The captain, initially thinking the sergeant was kindly helping the air quartermaster (AQM), was about to thank him when realisation dawned that the AQM only ever produced coffee with his hot water urn! What was the source of the unexpected beverage? With concern rising to alarm he leapt out of his seat and shot down the ladder into the freight bay where his worst fears were confirmed. A group of levies were gathered round a camping stove in the middle of the floor with a kettle of water heating for more brews of chai! In no uncertain manner the captain's anger and concern were conveyed to them, and the stove rapidly extinguished, cooled and stored.

"Flights of interest to the wider community on base, and beyond, gave us the opportunity to fly in, for the families, large supplies of fresh food from the Kenya cold store in Nairobi. Steak (whole fillets), pork, roasting joints and bacon were especially popular. When a flight was scheduled, and space was going to be available on the return leg, station personnel were notified and invited to submit an order. When received, the orders individually identified by customer name, were collected and passed to the crew. Via the good offices of the station staff at Eastleigh the Kenya cold store was alerted to the impending large order and prepared to satisfy it. We were met on arrival by the cold store staff who collected the orders and set about making them up into individual named packages. These were delivered direct to the aircraft on the day of departure, loaded and tied down and the altitude ensured that temperatures were kept low to ensure the freshness of the product on arrival.

"The scene on our return to Khormaksar was like something more akin to a famine relief flight to the tribes of East Africa. The aircraft was taxied to an area away from the squadron flight line, flanked by crush barriers holding back the eagerly waiting families. Once we had shut down and opened the freight-bay doors the

Unloading a heavy piece of kit at Dhala, always popular with the locals. [Len Clayton]

excited families were permitted to approach the aircraft and gather round the rear sill where the AQM picked up the parcels and called out the name. The lucky recipient whooped as if they had won a prize in the national lottery, came forward, identified themselves, took their much-wanted fresh provisions and headed delightedly for home to get them safely stored as quickly as possible. This procedure could be a lengthy process, but I can only recall one occasion when we encountered a slight hitch. A package labelled 'AC ***' was called out, but no aircraftman appeared to claim it. The package was left to the end and then taken to the officers' mess and placed in the freezers for safe keeping. The following morning the squadron adjutant received a phone call from a very irate officer in HQ demanding to know why the air commodore's fresh food order had not been delivered to his residence!

"The official working day on the station was from 07:00 to 13:00 and, after a demanding morning at the Uckers board, squadron officers assembled in the mess bar for a few beers before lunch and an afternoon 'zizz' to avoid the worst of the heat. There was a very strong beer-drinking culture, reflecting the times and the hot climate, and different squadrons gathered round their own tables to socialise and relax. Only bottled beer was available which was served chilled in pint bottles. The drink of choice was either Tennant's Lager or Carlsberg drunk from a standard handled pint jug, rather than the deplorable practice of later generations of drinking straight from the bottle. Personally, I preferred Tennant's.

"Entertainment and amusements, as we know them today, were non-existent. There was no TV, FM radio, internet, mobile phones, computers or social media, so we relied on two-month-old magazines for reading matter. We were also updated by two-week-old newspapers, flown out on commercial air services. Some lucky officers had friends among the RAF long-range transport aircraft crews who brought out the current day's newspapers.

"We had to rely on the Royal Mail for our air mail letter service to and from home. The most popular means of keeping in touch with friends and family was the 'Bluey', an exclusive-to-the-military single sheet, lightweight, foldable and sealable air mail letter form. This was afforded priority handling by the Royal Mail postal service. Packages came by surface mail and took weeks to arrive. For emergency communications there was a telegram service from a local post office, or one could pre-book a manual telephone connection through the military exchange.

"I was on the crew of Beverley XH110 captained by Fg Off Dickie Livermore, with Fg Off Andy Pryde as co-pilot. We were on a week-long detachment to Oman shuttling between Sharjah and Bahrain, with some sorties into the landing strips serving the local garrisons; these included Firq, a military base close to the town of Nizwa. Nizwa was dominated by its notably photogenic 17th century fort. On this particular day, after taking off, Dickie positioned the aircraft to get himself a picture of the fort, which would be quite unique and a talking point at the social gatherings back at Khormaksar. I positioned myself on the astrostep to view the scene from the astrodome; the aircraft was in a gentle climbing turn towards the fort, which was basking in the intense Omani sunshine. A range of mountains provided an evocative backdrop. Dickie was enthusing volubly about the shots he was getting and when he had all he wanted, with the aircraft turning more steeply with about 30 degrees of bank and not climbing, he announced to Andy over the intercom, 'I have control'. After the briefest of stunned silences Andy responded with words to the effect, 'you always had!' Dickie immediately grabbed the stick, levelled the wings and resumed the climb.

"Once the tension on the flight deck had subsided a discussion ensued to analyse how the situation had arisen. The conclusion was that Dickie, pre-occupied with getting into the right position for his intended photo session had thought that he had passed control to Andy; or that he done so in such a way it had not registered and been acknowledged. Andy, unaware that he was now supposed to be flying the aircraft, had been equally focussed on the photographic opportunity presented to him. So neither pilot, equally engrossed in taking photographs of the fort, was aware that no one was actually flying the aircraft. Thankfully, XH110, being well trimmed and naturally stable, and not party to the verbal exchanges on her flight deck, had been happy left to her own devices to play her part in framing the desired photographs. She serenely continued along the trajectory she had been set on until the normal arrangement of control from the flight deck had been re-instated.

"By October 1960 my time on 84 Squadron was coming to an end; however, my life on the squadron was about to hit the low point of my tour. At 3 a.m., on Wednesday 12 October I was roused from my bed with instructions to report immediately to squadron ops where I joined a crew captained by the squadron commander, Sqn Ldr K H Perry. We were quickly briefed that one of our aircraft, XL151, was missing, presumed lost. It had been circuit bashing on a night sortie when an emergency message had been received in station ops; a Somali air force C-45 Expeditor was overdue on a flight from Somalia to Aden. Rather than call out the duty Shackleton search and rescue (SAR) crew it had been decided to utilise XL151 which was already airborne, to search for the missing aircraft. It was flying low level, with landing lights on, in the hope of spotting the, presumed, downed aircraft. This would have been the aviation equivalent of trying to find a set of dropped car keys at night with the help of a cigarette lighter and ran counter to all recognised SAR night-search procedures. It was to prove fatal.

"We got airborne and headed for the calculated search area and, shortly after first light, found our lost aircraft little more than 20 miles north of Khormaksar. XL151 had been flying low level, as briefed, but failed to take into account the undulating nature of the sand dunes in that area and had flown into the rising slope of a dune. The nose and freight bay had borne the brunt of the impact and were totally destroyed. The mainplane, complete with all four engines, was fully intact and lay parallel to the line of flight. Nestled alongside it were the fully intact boom, tailplane and fins. Remarkably, there were no signs of any fires. We descended to low level to survey the wreckage for possible survivors; there were none. We climbed back up to 1,000 feet and orbited the wreckage, giving the RAF Regiment personnel and accident investigators who were approaching overland by truck a reference point at which to aim. We were relieved by a 37 Squadron Shackleton and returned to base."

The accident claimed the lives of Flt Lt Ronald Evans, LAC James Henthorn, Fg Off Michael Pike, Flt Sgt John Smith, SAC Eric Walter, Fg Off Anthony Weet and SAC Keith Wreford.

"A somber air of grief and disbelief hung over the entire squadron when we passed on the sad news. In addition to the operating crew the aircraft had also had on board two of our young groundcrew airmen, who had gone along for the ride and to enjoy some flying experience – the loss was felt right across the squadron. At five o'clock that same afternoon the entire squadron paraded in the British Military Cemetery in Ma'alla for the funeral service when our deceased comrades were laid to rest. No trace of the Expeditor was ever found. It was concluded that it must have filed a dummy flight plan to leave Somali airspace and then overflown Aden to an undisclosed destination in Yemen.

"I flew my last sortie with the squadron on 27 October 1960, and then it was time to pack my trunk, dispose of my car, submit to the farewell ritual dunking in the mess fountain, leaving behind some wonderful friends and a host of mostly happy memories."

David then converted to the Hastings at Dishforth. He spent two years at Abingdon on the Transport Support Element before going to Nicosia in 1963 as wing signaller and standards officer for the signallers of 70 Squadron Hastings.

Len Clayton and his Beverley at Thumier in 1964. [Len Clayton]

LEN CLAYTON

"The first approach and landing of an 84 Squadron Beverley at Thumier (later renamed Habilayn) after completion of the airstrip by Royal Engineers in 1964. The captain was Flt Lt Andrus, and it happens that I was on the crew of the Bev that day, the 22nd of May. The importance of the Beverley's reverse pitch propellers for short landings was certainly needed here. Habilayn became a massive base in the Radfan campaign."

DAVID DRINKWATER – AIR ENGINEER

> *Dave graduated from Halton's apprentice school in 1960. Following tours in the UK and Germany he applied for air engineer training. On completing training, the choice was Argosy, Shackleton, Hastings or Beverley. He thought the Beverley looked as though it would be the first one to finish RAF service – so the Beverley it was.*

"On my first trip away to Aden we blew a cylinder head. That meant that while the rest of the crew were living it up in the bar, my 'screen' (new crew member) and I were undoing red hot bolts and fitting a new cylinder head. Of course there were engine runs to do afterwards, and it was very late when we finally finished and hit the mess.

"Another incident involved us landing at a desert strip. The Beverley was going to be replaced by the Andover, and we were familiarising Andover pilots with the terrain. As we approached the desert strip our pilot told the Andover captain, who was present on the flight deck, that it was 'most important to maintain speed towards the end of the strip after landing'. Just before the end the aircraft should use its momentum to complete a 180-degree turn, thus facing the opposite direction for the next take-off. Well of course the inevitable happened and the nose wheel turned, but the aircraft didn't and we dug into soft sand with the aircraft canted at an angle. We had a bulldozer on board which was to be used to re-grade the strip before our subsequent take-off. Unfortunately, the back doors couldn't be opened because the micro switches controlling the auxiliary power unit were broken due to the angle of the aircraft. Eventually, after a lot of spadework and the application of some electric string to the micro switches, I managed to get the rear doors open and the bulldozer off the aircraft.

"We needed to get airborne before the sun disappeared behind the sand dunes, but we also needed the outside air temp to drop so that we could achieve enough take-off performance before we ran out of desert. The next hour or so saw me out on the strip whirling a 'wet and dry' thermometer round my head whilst holding an anemometer in the other, pausing only to consult the operating data manual. This book had hundreds of tables which, when consulted in the right order and using the parameters given by the temperature and wind speed (plus many other factors), gave some indication as to how low the temperature had to drop for us to clear the sand dunes at the end of this desert runway on our take-off run. The signal to start engines was the sight of me sprinting back to the aircraft as the conditions eventually complied with the requirements – we made it."

After lengthy tours on the Hercules, instructing, and as flight engineer on the Battle of Britain Memorial Flight Lancaster, Dave retired in the mid-1980s.

CHRIS MEAD – NAVIGATOR

"I was posted to 84 Squadron Khormaksar on 10 March 1964. My first operational flight was on 18 March to Nairobi. We returned on 19 March and the next day went to Ataq, a village in the desert to the north-east of Khormaksar. From that day on there were very few days when I was not flying. We were always aware of events that were occurring 'up-country' in places that we were operating into on a daily basis.

"Our Beverleys operated mainly into airstrips in the desert and mountains. The aircraft's rugged construction was ideal for such operations because it was unpressurised, the fuselage was high off the ground, and it had a large, fixed undercarriage. Moreover, it had short take-off and landing capability, so we could get large loads into and out of small airfields. We also had sufficient range to go direct to Nairobi in the south, and Bahrain in the north.

"However, there were occasions when re-supply had to be done by air. Again, the aircraft was perfect for such tasks as the rear doors could be removed before the flight so that large loads could be despatched on parachutes out the back. As the navigator it was not just my job to map read us to our destination (there were no radio aids). It was also, during an airdrop, to guide the pilots to the drop zone and, at the appropriate moment give a five-second warning, 'red on', then call, 'green on' for the despatch. At that point if we were releasing paratroops, the loadmaster would direct them out of the door. During an airdrop I had to leave the flight deck and position myself in the nose window downstairs.

"When we were tasked to airdrop supplies to forces on top of Jebel Wadina, Oman, we had an escort of two Hunter ground-attack aircraft from 43 Squadron. Their role, as we approached the tiny drop zone on top of the jebel, was to fly either side of us and strafe the mountain side with rockets and cannon to deter the rebel forces.

"My tour on 84 Squadron was full of events, many of which could have come from an RAF version of 'Dad's Army'. Within a month of my arrival on the squadron, we were briefed on a paratroop drop on the island of Pemba, to the north of Zanzibar. The plan was that we should drop the paratroops and then circle until it was confirmed that they had secured the airfield – at that point we would land. This was because the aircraft did not have sufficient range to divert anywhere else. The reason for this operation was that Tanganyika and the islands of Pemba and Zanzibar had joined to form an independent republic. The operation was called off when it was discovered that there were Russian anti-aircraft guns lining the drop zone which would have been pointing in our direction during the drop.

"A few months later we were tasked to transport ammunition up-country to Beihan. On take-off the aircraft struggled to get airborne. On arrival at Beihan it was discovered that the weight stencilled on the side of the ammunition box was that of the box only and did not include the much heavier ammunition weight. The aircraft had struggled on take-off because it was overweight.

"Operating into Mukeiras (on the border with Yemen) we were tasked to load a fire engine into the aircraft and take it to Khormaksar. Again, the aircraft struggled on take-off. When we arrived in Aden, we were advised that the fire engine had not been emptied of water, and once again we were overweight.

"The Hadhramaut Bedouin Legion (HBL) operated in the desert ('The Empty Quarter') to the north of Riyan. We were tasked with supplying a platoon via a strip in the desert defined by an oil drum. The platoon was headed by a British officer who, some weeks later, was murdered by an Arab member of his platoon.

"Other destinations included Djibouti, Addis Ababa, Salalah, Masirah, Kuwait, Mombasa, Mandera (on the northern border with Somalia), Socotra Island and Perim Island. Flights in and out of Mandera were particularly hazardous – either from giraffes that had to be herded off the runway, or from Somali rebels who would fire at the aircraft from across the border.

"In November 1965 I was detached with Pat Kemp and crew to Eastleigh. From there we had to fly to Ndola in Zambia, and then to Elizabethville (now Lubumbashi) in the Congo. This was in support of the United Nations during what was known as the Congo Crisis. In December, during the Rhodesian Crisis, we returned to Zambia in support of 29 Squadron Javelins from Akrotiri, Cyprus. My last operational flight with 84 Squadron was on 22 December 1965 to Mukeiras. At the end of December, I was posted back to the UK to 242 OCU Thorney Island as a navigation instructor. In March the following year (1966), I was selected to undergo conversion training to the Hercules (with which the RAF was about to be equipped)."

ANDOVER

Andover C.1 XS611 Gulf Comms Flight, Muharraq 28 June 1970. [Robbie Shaw]

84 Squadron moved to Sharjah in August 1967, re-equipping with the Andover C.1. The squadron later moved to Muharraq before disbanding on 1 October 1971. The only other Andovers to be permanently based in the Middle East were examples of both the C.1 and CC.2 with the Gulf Communication Flight.

ARGOSY

The Armstrong Whitworth Argosy was designed to replace the Handley Page Hastings, and 56 were ordered, entering service in February 1962 with 114 Squadron at Benson. At the same time 105 Squadron also reformed at Benson, moving out to Khormaksar in June. The squadron moved to Muharraq in August 1967 and disbanded on 1 February 1968.

JOHN JAMES

"I have many fond memories of the Argosy, which was very reliable and pleasant to fly. It only let me down once when a series of inverter failures en-route from Matsapha to Cheleka (Blantyre, Malawi) brought us to a grinding halt. The only passenger on board was the airport manager, who had been on an air traffic control (ATC) liaison visit to Swaziland. He insisted the crew was shared out amongst the five expat families employed at the airport. Khormaksar despatched four new inverters to Lusaka via Nairobi on East African Airways; they were transferred to a Zambian air force Beaver, which had an engine failure, and forced landed in the bush. A second set of inverters eventually turned up ten days later, bringing to an end a most enjoyable stay.

Argosy C.1 XN820 105 Squadron at Riyan, 1966-67. [Ian Macmillan]

"I had an interesting experience in Masirah. We operated a thrice-weekly schedule to Riyan, Salalah and Masirah. Departing Aden at 07:00 there were three one-hour-and-30-minute sectors, with one-hour turnrounds at Riyan and Salalah, before arriving at Masirah for a night stop. Scheduled arrival time was 13:30. The officers' mess bar always closed promptly at 14:00, but if we were on time, it was possible to sink a quick cold beer before the shutters came down. I will always remember the disapproving looks from behind three-week-old newspapers as an Argosy crew rushed through the anti-room at 13:55. On one occasion the bar closed early and the barman refused to serve us when we arrived at 13:50, so on our next trip we were determined to beat the system. Khormaksar Air Movements did a brilliant job, and we departed with a full complement of passengers, freight and mail 30 minutes early. The turnround times at Riyan and Salalah were halved and we headed for Masirah with an ETA of 12:00, 30 minutes before the officers' mess bar was due to open.

"We approached along the south-east coast of Masirah at very low level, intending to catch out ATC. As we rounded a rocky outcrop at 100 feet, we surprised a submarine sitting on the surface, about half a mile ahead and 100 yards from the beach. It crash-dived in a mass of bubbles and sat on the sandy bottom, fully visible in the shallow blue water. We climbed to 1,000 feet and reported our find to Masirah. 'Keep it in sight' they said, 'we will inform HQ MEAF'. Five minutes later we were told a Shackleton was being scrambled from Aden, and we were to remain airborne over the 'target' until it arrived on task. With just over two hours fuel remaining this was impossible. To cut a long story short, we landed at Masirah at two o'clock, just as the bar closed!

"The airfield perimeter patrol Land Rover was fired on by automatic weapons several times during the next few weeks, fortunately by a hopeless shot. An intelligence officer told me later that Baghdad Radio had been heard boasting about supplying gallant freedom fighters to oust the British occupiers of Masirah Island. So we found an Iraqi submarine, but failed Plan A.

"During my time on 105, the direct Khormaksar to Muharraq passenger schedule (five hours) that overflew Saudi Arabia was an all-day affair. The extended turnaround allowed enough time to grab a taxi to the Manama fish market and buy ten pounds of big juicy prawns. As they were uncooked, Paddy Whelan, my loadmaster, boiled them all in the hot cup on the way home, otherwise they would have gone off. The smell in the cabin was most embarrassing!

"I had a strange experience on one return flight. It was dark when we left Bahrain, passing over Doha in the climb to flight level 200 (20,000 ft) – the sky was clear and the stars were twinkling brightly. At around FL150 we ran into severe clear air turbulence; although it only lasted a few minutes, it was very choppy. Once we had levelled off the navigator set up his sextant to take a top of climb (TOC) fix. 'I can't see any stars!' he exclaimed. 'They were up there a few minutes ago.' I leant closer to the windscreen and sure enough the sky was pitch black, while down below a multitude of lights stretched along the Qatar peninsular as far as the eye could see. The pattern of lights was vaguely familiar, much like the stars. Surreptitiously, I lifted my cigarette packet, which was lying on my cup holder, and dropped it to confirm we were the right way up.

"A few minutes later we ran into another short spell of turbulence. At the same time the galaxy of lights sitting on the desert slowly rose to their rightful place in the sky. I visited the Met Office at Khormaksar the following day and described the experience. Apparently warm air from the Saudi desert funnels down the Qatar Peninsular, lying above the cooler gulf air and causing a powerful inversion. The resulting refraction would explain the star phenomenon.

"There was a bloated 'country club' on 105, whose members were never support-flying qualified and hardly ever flew to the Gulf. Nairobi was their domain. If I remember correctly only four crews were qualified to drop paras, medium-stressed platforms and one-ton platforms in my time. Those four crews were meant to be rotated but never were. We formed a formation team and called ourselves the 'Thunderboxes', practising low-level close-formation flying covertly until we were good enough to play the Hunters at their own game. On our debut I was leading when we approached at 100 feet for a run in and break on the easterly runway at Khormaksar. The 105 Squadron building was close to the threshold of runway 08, so the boss would have had a grandstand view. Apparently he turned incandescent as he watched four Argosies flash past his window and break sharply to the left in five-second intervals. When we returned to the squadron we were intercepted by the navigation flight commander. He was praising our performance effusively when the boss appeared looking very unhappy that his planned bollocking had been shot down in flames.

"105 Squadron took over the Mombasa leave run contract from Aden Airways in July 1965, when security on the civil side of Khormaksar was deemed to be unsafe. Five hours each way and two hours on the ground was a long day, but (Aden Airways) crew lunches in the terminal restaurant were very good."

IAN MACMILLAN – NAVIGATOR

"I arrived in Aden in September 1966, a first-tourist nav joining 105 Squadron. I went out on a 12-month unaccompanied tour, as all married personnel were doing by then, and that was just one sign that the UK's time there was nearing an end. The security situation off base was seriously bad, particularly in Crater and Sheikh Othman. It came to a climax one day in June 1967 when armed rioting in Crater got out of hand, with around 20 deaths amongst army personnel (mainly Northumberland Fusiliers, if I remember correctly). We heard from an RAF doctor, sent in to help recover the dead, that some truly dreadful things had happened that day. Control was lost for ten days or so until Lt Col Colin Mitchell took his Argyll's battalion into the town and re-established control using a very firm hand. Shortly after that 105 Squadron's time in Aden was cut short and we moved north to Muharraq in Bahrain. In the end the UK withdrawal from there was completed in November 1967.

"My first trip, screened of course, was down to Matsapha for the regular re-supply run to Francistown where an anti-UDI radio had been established. Landing back at Matsapha the aircraft lurched to one side. We corrected and taxied in to find both tyres on one side burst, and severe scorches on the other. No doubt a bit of brake on touchdown? So that was the end of re-supply runs until new tyres could arrive, and diplomatic clearance times meant that was at least a week away. The co-pilot and I blagged a flight to Johannesburg on one of the Aero Commander air-taxi aircraft that flew into Matsapha. A quick night there, then on by train to Pretoria, where we presented ourselves, all unbidden at the air adviser's door. Fortunately, he and his wife were the spirit of hospitality and the next day he flew us back to Matsapha on the ex-Queen's Flight Heron (still bright red) that was his personal aircraft.

"Another Argosy duly arrived with tyres and wheel-changing kit. I only mention this as I understand that, on a previous occasion, a flight laid on to bring a replacement windscreen from Khormaksar had arrived without it. With the aircraft came a signal from HQ MEAF, saying to get both aircraft serviceable and await instructions. These were not long in coming: two further aircraft were on their way and all four would be used to evacuate the army battalion based in Swaziland (1st Royal Irish Fusiliers) to Durban. There they would embark on HMS *Fearless* for transit to Aden, and recovery from there to the UK. Sanctions were about to be imposed on Rhodesia by HMG; the reaction of South Africa and Portugal, still the colonial power in Mozambique, was uncertain. It was clearly felt that the British battalion could become something of a hostage if things went badly. Our commanding officer, Eddie Rigg, came down to be detachment commander, and I was made ops officer and general army liaison for Operation Lopen that followed. So the planned six or so-days trip extended over nearly four weeks before my return to base.

"We did a bit of Argosy flag-waving, with a fighter escort. On 31 December 1966, I landed after a late morning continuation detail, to find the nav section deserted save for a note saying I've been 'volunteered' for a task that had just come in. This turned out to be a leaflet drop at a number of dots on the map up-country, for which two Hunters would provide escort. So we all briefed together, and they caught us up en-route making diving passes as the leaflets were chucked out from the para doors. A good time was had by all; I don't think we were shot at, and I can only hope that some leaflets reached their intended readers. I kept a copy for my logbook, and, to this day, I still have no idea what they were about.

"There were other interesting drops adding colour to the route task in that last Aden year – one to an army expedition on Socotra and, only days later another to drop rations and mail at Salalah, which was temporarily closed after flooding (we'd had flooding in Aden too from the same storm system, as I recall). Of course there were relatively routine army re-supply drops up-country to Mukeiras, Ataq, Lawdar, and Dhala.

"One of the things that differentiated the military Argosy from the civil version was the occasional dropping of two linked medium-stressed platforms with a Land Rover and trailer on each. Navs had only to call 'green on' at the right moment. He then hung on for dear life to the board on which he was lying up front for supply dropping, whilst the extractor chute fell, deployed, and started to pull the weight of a full freight bay out of the back. Upstairs both pilots had to prepare to deal with the immense and rapid change of trim about to occur as the second platform went over the ramp. This then threw the nav and his board up in the air for a moment before crashing back down. I have no doubt that someone can explain more fully the challenge involved in this mildly hair-raising procedure."

JOCK MANSON – PILOT

"We always seemed to have a 'hangar queen' in Aden. It was usually up on jacks in the corner and robbed for spares. Eventually the time would come to fly it back to the UK for heavy maintenance, so just about enough bits would be put back on again for the ferry flight. One such ferry flight showed how resilient the Dart engine was. They got as far as Sharjah on the first day. Now not every station had a stock of Dart engine oil, so the flight engineers normally took enough tins of the stuff to get them to the other end. On arrival at Sharjah the groundcrew chief said that they might not have any oil, but he would have a look. The crew told him to use some of his stock if it proved necessary. Next morning the flight engineer's stock of oil was still intact and the F700 (aircraft servicing record) showed that all engines had been topped-up, so it was assumed that the groundcrew had found some after all.

"They then got airborne and headed north across the mountains of Iran. On arrival at Tehran the flight engineer went up his ladder to check the engine oil levels. When he took the first oil cap off, a black foaming volcano of oil came gushing out; this phenomenon was repeated three more times. Further investigation revealed that although his stock of engine oil was still intact, his supply of Racasan (toilet fluid) had been considerably depleted! All four engines now contained Racasan. The Rolls-Royce man in Bahrain (Kenny Rogers, I think) and a team were flown to Tehran. All four engines were purged a couple of times, and all filters etc., were changed. After an engine run it was decided that absolutely no damage had been caused and the ferry flight to UK was completed without further incident.

"The other way that we used to go was via Bahrain, then over Kuwait, south of Baghdad, south of Damascus and then over Lebanon to Akrotiri. I did that route several times, but our biggest problem was that of diplomatic clearance. It went something like this; the Iraqi clearance was valid for four days or so, but you had to make the entry and exit points plus or minus two hours. The Syrian clearance was for a 48-hour period, whilst the Lebanese clearance was for 24 hours only. So if you had more than a two-hour delay from Bahrain then you couldn't meet the Iraqi requirement and so had to delay for 24 hours. This meant that the Lebanese clearance had expired and had to be applied for again – by which time the Syrian clearance had expired and so it went on and on.

"Salalah ran out of beer one weekend and I had to do an emergency re-supply from Bahrain on the Sunday morning. It was of such importance that we even had Saudi overflight clearance, so didn't have to go round Fahud. We had four pallets loaded with Amstel, and four pallets loaded with Carlsberg. The navigator worked out that if we went down in the Empty Quarter, we would not survive. It went something like this, first day you had to drink eight beers to meet your fluid requirement. Now it takes a pint of water to process an ounce of alcohol. Therefore, the next day you had to drink 20 beers, and so it was that you died on the fourth day with a smile on your face!

"When Rhodesia declared UDI, most of the aircrew on Khormaksar-based squadrons who would have been involved were assembled in a hangar and asked if they were prepared to take action against Ian Smith's illegal regime. The answer was a unanimous 'no'. I seem to remember a number of Canberra crews from Cyprus were also present. It was intended that 105 Squadron Argosies would have been used to drop paras to secure strategic rail and road points, then re-supply them. My contribution to the cock-up was to fly two large generators, delivered by Ace Freighters, from Francistown in Bechuanaland to Lusaka. These were to power Harold Wilson's folly – a propaganda radio station that was beamed at Rhodesia.

"On 8 November 1967 we took a Bristol Centaurus engine from Bahrain to Jeddah, this was in order to rescue Dick Barton (*not that one!*) and crew, who had lobbed into Jeddah with a failed engine while ferrying an 84 Squadron Beverley back to the UK. When we got to Jeddah we were a bit surprised to see that the Beverley was covered in graffiti. The aircraft was 'U' – uniform and this had been modified to 'UK AND/OR BUST'. There were several other symbols and messages about the fuselage. The old girl was headed for scrapping at Bicester and was only planned to land at RAF airfields en-route, so the lads in Khormaksar had gone mad with the paint brush. It certainly raised a few eyebrows in Jeddah, and the air attache wanted it out of there pronto.

"I remember taking a large triangular jack to Nairobi for a Shackleton which had to have a wheel change. The Argosy carried two ramps which were attached to the bottom clamshell door for loading and unloading. As the unloading of the jack seemed to be taking an age, I went back to have a look. To my horror, our man had

Argosy C.1 XP439 loading at Salalah, 26 April 1966. [John James]

one jack leg on each ramp, and the third leg supported by a plank of wood hovering in space between the two ramps; each end of the plank on top of an inverted bit of roller-conveyor. The plank was bowing ominously and looked set to snap. The large jack falling between the two ramps would have caused unthinkable damage. I asked, 'why are you doing it this way?' He replied, 'it's the only way to do it – the jack has three legs, and we only have two ramps'. I said, 'so why don't you turn the jack around a bit so that two legs can go down one ramp and the third leg goes down the other?'

"When I got to 105 Squadron in May 1966 there wasn't a lot of up-country work. The squadron seemed to rely on the new chaps arriving from the UK all fresh and signed up to do what little work there was while they were still current. I got checked out by Vic Blake and did my first up-country drop on 13 July 1966. The DZ was at a place called Musaymir which was surrounded by substantial hills. It was certainly an eye-opener to me who had only recently arrived from the UK – Salisbury Plain it certainly wasn't. Not only that, but it was a bit higher and a hell of a lot hotter!

"I learned a lot from Vic that day. I seem to remember that we had a speed limit of 115 knots when the clamshell doors were open; above that speed the old girl started to vibrate in a noticeable fashion. Needless to say, an engine failure at those heights and temperatures, with the doors open, would have got your attention in a major way. So it was that Vic taught me to ignore the run-in instructions etc. on the op order, but to start with an escape route from which you would survive an engine failure and then work backwards. It was always better to stick your wingtip into the hills when you had four engines running and the doors were shut and then give yourself the maximum amount of room when things turned unpleasant.

"The Argosy was generally speaking quite a pleasant aircraft to fly. The only thing that I found took a bit of getting used to was the marked nose-up change of trim on finals when landing flap was selected. A good push forward was needed on the control column to stay on the glide slope, but this was just one of life's great aviation idiosyncrasies. I don't remember it being difficult to fly on three engines. In those days we used to really shut the engine down, and feather the prop, in training (normally No.4 – the critical engine). Nowadays, (quite rightly) the engine would just be retarded to flight idle.

"On one of my Beihan trips we got back to the aircraft to discover that the auxiliary power unit (APU) had, most unusually, given up the ghost. The flight engineer changed the glo-plug, but it still would not start – night stopping at Beihan was not an option. Every night 'our lot' went over the mountain ridge, to the west of the strip, they met the assorted 'unclean' dissidents coming up the other side. If your aircraft was still on the strip then it was quite likely to be hit by a friendly little weapon called a recoilless rifle, which delivered an 11-lb explosive. This b*ggered up your aircraft and did your future career no good at all.

"We spoke to Aden on the HF radio, and they stressed the need to get out of there before nightfall. That left us with doing a battery start (I seem to remember that No.2 was the favourite engine for this procedure). Well, we got the engine running and we could even get it up to take-off power, but that was all we could achieve. There was an electrical relay on the Dart which needed at least 24v DC on the busbar before the relay would make and allow the generator to come on line. This we did not have and it was rapidly getting dark.

"So it was that the flight engineer (I think it was Andy Anderson) put his thinking cap on. He persuaded the army to get two batteries out of their vehicles which he then connected in series on the floor alongside the battery box. He then got some fencing wire and asbestos gloves and 'flashed' the combined current across the terminals of the aircraft battery. This was just enough to make the relay, and get the generator on line. The rest was easy, and off we went back to Neddy's for a cold one or two.

"Salalah suffered, and still suffers, from a local monsoon from May until about September. It meant that getting into Salalah was not easy. Because of the terrain, an approach could only be made from the south onto the 35 strip with a tailwind. The best time to get in during the monsoon was around 2:00 in the afternoon (period of maximum heating) when the cloud base might just rise high enough to make a landing possible. The best approach aid available was an ACR7 (PAR – precision approach radar without a glideslope). It was quite usual to break out of the low cloud over the sea at around 300 to 400 feet and then have to go through at least one other layer before finally breaking out at 'a rather low altitude'. When it was really bad, we had the additional help of a couple of 44-gallon drums full of scrap fuel. These were set into the 'bundu' on finals aligned with 35 and were then set alight to give us an orange glow and something to aim at.

"The airfield also had a published non-directional beacon (NDB) approach procedure which always made me smile. It made it very, very clear that flying north of the NDB was forbidden, because of the jebel which went up to 'several thousands of feet'. I could never work out how anyone could ever follow this procedure as the only way you knew you had passed over the NDB was when the needles 'dropped'. By then you were already in mortal danger according to the instrument!

"I was quite fond of Salalah, however removing the rebels from the hills was a bit of a problem. The b*****s used to come down the hill at night and launch all sorts of nastiness at the airfield. Our defensive positions were north of the airfield and locally known as porcupines. One night I was involved with a reinforcement flight from Bahrain. The Salalah guys had been in the porcupines fighting the 'unclean' for 48 hours. They had taken casualties which needed CASEVACing – and they needed help. I arrived at 03:00 (in the monsoon season) with the reinforcements and set about the usual ACR7 approach with the oil drums alight. I was told that the airfield was still under fire, but they had sent a Ferret scout car out to protect us while we landed.

"We finally came out of the last cloud layer at around 75-100 feet on 35 with a tailwind and threw the old girl on the ground. Very shortly afterwards I picked up the Ferret scout car in the landing lights; it was parked right on the intersection of 35/17 and 22/04. It was the shortest landing that I ever did in an Argosy. I would not have been the slightest bit surprised if the tail booms had come over the top. The commander of the scout car came from the Indian sub-continent. He had figured out that he would have the maximum defensive effect if he parked in the middle of the airfield. As best as I can recall, this resulted in having to change two wheels – we had to do it ourselves since everyone else was 'already occupied'.

PAUL H – ENGINES

"Oh joy, I spent nearly three years as an engine fitter on the Argosy's Darts and was on 105 Squadron from April 1962 to May 1964. Much fun with the beast, regular runs around the Middle East and down into Africa, we didn't carry much and didn't go very high (lots of limitations) but could carry a freight bay full of toilet rolls on a fortnightly basis from Khormaksar to Perim, soil from Kenya to Khormaksar for the boss's garden (AOC Middle East Air Vice-Marshal Johnnie Johnson) and small loads of passengers. It seemed to be a good VIP carrier but not a lot else. We used to load Hercules power plants for Valettas of 233 Squadron on a regular basis to fly up-country after their engine failures. We all had our 'own' aircraft as travelling groundcrew, an airframe, electrical and engine tradesman, went with the aircraft up and down the route ('jollies' they were, I usually ended up as tea boy). Mine was XP439, a lovely machine.

"We had an oddity in XP409 in that it had a nail embedded in the fuselage, starboard side just above the fuselage datum. The story went that when the new Coventry Cathedral was consecrated back in 1961, six big nails from the structure of the old cathedral were presented to six of Coventry's major industries, Armstrong Whitworth being one of them. The first entry in the aircraft F700 was 'nail in forward fuselage at station…'.

"The Argosy had RDA8 Darts on introduction to service, it wasn't exactly a sparkling performer, water methanol injection was used on every take-off. Filling that tank was a right pain, although in Aden we had local labour for those jobs. I remember the strengthened floor at the front of the freight bay; underneath it was the inverters and sundry other electrical gizmos. It caused some difficulties when the inverters failed with a loaded freight bay. It simply wasn't possible to open the rear clamshell doors to move the freight out to enable the floorboards (some 'millions' of screws all with worn heads) to be lifted. A fix was introduced to enable this to be accomplished. It was first introduced on XP409, an aircraft that had had an electrical fire in the battery box and had non-standard wiring which caused some head scratching.

"I was on one of the first trips to Matsapha. Us engine chaps had to check engine and gearbox oils soonest after shutdown; we normally went out of the cockpit escape hatch onto the roof and down onto the wings. We were surprised to find, very neatly going through the vortex generators and down the side of the fuselage, about half a dozen very neat holes. We had been shot at on our approach in. We never found any bullets inside or who did it. I had the unpleasant job of going through the rear cockpit door into the heat and humidity, down among the air condition pack, to try to find any damage but found none. The aircraft had the holes patched with

Argosy XP413 in the sea short of Khormaksar runway, 23 March 1964. [via Ray Deacon]

aluminium tape and returned to Nairobi low level with no pressurisation. Fg Off John Church, the junior engineering officer (JENGO) signed it off and went back with it, by request of the crew, with Bill Aspinall in charge if I remember correctly. We did have fun those days.

"My time on 105 came to an end just after XP413 was converted into a flying boat on the approach into Khormaksar on 23 March 1964 – a lack of ability to fly on only two engines on the same side. We quickly had it hauled up on the slipway at the marine craft section. It took just over a fortnight to dismantle ready for crating and shipping home, and it was well drained and flushed out. We had great fun drilling holes in the bottom of the fuselage to let the sea out prior to lifting the floorboards to flush the 'bilges' out with (very valuable) fresh water. It went back to the UK as deck cargo on the P & O *Oriana*."

JOCK MANSON PICKS UP THE STORY

"The Argosy in the water. The day that they ended up in the water in Aden was pretty interesting from the navigator's point of view. The cockpit escape hatch was right above the navigator's table. Taff refused to accept the fact that they had actually ditched (he was facing backwards) until the rest of the crew started to stand on his fingers as they went out. When he finally followed them, they were all sitting in one of the MS26 dinghies that were stored in the wings. Unfortunately, the dinghy had inflated between the booms of the aircraft, so they were sat there in their own personal swimming pool surrounded by the airframe.

"Taff stood on the wing and tried to persuade them that they really needed to get out and re-launch the dinghy away from the airframe; an MS26 dinghy could hold 26 survivors and was rather large and bloody heavy. So they all sat there in their MS26 watching XP413 – it showed no signs of sinking. It slowly dawned on them that the bottom of the fuselage was already on the bottom! Whereupon the chief cheerleader from the front got it in his mind that they should start saving as many radios and navaids from the radio rack upstairs as they could. This might help ameliorate the punishment to come from 'the subsequent court martial'. Now any of you who have ever been in a dinghy will know that there is no such thing as a dry dinghy. There will ALWAYS be water in the bottom. So it was that all of the radios etc. were completely ruined.

"From Taff's point of view, his biggest and most cherished item was the periscopic sextant. He handed it over the side to one of his friends who promptly dropped it, and it is still (presumably) on the seabed. XP413 was towed to the Khormaksar Marine

Britannia C.1 XL638 overshot landing at Khormaksar, 12 October 1967. [Author's collection]

Craft Unit and dismantled. It was taken home and rebuilt to fly again. As a celebration of its history, a Plimsoll line was painted on each side of the forward fuselage."

> *XP413 was rebuilt by Hawker Siddeley and returned to RAF service in May 1966.*
>
> *On 12 October 1967, Lyneham-based Britannia C.1 XL638 flying from Bahrain overran the Khormaksar runway on landing and finished on the salt flats before the causeway. Full forward thrust had been applied instead of reverse thrust after touchdown. The Royal Engineers could not pull the aircraft out from where it had come to rest so they first removed the cargo, then blew the fin and rudder off as the height was causing an obstruction/danger to aircraft movement. After spares recovery they proceeded to blow up the remains. A number of spares and controls from XL638 were used to refurbish the forward fuselage of another Britannia, G-ALRX, which had become a flight deck trainer at Brize Norton. It is now in the Aerospace Bristol museum.*

AVIONICS GUY

"We did the trial vehicle fits with the army in Bahrain. I think it was the Saladin or Saracen armoured car that was supposed to fit in an Argosy, but it wouldn't; regardless of what the designers and army said – 'but it must, it's shown on the drawing'! They would fit, but only with their wheels removed so that they could then be loaded onto a sled. Then we did trials with the low-back Bedford refueller, which had to be reversed in empty (we thought the idea was to fly it into remote strips ready to function). It fit in okay, but when it was loaded, because of the cab and engine gearbox at the rear of the aircraft, it put the centre of gravity right on the rearmost limit – fail again."

HASTINGS

The only Hastings squadron stationed in the Middle East was on the fringes of the area with 70 Squadron at Nicosia. One or two others were on the strength of the Middle East Communication Squadron at Khormaksar. However, UK-based Hastings squadrons were involved in supporting Middle East operations.

ALAN FOSTER – PILOT

"On 24 Squadron our regular trip was Colerne to Lyneham, pick up something, i.e. cargo or people, and then straight down to Malta. Sometimes we went on to El Adem, Idris or Cyprus. On a couple of occasions we were detached, once in Cyprus, and in 1964 when there was a serious political situation in east Africa with the mutinies in Kenya and the old colonies. At that time, Argosies were based in Aden, and there were two paratroop battalions up in Bahrain. They were moved down to Aden; the idea being that we had to reinforce or help the political masters there. The Argosies could do the para-drop but didn't have the range to get there and back again. There was also an aircraft carrier steaming flat out from Hong Kong to Dar es Salaam. Meanwhile we were sent out to Aden with 2 Para and 3 Para. The flight was a long one; Lyneham to Tripoli non-stop, then Tripoli to Khartoum and finally Khartoum to Aden – boy that was a boring trip. There and back was pushing 60 hours.

"We stayed in Aden while the political situation was being untangled and the carrier had arrived with Sea Vixens, marines, and so on. We then did re-support of the army in Oman with miscellaneous items; Land

Hastings C.1 TG533 242 OCU Dishforth, Khormaksar, 8 April 1958. [John James]

Rover wheels, toilet paper, bottles of beer, ammunition. That was from Aden, up the coast to various stations, Salalah, Masirah and then across to Bahrain. In each place it was stop, unload, load, have a meal and then press on. Then the navy and the marines got control and we came home."

HERCULES

The Lockheed Hercules C.1 entered service in April 1967. Given the anticipated short life remaining for the British in Aden, there was no consideration given to basing them there. Nonetheless, on occasion, UK-based examples found their way out there, as Chris Mead remembers.

CHRIS MEAD

"The situation in Aden had deteriorated even more during the time since I had left 84 Squadron in 1966. The protectorate was moving towards independence, and meetings had already been held between local leaders and the British Government. In July 1967 the unrest was highlighted by the uprising in Crater by armed police, resulting in the death of British soldiers. A short while later in a much-publicised operation, the Argyll and Sutherland Highlanders, under Lt Col Colin Mitchell, re-took the town and recovered the bodies.

"On 11 November 1967, we on 36 Squadron were detached to Muharraq for the evacuation of the British armed forces from Aden. We were warned on our arrival at Muharraq that casualties were expected. In the officers' mess, where we were resting prior to our flight, will forms had been placed on the coffee tables. A secret briefing then took place in an open-air cinema! We were accommodated in the Speedbird Hotel in downtown Bahrain, and our daily flight schedule was posted each morning on a board in reception. Fortunately, there were no casualties associated with the withdrawal.

"On one of the Hercules approaching the top of descent into Muharraq, the navigator decided to switch on his oxygen

Hercules C.1 XV192 Khormaksar, 8 September 1967. [Martin Henderson]

mask to energise himself after the long flight from the UK. Unfortunately he was smoking a cigarette at the time, and it ignited the oxygen mask, transforming it into a torch. Fortunately it was put out quite quickly and not too much damage was done.

"For the evacuation we would land at Khormaksar, load up with the engines running, then leave. I was the navigator on the very last aircraft (XV203) to depart Khormaksar on 29 November 1967. The captain was Flt Lt Ron Wright, an old friend from 84 Squadron. We landed at Khormaksar and taxied round to the control tower, opened the door for the last air traffic controller, then continued taxiing to the runway and took off immediately for Muharraq. We left Bahrain for the UK the following day."

HELICOPTERS

Fulfilling both light transport and SAR roles, there were four different types of RAF helicopter based in the Middle East. The Army Air Corps were also there with Sioux and Scout helicopters.

Aden Comms Flight Sycamore with 233 Squadron's Ben Hollis doing his dinghy drill. [Dean Pringuer]

SYCAMORE

The Bristol Sycamore was the first really effective helicopter in RAF service. At Khormaksar it fulfilled the SAR task with the Aden Protectorate Communication and Support Flight, which became 84 Squadron at the end of 1956.

CORNISH JACK – PILOT

"I did a three-month stint on the Sycamores at Khormaksar when they first arrived. Our first attempt at dinghy drill (the first with a Sycamore in Aden) was cancelled. The local shark population had got wind of it and gathered in our selected spot!

"The Sycamore power limitation made early SAR pick-ups a two-crew operation, pilot and nav/winchman. If circumstances demanded that the winchman needed to make physical contact, he donned a special headset. This plugged into a spring-loaded intercom lead (on a spool) so he could maintain contact with the pilot. To allow the pilot to keep an eye on what was going on directly beneath him, it was decided that a set of two convex mirrors should be mounted – one at pilot-eye level, angled towards the right oleo, where the second was angled toward the rescue scene. It was found that the Hillman Husky (then in service as a utility transport) hubcaps, suitably polished, fitted the purpose exactly. Thankfully, this system didn't last long, not least because the intercom lead produced ear-splitting resonance screams as soon as it was immersed. As an idea it was only marginally less useful than the 'Sproule net', which was intended to cope with the same problem, but was ultimately reserved for corpse recovery."

Belvedere HC.1 XG468 26 Squadron, May 1964. [Adrian Balch collection]

BELVEDERE

The Bristol Belvedere HC.1 twin-rotor helicopter arrived in Aden on 1 March 1963 when 26 Squadron relocated there from Odiham. However, their stay at Khormaksar was relatively short as the squadron disbanded on 30 November 1965. All its Belvederes were loaded aboard the aircraft carrier HMS Albion *and shipped to Singapore to join 66 Squadron.*

WHIRLWIND

Three Whirlwind HAR.10s replaced the Aden SAR Flight's Sycamores in March 1964, only to be usurped within a year or so by the later Wessex. As a result, the Whirlwind stories that follow relate to Cyprus on the fringes of the Middle East. 84 Squadron reformed with Whirlwinds on the island on 17 January 1972, with A Flight at Akrotiri and B Flight at Nicosia. Having been based overseas since 1920, at the time of writing 84 Squadron is still at Akrotiri, awaiting the arrival of Jupiter HC.2 helicopters.

GUY GIBBONS – PILOT

"All five Whirlwinds at Nicosia (1976-1980) were HAR.10s. As far as I know there was no difference (pilot wise) between HC and HAR Whirlwinds, the only obvious one being the rescue hoist (or the hydraulic pipework for it) just above the door.

Whirlwind HC.10 XP345 84 Squadron Nicosia. [Guy Gibbons]

Our UN Detachment was primarily support work – troop moves, underslung loads up to various UN posts along the line, and particularly water up to the mountain-top ones in the Danish (DANCON) area around Xeros and the Kokkina Enclave. We were almost always at max weight or more and had insufficient power. We also had winches to lift people into or out of those smaller observation posts without a helicopter landing site. The Whirlwind was underpowered, we had overweight loads, high temperatures, few refuelling sites and limited range – the best way to learn how to fly and operate a helicopter to its limits. Even on Chinooks I found I frequently used these techniques when operating close to max weight, when others were having problems.

"We did get involved in the odd rescue or two. Of note was 12 November 1977 for *Erturk 1* a Turkish ferry, which had an engine fire and was in danger of breaking up. There were about 117 passengers on board, but we got them all off with the assistance of the guys from Akrotiri who arrived about half-way through.

"When Turkey invaded the island, one squadron member was standing on top of the control tower at Nicosia taking pictures of the Turkish aircraft attacking the airfield. He suddenly realised they were flying straight towards him and firing cannons; he was slightly wounded by shrapnel. The tower controller (it was still run by the RAF despite being an international airport) was telephoned by an irate wing commander at Akrotiri. He wanted to know why they had closed Nicosia (it was under attack from aircraft as above) and were ordering him to reopen as they couldn't launch any Lightnings without a diversion, and Nicosia was their only diversion. The controller never got an apology. The intelligence cell (possibly RAF) told the officer commanding RAF Nicosia that the Turkish wouldn't invade as they had no capability. Meanwhile he was watching as parachutes were landing on the plain to the north. I remember flying the blue line (the boundary between Turkish and Greek Cypriot forces) and finding bullet holes in the rotor blades after landing.

"The only unit at Nicosia after the invasion was 84 Squadron (UN Det), which was parented from Akrotiri; its big comms section for the Middle East flight watch etc, had gone. So the RAF formally closed RAF Nicosia, I think it was 31 May 1977. Three or four days later, when I was the duty officer, I answered the phone to find I was talking to a very senior member of the Foreign and Commonwealth Office in London. He was virtually apoplectic and wanted to know who had authorised the closure of RAF Nicosia, and, even worse, promulgated it. I promptly (in good junior officer mode) passed him up the line and suggested he contact the AOC. It transpired (I later found out) that by closing RAF Nicosia AND lowering the flag without negotiation, we had broken the Status of Forces agreement with the government of Cyprus and they could now also take over the other sovereign base areas – Akrotiri, Episkopi and Dhekelia. The following morning the RAF Ensign was flying again!

"Whilst inbound early one morning I remember seeing a U-2 crash at Akrotiri. I didn't actually see the aircraft but saw the fireball and heard the shriek from the controller on the radio."

> *On 7 December 1977 the USAF Lockheed U-2 based at Akrotiri veered off the runway during take-off and demolished the ATC Centre. As well as the pilot, Robert A Henderson, the senior meteorological officer and four locally employed met assistants were killed. A number of RAF and civilian personnel also suffered injuries.*

JONATHAN PLUMLEY – PILOT

"I was posted to B Flight 84 Squadron in October 1976; however, this was changed just before I flew to Cyprus, and I would now be joining A Flight 84 Squadron at Akrotiri who needed a pilot who was SAR qualified due to a short notice posting to Oman of another pilot. I started there in January 1977.

"One rather windy day our first standby helicopter was called to a Greek fishing vessel which had put out a Mayday call giving the impression they were sinking. After several hours of searching, another helicopter and crew joined the search, this time aided by a Hercules which had just arrived from the UK and had picked up volunteers from Akrotiri to act as lookouts. The Greek vessel was found about 45 miles east of Cape Greco, but by now it was dark. The Hercules flew towards it and once there fired off green flares. This aided navigation for the Whirlwind, and we put the winchman on the deck of the fishing vessel, but the crew were adamant that they did not need to be rescued. The Hercules returned to Akrotiri to be rewarded with a champagne reception which, by the time the Whirlwind arrived, had all gone.

"In July 1978 following glandular fever I had to regain my flying currency having been off flying for several weeks. One requirement was my instrument flying proficiency, and this involved flying on instruments for one hour and completing two instrument approaches. The first radar approach went without any problems, but whilst going around from the second approach the engine did not produce enough power, and the rotor RPM started to decay. I immediately lowered the collective lever to regain the rotor RPM, and as we were at about 100 feet I prepared the helicopter for an engine-off landing. We landed safely, but the engine was still running with the power turbine inlet temperature rising very rapidly so we shut it down. We usually flew the Whirlwind with the parking brake on so as we ran onto the runway the brakes got rather hot and, as the brakes were smoking, our crewman ran away from the aircraft.

"The helicopter was towed back to the squadron and the engine examined. The squadron boss interviewed the two pilots separately, as it was clear that he suspected us of mishandling. Fortunately our stories matched perfectly, but worse was to come as the engineers could find nothing wrong with the helicopter. The squadron boss then asked me to do an air test, but I refused as I was convinced that there had been a serious malfunction. I stood my ground, as did all the other pilots, and the pilot flight commander suggested the engine should be changed. With that the squadron commander saw sense, had the engine removed and run on the engine testbed. Faults with the flow divider and inlet guide vanes were discovered. I never did get an apology or pat on the back for saving the aircraft from serious damage.

"On 3 July 1977 commander British Forces Cyprus (CBFC) needed to be flown to Larnaca to catch the Cyprus Airways flight to London. 84 Squadron went to considerable lengths to get him there on time. We were to fly him from Air House helipad at about 07:30. Two aircraft were prepared for the task so that if the first went u/s we had a spare. There was also a second crew available who could, if necessary, fly the second helicopter for us if we went u/s at Air House. The first aircraft started the first time, so we were now early for our task and flew to Air House where we waited. The crewman and I waited at the helipad, but we could hear a strange tinkling sound which came from a waiter carrying a tray. As he reached the helicopter, he said, 'the air marshal thanks you for being early and thought you might like some breakfast'! After breakfast CBFC joined us, and we flew to Larnaca. On arrival we carried his bags to the VIP lounge and waited until he had departed. He asked us what we were doing, and I told him that officer commanding 84 Squadron had told us to wait until he had left for London. He said we were not to wait as he had already taken up too much of our time and ordered us to return to base. We flew back to Akrotiri but on arrival we heard the ops 'phone ringing; officer commanding 84 Squadron asked why we had returned contrary to his instructions. We told him we were ordered to by CBFC!

"In 1978 there was a requirement to film the testing of a new parachute as it exited an Argosy aircraft. Unfortunately, the usual chase aircraft for the air-to-air photography could not deploy to Akrotiri where the trials were taking place, and a way had to be found to allow a Whirlwind helicopter to do the task even though the two aircraft were not speed compatible. One of our 84 Squadron pilots had the bright idea of arranging the timing so that the two aircraft were close enough by rendezvousing over a particular spot on the airfield at the moment of parachute release. This required very accurate flying and time keeping. The trial was a complete success."

WESSEX

As previously mentioned, 78 Squadron flew the Wessex HC.2 from Khormaksar from June 1965. The unit also maintained an SAR Flight detachment at Muharraq. The squadron moved to Sharjah on 13 October 1967, where it disbanded on 21 December 1971.

PULL UP A SANDBAG

COLIN BUTLER

"We landed in a Beverley at Hargeisa British Somaliland on our way to Eastleigh. When we were taxiing out we came to a sudden halt. A crewman had to get out of the aircraft again, not easy in a Beverley, to remove a very large tortoise which was chocking our nose wheel very effectively!"

Wessex HC.2 XR529 78 Squadron Sharjah, 4 May 1969. [Adrian Balch collection]

CHAPTER SIX

FAR AWAY PLACES WITH STRANGE SOUNDING NAMES

Whilst Khormaksar continued to be the single largest RAF station in the Middle East, the sheer size of the area of operations between the Mediterranean and the Far East Air Force (FEAF) meant that several other 'permanent' stations were needed.

AKROTIRI, CYPRUS

Motto – Acre Semper Acria *(The peninsula is always eager)*

RAF Akrotiri was constructed in the mid-1950s and was the base for operations during the 1956 Suez Crisis and the EOKA (translated from Greek as National Organisation of Cypriot Fighters) revolt in Cyprus. Initially part of the Middle East Air Force, hence its inclusion here, on 1 March 1961 it came under the control of the newly formed NEAF. However, it continued to play a very significant role in supporting operations in the wider Middle East.

BRIAN SHADBOLT – PILOT

"I arrived in MEAF on 28 December 1958 to join 13 (Canberra) Squadron after an epic 14-day troopship voyage, which should have only been ten days. We were offloaded from the troopship in small boats to a large, barbed wire compound on the outskirts of the little town of Limassol. EOKA were still being unpleasant, so being devout cowards we huddled into the middle of the compound surrounded

Canberra PR.7 13 Squadron Akrotiri, at Sharjah c.1961. [Brian Shadbolt]

by hundreds of soldiers. All the vehicles looked very strange as they had an angle iron contraption mounted on the front. This was for cutting the wires that EOKA suspended bombs from across the roads.

"Akrotiri was a construction dust bowl, the officers' mess was in cawood huts made of thin plywood with walls a couple of inches thick. 13 Squadron's dispersal was just south of the western runway threshold, and the squadron offices were in old railway trucks salvaged from the Canal Zone. The crew room was a small marquee, freezing in winter and boiling in summer. The squadron all posed for a photo while I was there, very much a one-off. I think this was the only time in my two-and-a-half years there that the whole squadron was in residence at Akrotiri. When I arrived, we only had three aircraft as EOKA had managed to get a small bomb into one of our aircraft when it was in the tech wing hangar for a minor service. I didn't get to fly a Canberra PR.7 until 13 February 1959.

"The Canberra colour schemes were completely random. The commanding officer tried to get them all in PR blue, but tech wing wouldn't oblige. We were constantly swapping aircraft. I personally took three back to Marshall's Cambridge (where I learned to fly gliders at 16) for night photo mods. We would then drop off a modified one to RAF Germany and take one of theirs back to Akrotiri. I think the German ones were getting low on fatigue life from too much time at low level.

"Our regular ongoing task was the Libyan survey, as apart from pre-war Italian maps of the coastal strip the country was totally unmapped. For this task there would often be one aircraft in Idris and one in El Adem. We spent an awful lot of time over the Libyan desert mapping. The first serious Libyan oil well was taken from our PR.7 at 400 knots. Look closely and you can see a set of tyre tracks – we were at about the driver's head height! A very brave nav was down in the nose with my camera. You could get very low over the flat stony desert, easing down until the shadow was looking quite close. The wingtip vortices left a spectacular dust trail.

"When starting a new area, we would fly N-S tie strips, about I guess every degree. The pictures would go to the Royal Engineers who would mark up the start points for each E-W run and then send them back to us. I seem to remember it was all done at 1:10,000 with 36-inch cameras at 30,000 feet. There was a fan array of six cameras, and at the back the 12-inch camera which covered the same area. That camera was still in use in 2005; from dodgy memory it had a pre-war Zeiss lens.

"There was a regular flight to the Persian Gulf. Routing was over Turkey to Lake Van then down over Iran to Bahrain, or Sharjah with its tarred sand runway. The Trucial Oman Scouts would need pictures for their latest skirmish. Then on to Aden which was not part of MEAF at that time. If we were unlucky, there would be quite a few sorties needed from Khormaksar as there was an ongoing, undeclared war all along the Yemen border. We had a regular run over Yemen. As they had no radar, we tried not to advertise our presence. Head out to sea and climb to find the contrail level, then drop down a couple of thousand feet before heading north. The person on the jump seat would go back and use the periscope to make sure we didn't start to trail. Routing was Hodeidah, Mocha, Sana, Taiz and then back to Khormaksar.

"As soon as we could we were off to Eastleigh and civilisation, we were trying to finish the Kenya survey as there were all sorts of gaps scattered around from earlier efforts by Lincolns. It was a very frustrating job as by the time the sun was high enough the cumuli would start bubbling up. We got to see a lot of Kenya at low level, burning off a lot of fuel. Eastleigh runway was about 500 yards of concrete, and then

Libya's first serious oil well from the nose of a low-flying Canberra. [Brian Shadbolt]

rolled murram soil. We were at 5,000 feet and it was quite warm, so take-offs were always a little tense until reaching safety speed. For longer flights we would position a couple of miles over to Embakasi, the international airport.

"When I was in Cyprus, MEAF consisted of Akrotiri, Nicosia, Troodos Radar and HQ MEAF at Episkopi. There was also a small air-sea-rescue set up in Limassol harbour. El Adem in Libya was also part of MEAF, but for some reason Idris, also in Libya, came under HQ Malta. MEAF seemed to quite often be forgotten by the paper pushers. We had two wheels-up landings onto foam strips after total hydraulic failures, and as a result the flare-bay jacks split. No-one had bothered to say there was a modification to replace them with a new model, which had been sitting in stores for a year. There was another drama when a signal arrived to say, 'do not use the survey camera until the drive motor has been replaced with a new flameproof version'. That meant we couldn't do anything, so the techies headed off to stores. Yes, we had had them in stock for two years, but as they were not issued, they are now in the dump. EOKA could get in to bomb our aircraft, but no-one could get into the dump! The contents were auctioned a couple of times a year to the local scrap merchants. Removing anything would be like stealing cash from Her Majesty's purse. Many favours were called in, blind eyes turned. It was a very secret operation, need to know. Very nobly the commanding officer led it with a couple of photo techies, who knew what they were looking for. Success, but then much postdated paperwork had to be generated (remember six carbon copies of everything) to legalise the work.

"Independence happened on 16 August 1960, so there were major upheavals with the formation of the sovereign British areas. Just before this, it dawned on the army, that if we ever needed to invade it would be a good idea to have pics of all the landing beaches. This, coverage of the coastline from 500 feet looking in at 90 degrees, was a fun job for us. Hundreds of short runs were involved. We got through the film very quickly, so back to base and new magazines loaded with engines running.

"When I left the squadron it was off to CFS, then to 6 FTS Acklington on Jet Provost T.3s and later T.4s. In July 1964 I left the RAF from there and went to Qantas."

MASIRAH, OMAN

Motto – Al-i' timad'ala al-nafs *(The reliance is on one's own self)*

Located on the northern tip of Masirah Island, RAF Masirah opened in 1943 as a staging post for flights between Aden and India, and it was also a base for anti-

submarine patrols. Closing in March 1977, it was the last permanently manned RAF base in the Gulf region.

JONATHAN PLUMLEY – PILOT

"I graduated from the Andover OCU in September 1972 and was posted to 46 Squadron as a co-pilot. I started flying in Masirah in May 1973 and only completed one Masirah detachment although I was scheduled for one in the summer of 1974. In May 1974 I was advised that I would be posted to the captain's course, but this quickly changed later that month, and I was posted to helicopters that July. This was all due to the dreaded defence review and I was one of the lucky ones to get a flying tour.

"The significance of May 1973 was that it was the time of the fuel crisis. There were severe restrictions on transport which hit us when trying to get to Brize Norton to fly to Masirah. There were four of us needing to get to Brize Norton, and although we applied for MT to take us there with all our kit, authorisation had to come from HQ

RAF Masirah, 1962-63. [Len Clayton]

46 Group; it was refused and we were told we had to use public transport. Our journey required us to use the nearest railhead at Emsworth, from there to Havant where we would change to a train to Basingstoke, from there we would catch a train to Reading then another train to Swindon thence by bus to Brize Norton! Our detachment commander took pity on us and asked officer commanding 46 Squadron if we could be flown to Brize Norton on a training sortie; this was granted as it did not require HQ 46 Group approval – even though we would be using much more fuel.

"We were flown from Brize Norton to Masirah, via Akrotiri, in a Britannia (either 99 or 511 Squadron). We were well looked after by the crew and had been allocated the best leg room seats on the aircraft. The detachment comprised two aircraft and two crews on a five-week rotation. On arrival in Masirah, we were greeted by the crew that we were replacing as they were flying home in the same aircraft, so the handover was short.

"The Twynham Hut (a replacement for the Nissen Hut) accommodation was for four occupants in single rooms but was basic, to put it mildly. A bed, which had old-style hospital-type long legs and feet in tin cans of paraffin or similar to kill bugs, a chair, a wardrobe and a chest of drawers. Windows were permanently open but covered in a fine gauze to keep bugs out, the ablution block was a short distance away but in addition to the usual facilities contained a drinking water cooler. The main mess building was a short walk away and had an amusing notice on one of the doors, 'TV Room' – except when you opened the door there was no TV, but a wonderful view of the desert. Another trick that was played on the unwise was getting a taxi to the 'Golden Flipflop' night club. New arrivals were told of the 'Golden Flipflop' but to go they had to be at the front door of the officers' mess at a particular time to catch the taxi. Naturally those responsible for the wind-up would watch the front of the mess to see if the newcomers were there to catch the non-existent taxi to the non-existent night club!

"The routine for the Andover detachment was straightforward as the routes we flew were quite limited, although sometimes we carried British Embassy staff to places such as Abu Dhabi. In general, we reported for sortie briefing no later than one hour before. We nearly always had up to five hours on the ground in Dubai, but slightly less in Muscat, so had time to see some of the sights. We also had a limited search-and-rescue capability, but I only recall using that on one occasion in the ten weeks. We flew to certain destinations usually on the same day each week. If I recall Monday was Seeb, Tuesday was Salalah, Wednesday Dubai, Thursday training day, Friday day off, Saturday Salalah, Sunday Dubai.

46 Squadron Andover detached to Masirah, at Dubai c.1971. [Jon Plumley]

"For Seeb (Muscat) we usually carried a large but empty 'coolbox' and brought it back full of meat for Masirah. For Dubai I do not recall us carrying anything but passengers, Salalah was usually a mix of freight and passengers but normally passengers only on the return, often just a small bag of mail. On one trip to Salalah we were full of freight and had room for just one passenger, the station commander Masirah. At the back of the aircraft there were just two seats, and one was the crash position for the loadmaster hence the station commander had to set next to him. Just after take-off the station commander came to the flight deck to complain that the loadmaster smelled of BO! The captain said that was the only seat available. Station commander tried to use his authority to override the captain but failed when we showed him the wording of Queen's regulations and air transport procedures. We kept it quiet that he could have sat in the jump seat.

"Our trips to Dubai, especially at the weekend, always seemed to coincide with the arrival of the British Overseas Airways Corporation (BOAC) flight from Singapore on its way to London. Whilst in transit we often heard them calling Dubai air traffic, but for some reason Dubai could not hear them. Naturally, as good professional aviators we offered to relay for them. Let us say that their callsign was Speedbird 123. We would then relay to Dubai saying, 'Dubai this is RAFAIR 678 relaying for Birdseed 123'! For some reason this action somewhat upset the Speedbird crew, so we tended to avoid them on the ground at Dubai; fortunately, we wore civilian clothes so were not obvious to the BOAC crew.

"On another trip to Dubai there was an incident with a 216 Squadron Comet carrying the foreign secretary to London, and an Iran Air 727 flying to somewhere in Iran. In those days Dubai airport only had one runway and an incomplete taxiway structure. However it did have turning loops at the end of the runway, but you had to taxi down the runway. On this occasion our Andover was returning to Masirah and given the status of the other aircraft we were number three to taxi and were instructed to take the first turning loop. The Comet was told to take the second loop and line up and wait, and the Iran Air flight was told to take the second loop in turn and stop at the holding point. Once we were in the first loop the Comet took off, followed by the Iran Air 727, we followed in turn and headed for Masirah (our route was well clear of the other two aircraft). Due to the limitations of the Dubai radar a basic procedural service was given relying on aircraft DME readings, altitude read back and rates of climb. The Comet had a lower rate of climb than the 727 who complained about his clearance as he was burning a lot of fuel being kept at the lower altitudes. The airwaves were getting somewhat tense with ATC asking repeatedly for rates of climb, altitude and DME for the Comet and 727, so my captain thought it might be helpful to offer our rate of climb. The other players could not see the funny side when we read out our rate of climb as 500ft/min, with theirs being about 1,000 ft/min for the Comet and over 2,000 ft/min for the 727! Our routeing and rate of climb were no threat to their safety.

"In the Masirah officers' mess the bar was naturally the place to socialise, especially as there were frequent changes to the crews with Hercules, Britannia and Belfast in transit to the Far and Middle East. Sometimes there were Comet, Vulcan and Canberra crews. One evening, when both Andover crews were present along with some Hercules and Belfast crews, we were about to order some drinks when the station commander appeared. He asked what drinks we would like. As a can of Double Diamond was the most expensive drink, we all naturally asked for that. The barman duly got the drinks from the fridge and lined them up on the bar. Looking at us rather strangely he asked whose bar book he should use. When we all turned round the station commander had disappeared. The following evening the same barman was on duty, but the bar was quiet as the visiting crews had departed. When nobody else was about the barman pulled out a bar book, left it on the bar and then disappeared out of sight. The bar book was the station commander's, and on opening it we could see it was empty. The next evening the barman did something similar, but this time it was the mess guests' bar book, which proved to be quite full of drinks mostly authorised by the station commander.

"One evening whilst in the bar, we sought the advice of the local RAF Regiment officer about going to the beach with an air rifle. He said there were some suitable targets there in the form of spider crabs, but we might also see turtles laying eggs or even some eggs hatching. Off we went in our Land Rover with suitable torches, the air rifle and plenty of pellets. We did see some turtles but walked further along the beach using our torches to illuminate suitable targets. In one puddle near the water's edge, we saw what appeared to be an inner tube, so whoever had the rifle fired several pellets at it. The 'inner tube' was clearly unhappy as it was a sea snake! We ran at a great rate back to the Land Rover and drove back to the mess. On arrival in the bar, we met the duty medical officer who asked what we had been doing. He asked how long it had taken to get back from the beach – we said about 15 to 20 minutes. He said that was a pity as they have the antidote for sea snake bite in the medical centre, but you must be there in under ten minutes from having the bite.

"Given the extreme heat and humidity in the summer months there were some medical incidents and events. The Andover suffered one major limitation in the heat and that concerned the air conditioning. It only worked efficiently when the aircraft was pressurised, and it could only be pressurised when airborne. This meant that the internal temperature was often more than 140 degrees Fahrenheit, hence starting and taxying took place in an uncooled environment. The temperature only became more comfortable after about 15 to 30 mins (sometimes the aircraft was pre-cooled by a cooling truck). Given that night-circuit flying had to be undertaken unpressurised and was flown once per month, there was the potential to lose a lot of sweat in the training time. This was normally with one captain and one co-pilot for one hour. One of the station medical officers became concerned for our health when he realised the conditions in which we were doing night training. He weighed us before the one-hour sortie, and we were given a gallon of dilute orange squash to consume during the sortie. After landing he weighed us again, I had lost 10 lbs! In the 10 weeks I was in Masirah I lost nearly two stones although I put that back quickly after my return to the UK.

"There was another incident involving the station commander. Soon after he arrived in Masirah, he got into the routine of his inspections. As he was unfamiliar with the layout of Masirah, the station warrant officer (SWO) suggested that the radio installations on the perimeter of the airfield should be inspected first. A suitable convoy of vehicles was chosen and the entourage set out to inspect the various installations such as TACAN, ILS, NDB etc. On arrival at the first installation, the SWO got out of the Land Rover and told the station commander to wait. The SWO went up to the door of the building and hit it hard with his pace stick. He looked at his watch, and after about 30 seconds he opened the door and invited the station commander to carry out his inspection. This routine was repeated at each installation, but on arriving at the third installation the station commander's curiosity got the better of him; he asked the SWO whether the procedure with the pace stick had some local significance. The SWO said it was merely to get rid of the snakes which curled up on the ducting within the buildings."

CRISPIN WILLIAMS – NAVIGATOR

Crispin Williams was a 6 Squadron Akrotiri Canberra navigator from 1965-1969

"One of the best ways to get selected for a good overseas trip was to wait until most people had left the squadron for the day and then write your name and possible overseas flight onto the 'planners' chinagraph board. If your writing looked anything like the planners, then there was a chance that he would think that he had written it to remind himself that you were due for a decent flight. Paddy Webber and I had tried this a number of times, without success, but we were persistent. In September 1968, just before one of our regular detachments to Sharjah we saw our names, along with our pilot John Armstrong and the boss's crew, assigned a 'ranger' trip to Kenya. Unbelievable – well, quite believable as we had heard a rumour of this flight a month or so before and had put our names forward, as it were.

"As always on these trips, it was up to us to work out how we would make the trip within the confines of the dates that we could be away from base. This was a 'plum' of a flight, so it was worth doing some work to make it even better. We would be starting from Sharjah and our likely staging posts were Masirah, at the top of the Indian Ocean, and Djibouti on the southern side of the Red Sea. We would have used Aden instead of Djibouti, but the Arabs who owned the place were not particularly friendly at the time. From Djibouti, then controlled by the French, it would be a long, single hop down to Nairobi International.

"First, we had to convince the boss that the flight down to Nairobi would be exhausting, and that we should spend more than 24 hours in town before heading home. He was easily persuaded. Our plan was to make a full low-level navigation exercise en-route to Masirah, then carry out another low-level exercise before departing for the Red Sea to arrive at Djibouti in mid-afternoon. The next day would be a straight transit. If we did this then we reasoned that we would have logged up around 12 hours for each aircraft, and that would be enough for us to take at least two, perhaps three days in Nairobi. Harry Ford, who flew with the boss was entirely happy with this and offered to do the diplomatic clearances, provided I planned the routes. The clearances were approved and we were authorised to arrive into Nairobi on the Friday at about lunchtime and depart mid-morning the following Monday.

"The transit to Masirah was easy, but exceptionally hot. The outside air temperature in Sharjah would have been in the region of 90 degrees Fahrenheit, which went up to something well over 110 in the aircraft before take-off. We had canopy sun hoods and, on a good day, an external air-conditioning unit with its elephantine trunk stuck through the open door, but these had to be removed before engine start. After starting the engines, the aircraft was 'buttoned up', and we cooked! We got airborne as soon as practicable and flew at low level, 250 feet or lower, until it was time to climb up for the short transit over Oman to Masirah. Blessed relief; with the climb came the cold soak of flying in lower outside air temperatures, and then it was time to descend into Masirah.

"Masirah is an island off the Arabian coast that was used by the RAF as a convenient staging post on the route to the Far East. The island was about 50 miles long and 20 miles wide and as hot and inhospitable as the mainland. However, the RAF bureaucrats would not allow the base to have air conditioning because it had sea breezes. Unfortunately, the sea breezes did not blow all the time, and it was often exceptionally hot. Within the RAF, Masirah was always thought off as a punishment posting for the difficult or unconventional, an impression that those who were posted here for six months happily encouraged.

"In addition to the RAF airfield there were about 12,000 locals spread through a number of villages, mostly in the north of the island – it was a desolate place. From the air about the only thing of interest was that none of the houses had roofs, so you could see straight down into them. The 'no roofs' rule had been introduced by the emir as a punishment for his people disobeying him in the 1920s.

Crispin's mount on the jaunt to Kenya, Canberra B.16 WJ776 6 Squadron Luqa. [Author's collection]

"Anyway, we arrived safely in Masirah and were soon cooling ourselves with a beer or two in the mess. It is one of the strangenesses of the services that the mess is always orderly, and the orderly room is always a mess."

Masirah was to be the final RAF station remaining in the Middle East, continuing as a staging post well after the withdrawal from Aden, until finally closing in March 1977. From there, Crispin flew on to the next far-flung place on the outskirts of Nairobi.

EASTLEIGH, KENYA

Motto – Shupavu na thabiti *(Tough and Strong)*

Set in the suburbs of Nairobi, the first residents of RAF Eastleigh were a detachment of Fairey IIIFs of 45 Squadron in 1929. RAF Unit Kenya was established on 14 December 1935. Eastleigh came into prominence as the major support base for aircraft involved in operations against the Mau Mau insurgents from 1953 to 1956. During this time the station was host to eight Lincoln bombers detached from the UK, and a variety of Austers, Harvards and Pembrokes. Meteor PR.10s from 13 Squadron were there from August 1954, and up to six 8 Squadron Vampires were regularly detached. 208 Squadron also flew their Venoms and briefly Hunters, from here. Eastleigh became a Kenya air force station in 1964 following the country's independence the previous year.

RAF Eastleigh's signpost. [Dean Pringuer]

Crispin Williams continues his Kenyan adventure. By this time in the mid-1960s, Eastleigh was no longer available and they landed at Wilson Field to the west of Nairobi.

CRISPIN WILLIAMS

"After our first airways call in Kenya, we descended together to see if we could see any elephants. Although we flew onward at around 500 feet, we only saw giraffes. Where were they hiding all the elephants? We popped up to a more reasonable height to request a descent into Nairobi and, following their instructions arrived safely at Wilson Field. We taxied in, parked up, post-flighted the aircraft, and reported to the BOAC desk who were our handling agents. An RAF engineer from the embassy met us. Having confirmed our return diplomatic clearance and ordered in-flight rations from BOAC, he dropped us at our hotel in town.

"The next morning, just as we were about to leave for our first African adventure, we had a call from the embassy. 'Had you been flying at low level to the north of the city and through one of the game parks?' he asked. 'Certainly not,' was the unhesitating reply. 'Ah yes' said the air attaché, 'a warden said that he had seen a couple of twin jets with RAF markings flying through his park. I thought that he must have been mistaken.' We headed for Lake Naivasha and forgot about the RAF. We were rowed around the lake and spotted birds that we had never seen before, took lunch on the lawn and watched a hippo slopping around in its pool.

"On the Monday morning, with our planning completed, we climbed on board the aircraft and, just before the door was buttoned up, a BOAC engineer handed us a couple of silver platters with neatly trimmed sandwiches on; oh, how the other half live. We taxied out for take-off. The children around the airport had a strange game that they shared with departing aircraft. The little boys sat on the boundary fence, close to the end of the runway, and held on like grim death as the aircraft ran their engines up before releasing the brakes and starting their take-off run. The boss went first and we watched as a dozen boys, sitting on the top rung of the fence, leant forward against the rush of hot air. Four of them failed and were blown off backwards. Amidst much shouting and waving of arms the boys picked themselves up and remounted the fence. We turned towards them before turning back on the very end of the runway. We ran up to full power, released the brakes and were on our way. We imagined, but never saw, the boys being blown away."

RAF Muharraq, 1967. [Author's collection]

MUHARRAQ, BAHRAIN

Motto – In sole laborate *(Work in the sun)*

The first operations from strategically important Bahrain were in 1924, and RAF Bahrain was established on 22 May 1943 as part of RAF Iraq Command. It was renamed RAF Muharraq in 1963. 152 Squadron operated Twin Pioneers and Pembrokes here from October 1958 to November 1967. The Air Forces Gulf Communication Squadron was also resident from 15 September 1967 to 8 August 1969, as was a Search and Rescue Flight (part of 78 Squadron) from 1969 to 1971. The Hunters of 8 Squadron were based here from September 1967 to September 1971, before moving to Sharjah. 208 Squadron Hunters were also based here from June 1964 to September 1971 when the RAF had to leave Muharraq.

JERRY POOK – PILOT

"RAF Muharraq shared the territory of Bahrain airport on the island of Muharraq, linked to the main island of Bahrain by a causeway. Bahrain lies just 20 miles off the eastern coast of Saudi Arabia, a low-lying patch of dust and sand floating in the shallow turquoise waters of the Persian Gulf. I had arrived at the hottest time of the year, when daytime shade temperatures rose to 40 degrees Celsius and more in oppressive humidity. Everything about the place reeked of the tropics: the palm trees and sand everywhere, the ubiquitous bougainvillaea in permanent flower around the base and the Bahraini Arabs, cool and mysterious in their traditional headdress and flowing white robes. Many of the women still wore the abaya, a gold-embroidered black cloak over modern dress. However Bahrain was the most progressive of Arab states and more and more women were wearing Western-style dress in public.

"The primary operational task of the Muharraq Hunter Wing was to defend Kuwait against Iraqi aggression; the Iraqis having tried their hand already in the early 1960s. At that time, British forces had moved rapidly to forestall an invasion of the disputed territory of the Kuwaitis, with whom we had a defence pact. We had to be ready to deploy north to Kuwait at any time. The Saudis would not let us overfly their territory, and so all of our peacetime training was carried out to the south and east of Bahrain. Additionally, some of the islands of the Gulf were disputed territory as far as the Iranians were concerned; they were bitter about the fact that the British government was now calling it the Arabian Gulf (to impress the Arab oil producers).

"208 Squadron was a great outfit, and I had heard of the squadron stalwarts before my arrival. The new boss was a swarthily handsome character with an engagingly eccentric approach, including a tendency to burst into operatic song at the drop of a hat. Only the squadron 'wheels' had an allowance to keep their wives in Bahrain; any other married pilots had to pay for accommodation downtown out of their own

Jerry Pook in a Hunter FGA.9 cockpit. [Jerry Pook]

resources. Life in the mess was simple and relaxed. We lived in single-storey huts with the luxury of air conditioning, the ancient wall-mounted units rattling away all night long to keep you awake on the rare occasions when you went to bed sober.

"I received a brief rundown on the local flying regulations from the squadron qualified flying instructor, who emphasised the dangers of going anywhere near Saudi Arabian airspace. The last RAF Hunter pilot to divert there had been removed from the cockpit at the point of a gun, causing a serious diplomatic incident. My squadron checkout was with the boss, a rather intimidating prospect. We walked out to the clapped-out squadron T.7 in the searing heat of an afternoon, the engineers having worked all morning to get it serviceable. Normally we never flew after midday in summertime, it was just too hot. 'Compass is U/S', the boss mentioned idly as we walked out: 'we've only got the standby'. The T.7 had been grounded for some time awaiting a G4 gyrocompass from the UK. This meant that there was no accurate heading information in the cockpit. 'It'll be OK,' he reassured me as we strapped into the burning hot cockpit: 'we're not going far.'

"I was not so sure. The horizon looked ominously obscure in the thick, leaden haze which blanketed the island. The low line of palm trees across the runway shimmered and danced in the heat, as if chastened by a strong breeze. We took off into classic 'goldfish bowl' conditions, the tenuous horizon disappearing completely as soon as we climbed away from the runway. The intention was to fly a quick medium altitude recce to the south down the Gulf as far as the Qatar coast, some 30 miles away, and then return for some instrument flying and visual circuits. If anything, the goldfish bowl effect worsened the higher we went. This was outside all of my previous meteorological experience. In European flying you could always climb above a haze layer, no matter how intense. There was no air traffic control radar available to help us. Knowing the sun was in the south-west, I rolled out to hold it in my two o'clock, checking below to see if I could pick up the east coast of the island as we headed south. The boss disagreed with my tactic, took control and rolled out heading to the right of the sun. The tiny standby magnetic compass swung wildly with the slightest change of bank angle. Visibility everywhere was atrocious. In the thick, yellow haze at 20,000 feet it was impossible to see if we were over land or sea. I was convinced we were heading west and said as much to the boss. By the merest chance the haze thinned somewhat to reveal a clear yellow line which could only be the Saudi coastline, just a few miles in front of us. The boss cursed, and I breathed a sigh of relief as he turned through 180 degrees to head back to Bahrain.

"I soon got used to the splendid tropical work routine, starting with a met brief at 06:30, followed by first take-offs at 07:00. Last take-off would be at about 12:00, and we would be in the bar by 13:00 to enjoy a few ice-cold beers before lunch. Afternoons of searing heat were spent lounging around at the pool, and at teatime we would wander downtown for a bit of shopping as the heat of the day moderated. Trips downtown were frequent, and in that age of gentler relations with the Arab world we felt free to mingle with the local crowds, shopping and browsing in the Souk with no fear of violence. Although there was mutual respect (we were here as part of a defence agreement with the Bahrain government), unsurprisingly there was little social contact with the locals. The language and cultural barriers were too strong, but I for one felt completely at ease among the Arab population.

"The Gulf flying was absolutely fantastic, and there was lots of it. From Muharraq we flew high-low-high sorties south-east into the United Arab Emirates territory, or across to Muscat and Oman, navigating on half-million-scale maps which each pilot had to illustrate for himself, there being no detail plotted inland from coastlines (in these areas the maps were just plain white paper). Fierce arguments raged amongst the old hands as to the exact location of the various features they had drawn on their jealously guarded personal maps. A classic example of this was the famous 'lone palm tree' plotted some 70 miles inland from the southern Gulf coastline, in the middle of nowhere. Occasionally we flew low-level departures from Muharraq, flying south down the Gulf of Bahrain to transit a low-level corridor over the sheikdom of Qatar. To the south and east of Qatar lay the vast open desert spaces of the United Arab Emirates, comprising Abu Dhabi, Dubai, Sharjah, Fujairah and one or two smaller countries. Along with northern Oman, this was a free-flying area for us, and almost totally unpopulated. For target navigation we had 1 in 100,000-scale monochrome maps, copied direct from air survey photos. They were good for topographic detail in mountainous regions, and with a lot of practice could be used for precise target navigation at low level over the desert.

"On my first mission into this region I led a pair of Hunters on a familiarisation exercise; one object for me being to check out the exact position of the 'lone palm tree' and one or two other features. In the crystal-clear heat of the early morning, we left the smooth, turquoise waters of the Gulf behind to set course inland from the rocky peak of Jebel Dhana, a favourite landmark on the southern Gulf coast. I had 'hacked' (started) the big Monte Carlo stopwatch as we crossed the coastline, to measure the ten minutes or so elapsed time to the palm tree. We soon cleared the rocky coastal terrain and settled down to a comfortable 100-150ft height over the sand dunes; low enough to be interesting, yet not so low that you had to use all your concentration for height keeping, to the detriment of lookout (the squadron laid on a 'bounce' for most missions and you were liable to be attacked at any time).

"Dust Devil right two o'clock – no threat!"

"Dust devils, or mini dust tornadoes, were a common sight, a ghostly spiral of sand moving through the desert. We called them on the radio for lookout practice. We had no accurate measure of height, and some people's idea of 100ft was far lower than others. The low dunes gave way occasionally to isolated patches of scrawny vegetation consisting of gnarled 'trees' just a few feet high. We crossed vast featureless salt pans where depth perception was impossible, the horizon shimmering misty gold like waves on a fabulous sea. These were dangerous areas, the lack of visual clues suckering you into flying too low. Periodically we flashed over a camel trail or 'road (approximate alignment)' as they were depicted on the map. Just a series of faint grooves in the sand, they were pretty useless for accurate navigation. After about eight minutes, a tiny object appeared on the horizon dead ahead – the lone palm tree. It stood barely 20ft high in the middle of nowhere, with no other distinguishable feature for miles. Having fixed the palm tree, I could see why it was a favourite checkpoint and rendezvous for formations broken up after being savaged by the bounce.

"On subsequent sorties we penetrated further south and east into the infamous Liwa Hollows, a moonscape of gigantic golden sand dunes interspersed with perfectly flat salt pans each one to two km across, all virtually identical. The Liwas extended hundreds of miles south into Saudi territory, forming the north-eastern boundary of the Rub' al Khali, the forbidding Empty Quarter of legend which stretched nearly 800 miles south-west to Aden. Here and there around the edges of The Hollows lay the occasional oasis, sparse patches of greenery and a few primitive dwellings. Borders were pretty vague in this desolate region, and we didn't bother too much about them. The interior of The Hollows was a 'Bermuda Triangle' for low-level navigation because the dunes all looked the same wherever you were. My first four-ship formation was an attack on a tiny target in the middle of the Liwas; a stone tower barely 15ft high, the remains of an ancient fort now buried deep in the sand. After some 10 minutes of switchback navigation the formation began the complex manoeuvring leading to a co-ordinated rocket attack, the aim being for each aircraft to dive on the target with minimum spacing from different points of the compass. We pointed hopefully into the salt pan, searching desperately for any feature which might be the target. No joy – a total balls-up by the leader, who had miscounted the

Jebel Hafeet. [Jerry Pook]

hollows on the long run-in, an all-too-common error. As we pulled out to reform, I spotted the tower in the next hollow – too late. To the east of the Liwas, lay another fascinating desert terrain consisting of immensely long and narrow salt pans separated by low sandy ridges barely 100ft high. You could fit a whole formation into one pan and fly straight for 50 miles or more. They were two to three km across, and it was like flying down a gigantic motorway cutting. These were favourite areas for bouncing, the bounce formation 'lurking' just over the ridge in the next lane, invisible to the target formation. When a navigational turn was called the bounce would hurtle over the dividing ridge and be into the formation like a fox among chickens. A dirty trick – although splendid sport for everyone concerned.

"At the extreme eastern end of the desert area lay the famous oasis of Buraimi, then still a smallish series of hamlets scattered amongst the patches of greenery. A few miles south lay the Jebel Hafeet, an eight-mile-long humpback rock feature rising 4,000ft from the flat desert floor, like a gigantic, crashed Zeppelin. This was a favourite navigational feature and letdown point for us approaching at 35,000ft from Bahrain, being easily visible from 100 miles away. At low level you 'hacked' the stopwatch at the jebel and headed south-east for about five minutes, en-route to the mountains of Muscat and Oman. In front and to the left you could see the gigantic impenetrable mass of the Fatah range, a sheer wall of rock rising 3,000ft from the smooth desert floor. Closer in you could make out your turning point, the deep slash of the Al Fatah Gap, the entry point for the mountains. Your formation closed up automatically into the compact arrow configuration as you turned to dive through the gap. In a flash you had left the bright, wide-open spaces of the desert and were flying through an impossibly rugged terrain of deep, sandy-floored wadis and towering razor-sharp ridgelines which extended a hundred miles north to the Strait of Hormuz. This was an excellent training area strewn with Arab dwelling-forts, many of them of vast size having been extended, defended, conquered and re-occupied many times over the centuries. These majestic, bleached mud constructions were favourite targets for simulated attacks, and we had an extensive target library of photos of them back in the squadron.

"There was good-natured rivalry with 8 Squadron and we tended to stick together on base and on regular launches downtown, either to the Gulf Hotel (The Hilton was not yet built) or to the Malcolm Club in downtown Manama. The usual means of transport was on the back of someone's motorbike, often three-up! Every night at about 20:00 a warm layer of dew would settle on the rubber-stained dusty roads, turning them into lethal skid pans on which no tyre would grip. In these conditions the sober motorcyclist negotiated each roundabout at five mph or less, both feet planted firmly on the ground, with all passengers assisting. Cars were not popular, the heat of the day turning them into ovens after a few minutes' exposure to the sun.

"We had the same problem with the aircraft on the line, although we used specially designed umbrellas most of the time to shade the cockpits. In spite of this, the ejection seat pans would have burnt the skin through our thin flying suits, had we not used real sheepskin seat covers for protection (Messrs Martin-Baker would have had a fit). The stick and throttles were too hot to touch without the protection of flying gloves. The dangers of heat stress were constantly emphasised by the medics. We had a strict rule that we had to get airborne within 15 minutes of climbing into the aircraft – there was no cooling on the ground, and you would be saturated with sweat after that time. Taxiing the two miles or so to the runway threshold was carried out at breakneck speed, with bared arms hanging out of the cockpit to achieve some cooling effect. Only after the gear was locked up could you feel a deliciously cool blast of air as the cockpit air conditioning switched on; this equipment was only effective at medium and high altitudes.

"At low level over the desert the air temperatures could be 60 degrees Celsius and more. Cockpits just grew steadily hotter in these conditions – the cockpit air conditioning being totally unable to cope – and you sweated buckets to compensate. After an hour of low-level flying, the luxury of cold air as you climbed for the stratosphere was indescribable. We marvelled at the fortitude of our predecessors on Vampires and Venoms who flew low-level in these conditions without any air conditioning at all.

"The flying, almost invariably in formation, was very competitive. Initial sorties were flown as wingman, following an experienced pilot to see how it was done and build up familiarity with the operating area. Later the new pilot would be given an air task requiring him to lead a formation (usually four) carrying out simulated attacks on two or three smallish targets anywhere in our low flying area of operations, whilst at the same time fighting off a bounce who could attack at any time. The bounce would have full details of the formation's route and their radio frequencies. It would take off before the formation, and a favourite tactic was to lurk at high altitude over Muharraq, waiting to see the target formation get airborne. Then the bounce – often a pair of aircraft or more – would 'stalk' the formation from above 30,000ft, hiding in the deep blue many miles above before swooping down almost supersonic to attack when the formation was occupied in a turn or attacking the target. No problem 'dropping bangs' (i.e. going supersonic) over the desert. The leader would have to work out all the details of the attack and routeing to and from the target, plan and brief the mission, including tactics against the bounce, and be debriefed on his performance after landing. There would always be an experienced pilot in the formation, often one of the flight commanders.

"During my squadron work-up I came closer to death than on any other occasion during my whole flying career. The weather was brilliant and calm with a hazy horizon at low level. I was flying as number four, wingman to the deputy formation leader. We were on a high-low-high bounced strike, and for once there was only one bounce aircraft, flown by a squadron pilot I disliked intensely. I was already starting to fancy myself at combat and once again felt that tremendous surge of adrenaline as I picked up the bounce, a mere speck in the deep blue vertically above us, as we descended through 20,000ft over the sea south of Yas Island. In spite of my early pickup and warning call on radiotelephony, the bounce was soon in the middle of our twisting and turning formation. Determined to keep contact with my adversary, I committed the cardinal sin of losing my element leader within seconds of starting the fight. Desperate to regain some kudos, I threw myself at the bounce while shouting on the radiotelephony that I would soon be 'claiming' him. On hearing this the rest of the formation promptly departed at warp nine heading for Jebel Dhana, abandoning me to my well-deserved fate. My personal duel with the bounce dragged on for several minutes, and it became uncomfortably clear that I was nowhere near to getting a kill. Unbeknown to me the bounce was setting me up for a run-out and, having skilfully manoeuvred me away from the last-known position of my companions, he suddenly disengaged in hot pursuit of my erstwhile formation. Incensed at the way I had been duped, I dived frantically for airspeed, simultaneously 'skylining' the departing bounce as a dwindling speck just above the horizon. Throughout the engagement so far, I had not checked on my height, and I fondly imagined that I was still at least 10,000ft above the sea. My whole attention was rivetted on the tiny speck on the horizon as my aircraft began to hum with the

Hunter's famous 'blue note' at high airspeed. I couldn't afford to look in the cockpit – if I lost visual contact I knew I would never pick him up again in the haze. After a minute or two the horizon in my peripheral vision slowly began to change colour. Through the thunder of the 600 knot airflow, I dimly became aware of a tiny voice in my brain repeating the same message over and over again. In a flash, and barely in time, I awoke to the awful reality – *CHECK YOUR HEIGHT*!

"I was in a shallow dive with the altimeter slowly unwinding through 200 feet. The sea was like glass and could have been 200 or 2,000ft away – it was impossible to judge. Just a few seconds more of doziness and I would have flown into the water at maximum speed. I pulled up violently to get away from the treacherous water that had so nearly smashed me to oblivion. Severely shaken, I flew slowly home to receive a well-deserved bawling-out for failing to stick in formation. I was too ashamed to tell of my near disaster.

"Squadron life at Muharraq was idyllic for a bunch of young bachelors on a day-fighter/ground-attack wing. Our squadron offices were air conditioned and located just a few yards from the aircraft flight line. I discovered that our squadron engineering flight sergeant was an old acquaintance from Valley, where he had been an excellent ground school instructor. In the squadron there was constant good-natured rivalry and practical 'jokery' among the junior pilots. The flying was so good that it was difficult for people to unwind on the ground, and so we took refuge in constant mickey-taking and banter. I soon learned to avoid asking serious questions of fellow junior pilots. If you asked where a particular individual was, for example, the inevitable answer would be, 'he's on the roof with a rat in his mouth, singing "Death to Mussolini!"' Quite where this obscure and perverse answer came from no-one seemed to know – it was just a 208 Squadron tradition. I still use it to this day if someone is asking particularly stupid questions.

"As well as bounced low-level strikes we flew a lot of pure combat missions, with as many as eight or ten aircraft in action. Sometimes it was four versus four, sometimes four versus six. The Persian Gulf climate, although predictable for weeks on end, was vastly different from European weather. The problem of deep haze layers made combat very difficult as it was easy to lose orientation with no horizon visible. However, the usual weather pattern was of gloriously clear conditions everywhere, with occasional layers of cumulus building up from a base above 15,000 ft, far higher than you would find at home. These clouds were ideal for hiding behind during medium-altitude combat. I started to wear Polaroid sunglasses in flight, (strictly forbidden by the medics), to help to see through the murk. They were very effective in haze, although I used to get some extreme 'psychedelic' colour effects caused by the many layers of glass in the armoured windscreen. During these big combats it was absolutely vital that formations stayed together and maintained discipline. Wingmen had to stick, search and report, the primary duty being to hang on to your element leader whatever he did. Loose aeroplanes falling out of formation became a menace, the leader unable to work out who he was talking to on the radio. During combat you would often be manoeuvring several miles apart from each other, the aircraft of your supporting element mere specks in the distance. R/T discipline was rigid, and there was no room at all for over-excited shouting into the mike. One of the biggest problems was keeping tabs on who was who. We had various tricks to positively identify an aircraft some distance away, one of which was to call him to 'roll'. On receiving this call, he had to carry out a 360-degree snap roll immediately in order to be visually identified by the rest of the formation.

"The biggest problem facing a wingman at low level was simply staying in contact with his element leader and not flying into the ground. You are flying at about 100ft at 420 knots, trying to follow another Hunter just a couple of hundred yards in front. You are expecting to be bounced at any moment (lookout was continuous – you could never relax) and your primary area of lookout is behind the opposite pair of the formation, cruising a mile away from you. To pick up a bounce, you have to

208 Squadron Hunter FGA.9 at low level. [Jerry Pook]

search deep in the six o'clock of the formation, twisting your head around almost through 180 degrees and holding this uncomfortable position for five seconds or so while you make sure your eyes focus at infinity. You are now travelling at 420 knots, barely 100 feet above ground and staring behind you for long periods, unable to look where you are going. When you look forward again you hope, firstly, that you are not just about to fly into the ground and secondly, that your leader is still there. To survive and become efficient at lookout in such conditions you needed the good old 'sixth sense' of situation awareness that warned you what was going to happen next. During the brief moments when you looked ahead you would check for any forthcoming obstacles which you knew the leader would be dodging around and estimate how long it would be before he would need to turn. When any radio call was made you would immediately check your leader to see which way he was going to turn. Most difficult of all was flying in arrow formation as a four-ship, while the leader manoeuvred through narrow valleys in the mountains. In this you moved up even closer on the lead, to 50 yards or less between aircraft, slightly above him, and you also had to stick to your side of the leader's fore-and-aft axis, i.e. if you were number three on the left side you had to stay that side whatever the leader did. This meant that when the leader rolled into a hard turn towards you, you had to put on an immediate bootful of bottom rudder to drop the nose and allow you to keep sight of the upper surfaces of No. 1 and No. 2 in front and below you. The great temptation was to drop below the lead and lag the turn, thus keeping him in sight more easily – but this was a lethal trap. Remember that the lead would fly as low as he wanted, and anyone dropping below his flight path would be 'creamed' on the next piece of rising ground. After 20 minutes of hanging on in this formation all of you were exhausted and dripping with sweat; at times I found myself thinking, 'a chap could get himself severely killed doing this'.

"Our standard operational readiness exercise was called 'hot rod'. When this was called, at short notice the sweating armourers would immediately arm up most aircraft with armour piercing SNEB (Société Nouvelle des Établissements Edgar Brandt) rocket pods, and 480 rounds of 30-mm high explosive/incendiary ammunition. Some aircraft were left armed with guns alone, to act as fighter defence of Bahrain. Pilots were split between attackers and defenders. As attackers we would launch off in fours down the Gulf to Jeb-a-Jib range near Dubai, where the army would lay out a line of scrap trucks for us to smash up – cans of petrol being left in them to make them burn better. We would carry out a formation attack, four at a time, under the control of our excellent forward air controller, a current Hunter pilot. All rockets were fired together in a half-second burst. On a re-attack we would fire the guns two at a time, each round exploding in a pinpoint of light on the ground. With a good burst you could completely destroy a truck in under a second. We weren't supposed to fire all four together because of the tremendous recoil (many of the cockpit circuit breakers would trip). I tried it once, briefly – the aircraft seemed to hit a brick wall as the guns fired. After the attacks we would head back home to act as 'bombers' and targets for the fighters defending Bahrain, attacking from all sides under the control of Romeo radar, our local air defence radar. As one of the 'fighter' pilots back at Bahrain, life was also pretty exciting. We teamed up as pairs and went out to the line to 'cock' our aircraft, i.e. prepare all switches, levers, straps, etc., for as quick a departure as possible. Then we went back to the squadron to lounge about in the coffee bar waiting for the 'scramble' order on the squawk box. It was good old Battle of Britain stuff, and great fun if there was plenty of action. This was the day fighter part of the DF/GA role. The squadron squawk box would click on:

'Gold scramble!, gold scramble!: vector 150, angels 250'. Game on!

"We run to the squadron gharry (transport) and hang on the back, the squadron driver breaking all speed limits on the short journey to the flight line. After a start-up and take-off at maximum speed we head 150 degrees in the climb to 25,000ft, Romeo radar giving information on the incoming raid. Because we had no on-board search radar, we had to work out our own interceptions, Romeo just giving us bearings and distances to the raid. You did this by means of a simple interception graph on your kneeboard, the aim being to roll out just half a mile behind the attackers. Occasionally we intercepted Vulcans, visible from miles away as they cruised at extreme high altitude. Our only technique to shoot them down was the 'zoom climb' in which we pulled up into a vertical climb well ahead of them, hopefully to get them briefly in the gunsight at maximum range before we ran out of airspeed and stalled out. Often, we were visited by Canberra PR.9s from Malta, carrying out photo surveys of Oman. They were full of 'bull' about their manoeuvrability and impressive rate of climb, claiming that we wouldn't get near them in a combat; one day I tried it out, intercepting a PR.9 over Yas Island. After a lot of low-speed milling about I managed to get some quite pretty gun camera film of the 13 Squadron flight commander. I sent back some prints to their squadron in Malta.

"In the new year we heard details of the timetable of the final disbandment of 208, leaving 8 Squadron to hold the fort for a couple of months before they too went home, to be reformed as a Shackleton squadron. Our splendid wing commander ordered that 8 and 208 should amalgamate their flying programmes to produce more big-formation flying. For the rest of our time in Bahrain, we could always guarantee enough aircraft to launch eight-ship attack formations, often with a four-ship bounce, leading to the most almighty fun 'punch-ups' in flight.

"By the end of September 1971 my all-too-brief tour in Bahrain was over. We put away the squadron standard at an emotional disbandment ceremony at which I was the standard bearer. I had already heard that I was to get my first choice of posting again, to the new Harrier OCU at RAF Wittering. I was nominated for the last UK ferry of 208 Squadron, to be led by the new boss. The third pilot was a fiercely keen and talented young New Zealander who had recently joined the squadron.

"We set off from Bahrain with the last three 208 Squadron Hunters. After our weary arrival at Kemble, I spent a few days in Dawlish and then headed for Wittering in my green MG Midget. In just over 18 months I had flown 420 hours on the Hunter, and it had been action-packed stuff. Amazingly there had been no accidents on the Desert Hunter Wing in that time. From what I had heard of the Harrier, the flying was going to be even more interesting." [1]

Argosy C.1 105 Squadron Khormaksar on turnround at Salalah. [Ian Macmillan]

SALALAH, OMAN

Motto – Nusoor fee ard sadeeoa *(Eagles in a friendly land)*

Situated 650 miles from Aden in the coastal plain of Dhofar, in the Sultanate of Muscat and Oman, Salalah was constructed as a staging post in 1928. It was a regular refuelling stop for Valetta, Beverley, Argosy, Dakota and other aircraft operating on the Aden-Masirah-Sharjah-Bahrain route, and had accommodation for a limited number of personnel for overnight stops.

CORNISH JACK

"Riyan and Salalah had particular 'value' as 'punishment postings' for junior officers who had committed misdemeanours (especially the 'social' variety). One of our 233 Squadron skippers was thus posted as deputy officer commanding Salalah. The officer commanding himself was a deeply disliked flight lieutenant who insisted on all the parades and general 'bull' of training camps. This was at a time when National Service was coming to an end, and one such airman was given a going home party in the combined mess on the night before his departure. Much 'falling over juice' was dispensed, with some 'extras' for the less well-regarded officer commanding. Very late the next day, when he woke up in his room – there was no daylight! During the night 'persons unknown' had bricked and boarded up his door and window.

"I became aware of this on the next day when we flew in. On our first radio contact I was given all the airfield details, and a peculiar add-on: 'Don't stare at the boss when he meets you'. In addition to his unattractive character, this chap had a truly luxuriant handlebar moustache of which he was very proud. All was revealed when I opened the door on shut down – the officer commanding's heavily tanned face was disfigured by a stark white upper lip. In addition to the 'entombing' of the night before, just half of his pride and joy had been removed, thus leaving the final indignity to his own hand. The ensuing ruckus reached 'authority' in a form which made the problems clear, and he was quickly moved to pastures new."

SHARJAH, TRUCIAL STATES (NOW PART OF THE UNITED ARAB EMIRATES)

Motto – Min al-barr ila al-sama *(From the land to the sky)*

A very basic airfield existed at Sharjah in the 1920s.; however, it really started life in 1932 as a landing ground for Imperial Airways Handley Page HP.42 services

Sharjah gate. [Author's collection]

to India, with RAF aircraft starting to adopt it the following year. Throughout World War II it was used as a base for anti-submarine patrols, and as 44 Staging Post. Among the squadrons based here were 84 and 244, with Blenheims. Sharjah's geographic location ensured it remained an important station in the postwar period, but it was little used in the immediate aftermath. However, unrest in the region brought a detachment of 6 Squadron with Vampires in 1952. This was later followed by 8 and 249 Squadrons with Venoms, then 8 and 208 Squadrons with Hunters. Both those Hunter squadrons, plus similarly equipped 43 Squadron, regularly used Sharjah for their armament practice camps, for which the Jeb-a-Jib range was some 50 miles away. It was also the home of 78 Squadron Wessex from October 1967 to 21 December 1971 when it disbanded. After having to leave Muharraq in September 1971, 8 Squadron moved to Sharjah where it remained until December of that year.

JERRY POOK

"On 208 Squadron, we would often land at Sharjah on the Gulf coast some 250 miles to the east to stay the night. Sharjah was a splendid place, occupied by men only; no-one was allowed to bring wives or girlfriends there, not even the station commander. The only female on base was the civilian met man's wife, who had a disturbing tendency to come into the bar wearing the shortest miniskirts. Other units on base were 210 Shackleton Squadron and the Andovers of 84 Squadron, plus Wessex helicopters of 78 Squadron. 84 Squadron were even madder than we were. They had seen the film *The Great Escape* in the camp cinema and had formed an escape committee to tunnel their way out of their accommodation hut. They did it in fine style, just like the film, tearing up the floorboards and digging through the sandy soil towards the officers' mess bar. Various squadron members would wander into the bar patio area to stand around, in seemingly innocent conversation, while surreptitiously emptying pocketfuls of sand into the goldfish pond. Eventually, realising that escape was impossible, they turned the excavation into an underground squadron bar for late-night drinking.

"Both us and 8 Squadron, our rival Hunter outfit at Muharraq, spent a lot of time at Sharjah. We held regular armament practice camps there, using the desert ranges of Rashid and Jeb-a-Jib just over the border in Dubai. Additionally, there were army co-operation exercises and some operations with the British-officered Trucial Oman Scouts and the SAS, the latter spending a lot of time rushing about the desert with their Land Rovers painted a fetching shade of pink. Known as 'desert pink' it was a surprisingly effective camouflage colour almost invisible from the air.

"My favourite fun-flying area lay in the mountains just 50 miles or so north-east from Sharjah, in the Ruus Al Jibal, where razor-sharp ridges alternated with deep wadis in a mathematically regular pattern for a distance of 30 miles or more. For casual amusement you could fly a switchback white-knuckle route at right angles to

208 Squadron flight line at Sharjah with 210 Squadron Shackletons in the distance. [Jerry Pook]

the grain of the terrain, diving steeply into each wadi and pulling 7G to climb almost vertically up the next rock face. Well before you reached the top you rolled inverted and pulled 7G once again to zoom tight over the ridge – the rock face just a few feet above your head! When pointing straight down into the next wadi – still just a few feet clear of the rock – you rolled upright and began the next 'switchback'. Truly a sport of kings, although moderately dangerous if you overcooked it." [1]

JONATHAN PLUMLEY CONTINUES

"My first trip to Salalah was a voyage of discovery as we were subjected to quite severe restrictions whilst on the ground. Normally, if the wind permitted, we would approach Salalah on the northerly runway coming in from the sea over Salalah town. We would normally depart on the south-westerly runway. We were only permitted to have one military transport 'plane on the ground at any one time, unless you were departing and the other aircraft was arriving. Transport aircraft were parked in a revetment made up of concrete and sand-filled oil drums. We were not allowed to stay in the aircraft while it was unloaded or refuelled. The crew had to observe the aircraft from a safe place such as the control tower, and we were not to be on the ground for more than 45 minutes!

"Being a naïve co-pilot (I had been qualified on the Andover for just nine months) I could not understand the restrictions at Salalah. While we were waiting in the tower, I asked the warrant officer in charge why we could not wait in the aircraft, and why we could only be on the ground for 45 minutes. He said, 'come with me laddie!' He showed me a large crater at the rear of the tower and explained the mortar attack that they had suffered recently. Subsequently I discovered this was associated with the Dhofar Rebellion and the 46 Squadron detachment was supporting British and Omani forces although we did not realise it at the time. The expert analysis of the local situation revealed that the rebels had the capability of launching mortar attacks on Salalah airfield, but they would need about 45 minutes from deciding to attack to getting close enough to launch a mortar that could reach the airfield."

MICK SPEAKE – GROUND PHOTOGRAPHER

"In 1971 I got the 'shocking' news that I had been selected for a nine-month unaccompanied tour to Muharraq, working on 8 and 208 Hunter Squadrons. However this was short-lived as after a few weeks I got posted to 210 Squadron Shacks at Sharjah, the last tradesman to do so before the squadron was disbanded; they had just three MR.2 Shacks. The front cannons had been removed, toothless wonders I thought at the time. I will never forget the Argosy 'whistling tit' flight down to Sharjah. I had severe Bahrain gut at the time, and there was just a urinal for our use; I didn't know if there was a proper toilet in the flight deck area, maybe I should have asked. Anyway we got to Sharjah and one of the airmen, whom I knew, met me with the squadron Land Rover. How I made it to the arrivals toilets I will never know, but the relief was beyond belief!

"After a couple of weeks or so, there were just three photographers at Sharjah, a ground photographer (whom we didn't have much to do with), Dan, an air photographer and me as the corporal air camera fitter on the squadron. Dan and I took turns to do the 'clickie' before flights every morning and mid-afternoon seeing-ins and film down-loads, then processing the films and printing. Amongst the line equipment was a large-diameter hose (part of a refrigeration unit) which was pulled through the rear door of the aircraft. Unfortunately the cameras were right at the back of the fuselage, so you sweated buckets there when changing film magazines – trying not to drip sweat onto the camera's glass platens.

"It was common knowledge that the daily sortie, by a single Shack, was to check on the Russian Kotlin destroyer anchored some way into the Gulf. Although our Shack flew in very low, the Russians would be waiting and when the photos were developed you could see the ship's guns and missiles trained on the aircraft as it circled.

"One afternoon one of our aircraft landed and the tail wheel broke right off. It carried on taxiing off the runway, and then stopped for a make-shift trailer rig to eventually be attached to its rear to then make a rather shame-faced journey back to the hangar pan. Over the next couple of weeks, the riggers hoisted up the rear of the fuselage and repaired the undersides of the twin fins; these had been scraped away as the aircraft had landed and taxied. Of course there was a lot of squadron mickey-taking, chiefly that the aircrew hadn't realised at first that the tail wheel had broken off and it had only dawned on them when the attitude of the aircraft seemed a bit more inclined than usual.

"On the squadron we had an occasionally grumpy engineering officer. The lads thought up a wheeze to cheer him up on his birthday, with the aid of our cross-eyed Arab cleaner, Ali. He was a pleasant and very obliging young man, but you never knew if he was talking to you or not. Anyway, the lads taught him to sing, 'You Are My Sunshine'. On the morning of the engineering officer's birthday, Ali was propelled into his office and proceeded to sing, with a very quavery voice, his well-rehearsed song. After a few seconds of this all we heard was, 'Ali, f**k off out of my office!' Everyone outside burst into laughter as Ali beat a hasty retreat, followed by the engineering officer who could do little else but join in our merriment.

"The best memory I have of the Hunter-equipped 8 Squadron was its arrival at Sharjah for the last few weeks of the station's existence. We were all waiting on the line to see them fly in. They did so in spectacular fashion, line abreast at zero feet and seemingly maximum speed, with the desert dust swirling up behind them with the jet-wash. Absolutely awesome!

"Eventually the end of November dawned and Harold Wilson had decreed that the Gulf stations would close. This was the only thing for which I am grateful to the Labour Party. Some of our groundcrew transited back with our faithful old Shacks, while the rest of us piled into an RAF VC10 and lorded it all the way back to a wintry UK. Pat, our little daughter Coral and I met up on Swindon station to have an emotional and joyful reunion, and then travel up to London for the weekend, which was really ace." [2]

CRISPIN WILLIAMS CONTINUES

"We visited Sharjah frequently; it always felt as though it was just outside the civilised world. The town of Sharjah was small and poor, with just a single three-story building. The ruling Sheik lived in a tumble-down palace on the main square, which, in those days, was still rough sand. In the square were a couple of old cannons that had probably been standing there for a hundred years or more.

"Punishment in these Arab countries is direct and obvious; there is a belief that to keep someone in prison is inhuman, and I tend to agree. There were occasional public whippings when the unfortunates were tied to these cannons. All the men carried ancient rifles on their backs and knives in their belts. The curved knife of Sharjah is called a khanjar, and it was one of the symbols of the Trucial States. Peace was kept by the British-officered Trucial Oman Scouts, or 'tossers' to their friends. The TOS were a small, but elite force, that lived on the high ground by the airfield; from there they policed the states with the aid of a mixture of camels and Land Rovers. Although the force was small it had immense influence. Some officers who would have risen to colonel or higher in the British army chose instead to spend their entire careers in the force, accepting that they would never rise higher than captain."

Shackletons were first deployed from 228 Squadron to Sharjah from 1957 to 1959 to help tackle political unrest in neighbouring Oman. Aircraft from 37 Squadron at Khormaksar arrived briefly in 1967 before the unit disbanded, to be replaced by a Maritime Detachment (MARDET) operated by UK-based squadrons in rotation. This continued until November 1970 when Ballykelly's 210 Squadron was relocated to Sharjah, remaining there until it too disbanded almost exactly a year later.

BILL TYACK – NAVIGATOR

"37 Squadron was disbanded when Britain withdrew from Aden in 1967. Thereafter the maritime air presence in the Arabian Peninsula, and Persian/Arabian Gulf, was provided by Shackleton detachments from UK squadrons based at Sharjah. On the eastern coast of the Gulf 80 miles south of the strategically important Straits of Hormuz, Sharjah was one of seven Trucial States that became the United Arab Emirates in 1971. British treaties with the Trucial States dated back to 1820, and the British military presence provided the states with a measure of protection against the territorial ambitions of large neighbouring states such as Iran and Saudi Arabia.

"Our 42 Squadron crew was detached to Sharjah, from St. Mawgan, during the summer of 1969 and was captained by Dave 'Bog-H' Baugh. We collected Mk.3 XF701 from Kinloss and flew out to Sharjah via night stops in Gibraltar and Luqa,

Shackleton MR.3 WR983 of the Kinloss Wing overhead Sharjah. [via Jeff Peck]

and a refuelling stop at El Adem in Libya. After taking off from El Adem, in hot conditions, we had to use both Viper jets to help drag our fully-loaded aircraft up to the minimum flight level on Egyptian airways of 10,000 feet; we then needed to burn one Viper continuously to maintain that level.

"Sharjah in the 1960s was a desert sheikhdom with few roads, and almost no infrastructure. Sharjah town, the capital, consisted of a 19th Century fort and a couple of rows of buildings along the creek. Local tribesmen, straight out of 'Lawrence of Arabia', visited the bazaar dressed in flowing robes with khanjars in their belts, and antique muskets over their shoulders. It was just before the AK-47 became the weapon of choice for everyone in the region. There was sufficient local atmosphere to satisfy those romantic souls who had grown up reading about T E Lawrence, Gertrude Bell, and Wilfred Thesiger who had undertaken his famous crossings of the Empty Quarter only some 20 years earlier.

"The Shackleton detachment shared the airfield with a permanent detachment of Hunter FGA.9s from 8 Squadron, and Wessex helicopters of 78 Squadron. Of course it was an all-male station, apart from a lady from one of the charities who ran a canteen. She lived in her own secure compound in the officers' mess. It was rumoured that shortly after her arrival she was admonished for hanging her washing out to dry, because it was feared that this would excite the troops! Entertainment on base was limited to sports such as soccer and tennis, despite the sweltering heat, and the occasional film night in the messes. To relieve the boredom, some of the more senior aircrew officers who were familiar with North Yorkshire from tours at Topcliffe, Leeming and Acklington used to celebrate market days (Ken Maynard and Tony Hinds were the ring-leaders). It turned out that each day of the week was the market day in at least one North Yorkshire town. The significance of this was that, in those days, the Yorkshire pubs were open all day on market day. Someone would announce, 'Today it is market day in Ripon', and the worthies would settle down after lunch with a crate of beer and tell tall stories to one another. Expeditions further afield were limited by a lack of transport. However, one trip, a fishing trip in an Arab dhow, was memorable for the wrong reasons. I felt fine on the journey out to the fishing spot, but once the engine had stopped the dhow started to wallow in the swell. I was soon leaning over the side to delighted cries of 'ground bait!' from my companions. For the remainder of the 12-hour trip, while my friends enjoyed their sport, I lay comatose, and increasingly dehydrated – there was no shade, and I could not even keep water down. That trip taught me more about the challenges of survival at sea than any sea survival course.

"The Shackleton detachment had three main tasks; Operation Bronze, Operation Turquoise, and we also had to practise the capability for ground support operations in a counter-insurgency role. We would fly occasional sorties to exercise with Royal Navy ships in the area. Every sortie was tasked to check that the Sharjah flag was still flying on the Greater and Lesser Tunb Islands in the eastern Persian Gulf. These were specks of land totalling some 12 square kilometres in area, with a small population of Arab fisher folk. They lay 17 miles south of the Iranian Qeshm Island, and about 44 miles from the Trucial coastline. Ownership of the islands had been disputed between Iran and the Arabian sheiks for centuries; in the 1960s they were under the control of Sharjah, but claimed by Iran. The first Hunter sortie of the day overflew the Tunbs to 'show the flag' and check that the Iranians had not invaded during the night. Later Shackleton overflights reinforced the protecting power's presence. In late November 1971, two days before the British treaties with the sheikhdoms lapsed and the United Arab Emirates was formed, Iranian forces invaded the Tunbs and ejected the Arab population.

"Operation Bronze was a maritime surveillance of the Gulf, using a radar/visual search to report vessels of interest to the British Forces Gulf headquarters in Bahrain. A 'bronze' was one circuit of the Gulf, and a 'double bronze' was two circuits. These were rather tedious. Visibility was poor, especially in the heavily-polluted northern part of the Gulf, while the heat and humidity flying at 1,000 feet were debilitating. We flew with urns of squash, that started out ice-cold, and each member of the crew took turns at supplying everyone else with a constant supply of drink.

"Operation Turquoise was much more interesting, a visual search of the Omani coastline to interdict arms smuggling. In the late 1960s two Marxist groups, the Popular Front for the Liberation of the Occupied Arabian Gulf (PFLOAG) in Dhofar Province to the south, and the National Democratic Front for the Liberation on Oman (NDFLO) in the north, were fighting the Sultan's forces. Britain provided military support to the Sultan that ultimately led to the defeat of the rebels in 1976. Meanwhile the rebels were supported by the usual suspects – China, Iraq, Russia and Yemen – and were receiving arms shipments via small boats which landed at remote spots on the coastline. We undertook our reconnaissance by flying through the Straits of Hormuz, and then descending to fly at 100 feet along the shore looking for suspicious boats or signs of landing. With two pilots, nose gunner, bomb aimer, two beam lookouts and one in the tail we could bring seven pairs of eyes to bear on the task. Flying as far south as fuel would allow, we then returned the same way but positioned about a mile out to sea. Anything suspicious was reported by high frequency radio to the Trucial Oman Scouts. The Scouts, as a result of a report from our crew, were able to intercept a group of arms smugglers.

"British military support to the Sultan took several forms, these included special forces, RAF Regiment field squadrons and RAF pilots flying Omani Strikemaster aircraft in the close-support role. The Shackletons were held in reserve as a 'big stick'. The MR.3 could carry 12 1,000-lb bombs, while the MR.2 could carry 15. All navigators had to qualify at bomb-aiming from medium level (around 12,000 feet); to this end the aircraft were fitted with a variant of the World War II Mk.14 bombsight. However we did not drop any weapons in anger during my detachment. We did find a bullet hole in our aircraft after one sortie, but we judged that this had more likely originated from a wedding celebration rather than a hostile act!

"Apart from one or two ports, such as Muscat, there was virtually no sign of human habitation – it was a wild and beautiful coastline. We would spot a couple of fishermen launching a small boat, or a single man standing in the water casting a net apparently miles from anywhere. Every so often we passed a beau geste-style fort, many of which were originally built by the Portuguese in the 16th Century. It was astonishing to think that at the same time as Neil Armstrong was making the first footprints on the moon (20 July 1969), we were looking for footprints in the sand on the coast of Arabia. On reflection, this was a fascinating few months for me when I was part of a short chapter in Britain's long involvement in the Gulf. It gave me glimpses of a way of life that has all but disappeared as a result of the oil money and tourism that have flooded into the region." [3]

FURTHER OFF THE BEATEN TRACK

A selection of the rather more remote airfields and undeveloped airstrips frequented by MEAF aircraft.

DHALA

The Emirate of Dhala was part of the British Aden Protectorate, which became part of the Federation of South Arabia. Dhala airstrip was 100 miles north of Khormaksar.

'CAPOT' – ARMY

"A Beverley landing at Dhala in about 1962. Our trip to Dhala was to celebrate the completion of an airstrip lovingly constructed by a small crew from 5004 Airfield

Dhala airstrip 100 miles north of Khormaksar. [Dean Pringuer]

Construction Squadron. For about two years an elderly flight lieutenant had masterminded the job, which involved hacking out large pieces of rock, crushing them, spreading the material, rolling it, sealing it with tarmac, and so on.

"A Beaver appeared and landed, with all sorts of brass from Aden. Then a Beverley hove majestically into view, circled once and carried out a stately approach and perfect touchdown. As it rolled out waves developed in a V-pattern in the tarmac

Beverley C.1 landing at Dahla, 1962. [Capot]

along the length of the nice new strip, leaving a pleasing corrugated appearance! The commander in chief turned to the flight lieutenant and remarked that his future for another two years was now defined. He then climbed back into the Beaver, which departed from a convenient smooth piece of ground.

"That evening the generator broke down during a film the flight lieutenant liked and...he went doo-lally threatening us all with a loaded .303 rifle. 'You barstewards!' he yelled, pulling at the trigger with the safety catch still on, 'You did it on purpose!' Sadly he was shipped out next day by three-tonner, securely fastened down, and the crew went back to work. I have no idea what happened to the Beverley."

JOHN LENNARD – NAVIGATOR, VIA HIS SON RICHARD

"John was a flight sergeant navigator on the Twin Pioneers of 78 Squadron between November 1958 and November 1960. On 9 February 1959 he flew a special flying patrol (SFP), prior to which his Twin Pioneer XM286 had special communication equipment installed by a civilian engineer. The aircraft took off at 23:20 hours captained by Fg Off Forester with John as navigator. They climbed to 12,000 feet heading north over Dhala. No lights were allowed and they maintained radio silence. They then flew over the Yemeni border with the newly installed equipment picking up radio transmissions from the ground and re-transmitting them direct to London. The sortie lasted for an hour and 35 minutes."

DEAN PRINGUER – NAVIGATOR

"On 233 Squadron Valettas I visited many strips up-country in Aden Protectorate, including Dhala, Mukeiras, Ataq, Lawdar, Ghuraf, Gatn, Nuqub and Beihan. Dhala airstrip was 100 miles north of Khormaksar and had to be approached from the east as there were 2,000-feet high mountains looming at the far end of the runway. I think it had an oiled runway surface, I don't remember any paving and they may have sorted out the 'hump' it had. We would often take the air officer commanding Middle East and other senior RAF officers for a spot of fishing. We night-stopped on occasion, feeding ourselves from flight rations and sleeping in accommodation not befitting a fastidious 'truckie'."

KAMARAN ISLAND

Approximately 200 miles north of Perim Island off the southern tip of the Arabian Peninsula, Kamaran is the largest Yemeni island in the Red Sea, strategically located at its southern end. At this time it was a British protectorate.

Kamaran – last outpost of empire. [Dean Pringuer]

RAY CARRAN – SIGNALLER

"On 20 October 1966 crew six of 204 Squadron Ballykelly was deployed to Khormaksar, Aden to update our competency in medium-level bombing and gunnery. Since forming as a constituted crew, four months previously, this was a pleasant break from the routine of anti-submarine warfare (ASW) exercises and crew training. We took off in WR952 having been tasked to drop our 25-lb practice bombs, and shoot off our 600 rounds of 20-mm cannon on the range to the north-west of Khormaksar. Everything was going according to plan, with a modicum of success from the bombing, when a call came in for us to report our fuel state and prepare to be diverted to an SAR task.

"We had enough AVGAS to satisfy at least the initial requirements. We were told that an RAF Dakota heading for Kamaran Island had failed to report in. As relative strangers to this part of the world we asked for further information on the island. Eventually we located it about ten miles off the Yemeni coast. The Yemen was hostile and we had to avoid overflying their territory, so we set heading to 'on-top' Perim Island. We prepared to carry out a 'creeping line ahead search' along the assumed track of the Dakota.

"As we came abeam the Yemeni town of Hodeidah we became the target of interest for a couple of MiG 17 Frescos, which were home-based there. They flew alongside, and then carried out close inspections of our underside, topside, right and left sides. Our reactions to this attention were firstly to head for the water to give them one less aspect to look at, and at the same time try to get in the lee of some of the islands dotted about. As we did this one of the MiG 17s flew directly under us and pulled vertical right in front, so we had no option but to fly through his jet wake. That was quite scary and prompted a response from our air electronics operator Bill Checkley, that if he did that again he would give him a burst of 20-mm cannon! That was a sort of throw-away remark uttered in times of tension, but it typified the feelings we all had towards our aggressors. After several passes and 'close encounters' lasting about 20 minutes, the jets departed and we, very shaken, continued on our search. All of the goings-on were reported to our control, and we were told that the Dakota had reported the same thing, then gone off the air – consternation on board our aircraft. However, we put our feelings on hold and got on with the job in hand, assuming the worst.

"We flew north and eventually reached Kamaran Island. There, much to our surprise, was a dirt runway with a Union Jack flying in the breeze, and the RAF Dakota parked outside a small building. Our next signal to control was along the lines of 'what the hell is going on?' The reply was 'the situation is resolved; you can now return to Khormaksar'. Gee, thanks! Discussion among the crew now concentrated on how best to get past Hodeida on the homeward leg. We opted to go as low as safely possible to decrease the chance of radar intercept. It was a very relieved, if somewhat bewildered and angry crew, that touched down at Khormaksar. We were met by a wing commander from operations who wanted to know where our photographs were. On telling him that we had other things to worry about, he promptly gave me a dressing down on my lack of foresight. That did it for me, and I felt like demanding to know which fool sent us, an armed aircraft, on a SAR mission into what was potentially a hostile situation without having the sense to brief us on what was going on. It would have been an end to my promising career if I had done that. However, all I said was 'what do we have three squadrons of Hunters in Aden for, if we can't supply top cover to an SAR mission?'

"A highly charged debrief followed in which I discovered that control was fully aware of the Dakota's plight, but thought it wise not to tell us that Kamaran Island was a British protectorate, the Dak was on a 'milk run', and two Hunters were on runway alert in case something happened to us. We learned that the two MiGs,

Approach to Riyan airfield, 1962-63. P12 compass top right. [Dean Pringuer]

despite their Yemeni markings, were probably flown by Egyptians, and that, even if the standby Hunters had been scrambled, there was little they could do against MiG 17s! I know of at least one ex-fighter Shack pilot who fancied his chances in a Hunter against the MiG 17, however." [3]

MOGADISHU, SOMALIA, RIYAN AND RAS KARMA, YEMEN

DEAN PRINGUER CONTINUES

"In May 1962 we had a breakdown in an aircraft, flown by Flt Lt Williams and Flt Lt Locke, at Mogadishu, Somalia, while en-route from Khormaksar to Eastleigh. We had to keep an engine running for enough electrical power to call HQ MEAF for help by Morse key. As we did not carry groundcrew or a spares pack on these scheduled flights, pilots Ted Denham and John Williams brought in spares and groundcrew in another Valetta.

"In early July a local ruler, in a fort in the Hilyan area of Upper Yaffa, reported being besieged by rebel tribesmen. 233 Squadron Valettas did a number of supply drops to the garrison, supported by the Hunters of 8 Squadron and 208 Squadron. For supply drops there were only four panniers. There was space on the port side where I stood, off the rollers, and it was totally manual extraction. From the manual

Supply Drop Sequence c.1963 – red on. [Dean Pringuer]

Supply Drop Sequence – green on. [Dean Pringuer]

Supply Drop Sequence – parachutes deploying. [Dean Pringuer]

effort, displayed by the dispatchers, no momentum was built up and there was no danger of being swept along with the load. There was a load deflector barrier and a dispatcher in a 'safe' place. There was no gate to stop the load, it was merely held in place by hand. I remember the DZ was quite small, on a hilltop, which would explain our overshoots. We did not carry air loadmasters on 233 Squadron.

"On 27 September 1963 we were tasked to fly in VW195 to Riyan. Once there we were to collect a letter and a wireless telegraphy operator and take them to Socotra Island, Yemen, a flight of 300 nautical miles. The letter, addressed to the Sultan, was dropped in a weighted mail sack with parachute, on what appeared to be the main square in Hadibu, the capital. After the mail drop, we flew about ten miles west to the airstrip at Ras Karma, a disused World War II field. There was no air traffic controller here, it was completely deserted, and after a low pass to check the runway for goats and debris, we landed safely on the rough surface. Here we left the wireless telegraphy operator with food and water in the hope that the letter had reached the Sultan safely, been read, and that transportation had been sent to pick him up. He was to reinstate the failed communication link at Hadibu. I never heard the outcome save an intelligence summary which stated that the wireless telegraphy operator had repaired the radio and was not left to die in the desert!

"I was the navigator flying the Sultan of Muscat and Oman from Khormaksar to Salalah on 13 October 1963. The MECS VIP Valetta was unavailable, so he had to 'slum it' with us. The aircraft was 'tarted up' with VIP seats, and we had our air quartermaster on board to look after him. The Sultan was met by an Honour Guard of local tribesmen and a volley of shots for the Sultan on his arrival. Rumour had it that the Sultan would normally reward his crew with Rolex Oyster Perpetual watches. In our case nothing was forthcoming, probably due to the uncomfortable flight in a lowly truck.

"I never experienced an engine failure in 2,000 hours of Valetta and Hastings flying. This was a testament to the Bristol Hercules engines, although I believe there were a lot of serious teething problems that led to some crashes. We did a lot of formation flying, to use up airframe hours, before disbandment of 233 Squadron on 31 January 1964."

PULL UP A SANDBAG

BRIAN SHADBOLT

"At Eastleigh, my navigator found a puff adder curled up round his bag. It was dealt with using the long-reach CO2 extinguisher."

LEN CLAYTON

"On take-off from Mukeiras, a pot shot from the side of the strip hit the starboard tyre, puncturing it. Thankfully Flt Sgt Shannon managed to bring the Valetta to a stop safely before the cliff edge on the extreme eastern edge of the airstrip, overlooking Lawdar some 4,000 feet below – the ball shot was found inside the tyre!"

---

[1] *Flying Freestyle* by Jerry Pook
[2] *Shackleton Boys* 2 by Steve Bond
[3] *Shackleton Boys* 1 by Steve Bond

CHAPTER SEVEN

THE OTHER SIDE OF LIFE

Whilst air and groundcrew are the most obvious participants in aviation, there are so many other service roles which play their part. A few of them are detailed here, each highlighting a different aspect of the support required for flying operations. We also see something of what life was like for the wives and families.

View towards Crater from officers' mess non-air-conditioned accommodation [Dean Pringuer]

DAVID FORSYTH – SUPPLY AND MOVEMENTS OFFICER

Prior to his RAF service, David had been employed as a gillie on a grouse moor in Scotland. He found himself in Majunga in 1971 as the detachment supply and movements officer. As outlined in chapter four, following Rhodesia's UDI, Shackletons were deployed to Majunga to help maintain the Beira oil blockade.

"As a young flying officer I took over the grandly-named appointment of officer commanding supply and movements flight in Majunga, for the first eight months of 1971. It was a one-off, life-changing experience since competence in French was essential for both professional and social reasons. It laid the basis for a subsequent 30-year RAF career in which mastery of French was to play a significant part.

"The RAF Detachment Majunga existed from 1966 until 1972. Aircraft were provided initially from squadrons based in the Far East or Middle East, then later the UK. Aircrew and groundcrew did two-month stints, whilst a small number of cadre officers and airmen did six-month stints. The wing commander commanding officer did 12 months, accompanied. Views as to the relative success of the Shackleton

Majunga detachment line accommodation. [Dave McCandless]

deployment are mixed – but the episode did provide a unique opportunity for a relatively small number of RAF personnel to experience life in a French/Malgache culture, whilst staying overseas without the usual trappings of military infrastructure.

"The 'flight' consisted of a corporal, a senior aircraftman and 'moi' (this was a French-speaking job in a former French colony) – which was fine for the supply bit of the job. To cope with unloading, and loading, the fortnightly Britannia re-supply aircraft, the movements team had to be augmented by whichever senior non-commissioned officers and airmen could be persuaded to get involved in what was invariably heavy, hot and sweaty work. They were motor transport mechanics, administrators, cooks and anyone who did not move fast enough when my persuasive corporal was looking for reinforcements! We had neither a forklift truck nor much in the way of handling aids, with the exception of an apparatus known as a Britannia freight lift platform. This was specifically designed for lifting loads up to the height of the freight access door in a Britannia. 'Brits' were programmed for a leisurely 24-hour turnround and the air loadmaster generally stayed with the movements team to help, whilst the rest of the crew went into town for a 'cultural visit'.

WEIGHT WATCHERS AND 'MOI'

"Early in my stay it was decided to use Hercules instead of Brits, on what were called tactical turnrounds of 15 hours only, with aircraft arriving mid-afternoon and leaving at about 06:00 the next day. This departure time was important as the first leg back to the UK, from Majunga to Muharraq, was about 14 hours flying, near the limit of the Herc. To get off the shortish runway at Majunga, with maximum fuel on board, required a take-off in the cool temperature of the early morning. But this small civilian airport on which we were squatting operated from 08:00 to dusk. Airport air traffic control, met and fire crews were manned to allow take-off at 06:00 but the fuel supplier was not. That meant refuelling the Hercules the day before, sometimes before we had off-loaded all of the incoming freight and certainly before we had loaded the outgoing freight – most of which were aircraft and vehicle spare parts and tools. Unlike the Brits, we were unaided by the loadmaster. The Hercules' crews would abandon their aircraft to our tender mercies and went off to town for a 'tactical' rest, with an admonition to us to make bloody sure she was ready for the 06:00 take-off!

"A Hercules with maximum fuel is inherently tail-heavy – and from this flowed a sphincter-tightening episode. This particular afternoon we had to empty the aircraft and refuel it before re-loading. The on-board winch was unserviceable (nothing new there), so everything again had to be man-handled aboard either carrying it, or pushing and pulling it up the tail ramp if it was too heavy to carry. All was going well until I was told there was a last-minute item which simply had to return to UK for overhaul – a Shackleton's Griffon engine. These weighed, from memory, about 2,000 lbs and were normally mounted on an air-transportable stand. This was lightweight and had a horizontal bar set high enough to allow the stand to be pulled by the winch up the Hercules ramp, and over the hump where the ramp met the aircraft freight deck. A quick re-calculation of the aircraft trim sheet showed the aircraft, even with all that fuel and this extra weight right at the rear, would still be just within permissible limits. However, as Rabbie Burns had it – the best-laid plans and all that. Observant readers will recall that the aircraft winch was unserviceable.

"Initiative was quickly unleashed. We decided to run a chain from the engine stand into the aircraft, through a lashing fitment on the deck, and back out to the airport fire engine, vintage 1940s. Driving the fire engine, in thick clouds of fumes emanating from the exhaust and the burning clutch, away from the aircraft had the effect of pulling the stand up the ramp and into the aircraft. Decidedly dodgy stuff and written nowhere in any guide for loading aircraft. But my Cranwell training was not for nothing – I was indoctrinated in getting the job done, whatever it took.

"Re-enter Rabbie Burns – the best-laid plans etc. This last-minute unplanned engine for repatriation was not mounted on an air transportable stand, but on a normal stand for use in workshops. The horizontal bar at the base of this stand was right at the bottom, unlike its air-transportable brother. This meant that it could not breast the hump at the top of the ramp to enter the aircraft without grounding and sticking. Forcing it with our fire engine and chain lash-up would damage the aircraft ramp, and potentially render the aircraft unserviceable. The only apparent option was to fail to return the engine – which would be highly unpopular, as they were always in short supply, and could ultimately have an impact on Shackleton availability to meet the Beira patrol task.

"Then that accursed initiative reared its ugly head again. If we got the engine onto the ramp and then raised the aircraft ramp, the angle to be breasted at the top would decrease to the point where the stand could cross over without scraping. So… the fire engine moves away from the aircraft, and the engine on its stand crawls up the ramp. So far so good. The corporal activates the ramp control and the ramp begins to rise, great. But hang on, as the ramp rises the rear end of our tail-heavy Hercules starts to go down towards the ground. If that continues unchecked, we shall damage the underside of the aircraft, and it won't be able to leave as scheduled. End of promising young officer's career!

"Help was at hand from an unlikely source. A Shackleton had landed a few minutes earlier after a 12-hour sortie and was being worked on by a post-flight team. This was led by a chief tech who was, shall we say, struggling to maintain the lithe profile of his youth. Here was 20+ stones on the hoof, with another half a dozen chaps who would weigh in at about 12-14 stones each – getting on for 1,500 lbs of fully mobile ballast weight. Said team was easily persuaded to climb into the Hercules cockpit, thereby counter-balancing the weight of the engine stand by just enough to stop the Hercules sitting on its arse as we lifted the ramp and eased the engine into the freight compartment.

"In the slang of the day, we 'hacked it'. The Hercules load was completed and the trim sheet was closed off. Very early next morning the crew returned from their evening's entertainment in Madame Chabaud's 'leisure complex', over which it is best, dear reader, to draw a veil. Passengers were loaded, aircraft and trim-sheet were accepted by the crew, tyres were kicked and off they soared to Muharraq.

SOLIDARITY IN THE FACE OF THIEVES

"In Majunga, the adjutant/interpreter, the administration officer and the supply and movements officer shared a three-bedroom flat a few floors above the detachment's bureau. The flat had its own Malgache 'boy', Joseph, to keep house, and Miradgee, a Comorien cook (the reason for including this apparently unnecessary detail will become clear).

"Each bedroom was sparsely, but adequately, furnished with a single bed inside an all-enveloping mosquito net, a bedside table with light, a wardrobe, a chest of drawers, a table/bureau and a couple of chairs. Each bedroom had two doors: one off the central corridor and a sliding door which gave onto a balcony which ran the full extent of the flat.

"One night during my first week there, lying on my front, I began to dream that there was someone under my bed. But then I realised that I was not dreaming! I lashed out at the figure, only for my fist to be caught up in the mosquito net. The figure leapt up and exited the room onto the balcony, dropping things as it went. With me shouting in pursuit, half aggrieved and half scared, the figure ran round the balcony to the lounge, out the front door and down the stairs. I soon gave up. It was about that time I realised the figure was small, black, naked and covered in oil (I later learned this was to make it more difficult for a pursuer to maintain a hold if the thief was caught). The sum of losses was a toothbrush and toothpaste after I collected what the thief had jettisoned.

"I also realised that on hearing my shouts and the commotion, my two flat-mates had leapt to their feet in their rooms and locked their doors from the inside. So much for solidarity – clearly more of that amongst thieves than in the face of them. Miffed, I certainly was! Fast-forward a few weeks, and a changeover for another of the flat-dwellers. After his first night he awoke to find he had been robbed. He had not heard anything, but we found the front door open.

"Then I had a Eureka moment – who would know that there was a new person in the flat, and how was access being gained to this fourth floor flat? Suspecting 'inside' participation – the cook and housekeeper each had a key – I took Joseph to the balcony and made it clear that if we were burgled again, he would be taking the short route to the ground, over the rails of the balcony. Why Joseph? He was much the smaller of the two. No fool, moi. Bluff of course, but it worked. The next incomer to the flat was not burgled.

CANUTE I AIN'T

"On taking up post, as a 'permanent staff' officer, I had the luxury of my own assigned Land Rover – status indeed for a fresh-faced flying officer. In the UK, one would normally be a wing commander in command to merit one's own vehicle. After a few days I decided to explore on my own in my trusty Landie – which was actually quite aged and bashed. I left the airport and followed a sandy track along the coast through the area known as Amborovy. This was pretty much a deserted area during the week although there were beach houses dotted around which no doubt would be used at weekends and holidays. Then I saw on one house half a dozen native Malgaches working on a roof.

"After a few kilometres I saw, beside the track, a little gap which gave onto a steep, vehicle-wide path sloping down the cliff to the beach. After driving down that for 30 or so metres I was on a beautiful beach, with nary a soul to be seen in either direction. Out with newly acquired lamba, a thin multi-coloured cotton cloth about the size of a large beach towel, spread it on the sand and down onto it for a planned ten-minute kip in the sun to change my white, January legs into browner versions which would not betray my recent arrival.

"I awoke about an hour later to see things had changed dramatically. Black sky, thunder and lightning and heavy tropical rain pattering down and growing in intensity – and the tide was coming in. My Land Rover was now just a few yards from the incoming sea. Ah well, no sweat. Press the knob to engage four-wheel drive and up the slope we'd go – but disaster! Half way up, total loss of traction on what was now a wet, slippery track of that red clay from which Madagascar had earned its alternative name of the Red Island.

"Reverse and slide back down to the bottom and engage the low ratio crawler gearbox. Surely that would get us out of trouble? After all I had driven Land Rovers out of peat bogs in Angus when other, lesser mortals, had got theirs firmly stuck. But no better – half way up we lost traction again. We slid back down to what was now a very narrow strip of beach as the tide kept coming in, and it was getting narrower with each incoming wave. Oh sh.. how was I going to explain a flooded Land Rover in my first week? Would I be on the next flight back to the UK, with my tail between my legs, to participate on the wrong side of a court martial for losing the Queen's Land Rover?

"Then I remembered the workers on the house. Breaking the Malgache sprint record, I sprinted up the slope and along the track. With much gesturing and encouragement, I persuaded these worthies to follow me. They were bare-footed and in torn shorts and t-shirts. Back to the Land Rover, load two in the back, two on the bonnet to add weight to the rear and front wheels (a trick from the peat bogs which now seemed light years away) and two pushing. With much giggling and shouts of 'Alefa! Alefa!' (Go!), in a great spray of red mud we managed just, to reach the top of the slope.

"My relief was palpable. I emptied the contents of my wallet, probably about £10 worth of FMG (Francs Malgaches, known irreverently as French Machine Guns) with much repetition of 'merci, merci' by them and by me. Off I sped to the middle of town and our flat above the bureau. £10 was a small sum for me to pay to rescue my career from a potentially unpromising start, but would have seemed a fortune to those natives of one of the poorest countries in the world.

"Next day I shared my scary experience with Chief Tech Williams, the motor transport maintenance chief who, like me, had just arrived. He said the vehicle would be needing an overhaul anyway and took it off to the motor transport servicing tent. Later in the day he came to see me with a wide smile. In his delightful singsong Welsh tones, he said something like, 'No bloody wonder you could not get her up that cliff. The prop-shaft to the front wheels is missing so no front-wheel drive … oh and by the way, where there should be springs in the brake-drums somebody has put string – strong string mind you.' It was then that I discovered that RAF Majunga, supposedly a short-lived organisation, was the dumping ground for vehicles which were becoming surplus to requirements in the Middle and Far East, and of course, as these bases were closing, they got rid of their rubbish first.

CLOSE ENCOUNTERS OF THE STEERING WHEEL KIND – ENCOUNTER 1

"After unloading and reloading a Hercules at the airport we needed to drive the four or five miles back into town. We consisted of five or six senior non-commissioned officers and airmen. We also had a quantity of various goods to deliver to one or other of the accommodations which housed the detachment personnel. The complement of passengers meant we had to load the goods into one of those heavy, medium-sized trailers which were bought to be pulled by Land Rovers; I think they were called Sankey trailers. As I sat behind the steering wheel one of the lads told me he had hitched on and plugged in the lighting cable,' so off I went with a full passenger load and a well-laden trailer.

"The road between the airport and the town of Majunga was, for the most part, a dead straight and well-made road with a deep monsoon ditch on each side. The road was little used by traffic other than prior to, or just after weekly Air France Boeing flights from Majunga to Paris. These were in themselves social occasions when the airport bar did a roaring trade. We had gone only a few hundred yards, fortunately reasonably slowly, when there was a very loud, graunching noise from behind me. One of the rear passengers shouted that the trailer had come loose. Fortunately, on the straight road, it carried on in a straight line until it simply stopped by the tow bar digging into the road surface. It was hitched on again, this time properly, and no more was said. It could so easily have tipped and spread its load all over the road and the ditch.

ENCOUNTER 2

"There were relatively few roundabouts in the town but one, an iconic one, was formed by a very large baobab tree. Its girth was several metres and it was a most effective roundabout. Unlike in the UK, where priority is given to the vehicle already on the roundabout, French driving conventions of the day, still in play since

Madagascar had gained independence several years before, gave priority to vehicles entering the roundabout from the right. For more than six months I had diligently applied the French rules and had not had a close shave, never mind a bump.

"On the roundabout as night fell, I checked to my right and carried on. From nowhere, it seemed, materialised a Malgache on a bicycle, intent on claiming, quite justifiably, his priority. This bicycle had no lights and was travelling faster than I was. Somehow, by some gymnastic miracle, he leveraged himself off his bike which clattered to the ground, and onto the broad mudwing and flat bonnet of the Land Rover. I had a vision through the windscreen of a black face, white teeth and white fearful eyes. As I did my emergency stop, he jumped down, mounted his bike and shot off, apparently unhurt. A chastened relieved driver, I carried on to my destination breathing deep sighs of relief.

MOWGLI GOT US INTO THIS – OR – THE ITALIAN JOB

"For some reason it was the designated supply and movements officer who, before leaving for the island, had to attend the projectionist's course at Hendon. It transpired that he would have the additional task of being responsible for receiving three or four 16-mm films from each incoming fortnightly flight which staged through Muharraq. Then returning them on the next flight, thereby ensuring the services' Kinema Corporation's supply chain was unbroken. Films were more of a morale booster than readers today might imagine.

"Once in Madagascar I found that this arduous secondary duty extended to operating the projector for film shows in the officers' mess, and ensuring that throughout the two weeks each film rotated (pardon the pun) through the airmen's camp, the non-commissioned officers' accommodation and the officers' mess. The last named was on the first floor of a large block – which did not deter dozens of young Malgache kids from climbing on the petrol pumps and roof of the petrol station opposite, to boo and cheer very loudly the little bit of action they glimpsed through the open windows.

"The detachment commander during my time there, Wg Cdr Doug Cook, liked to entertain local personalities to drinks and the film in the officers' mess. *Jungle Book* was very popular, and he had invited the local manager of the AGIP Oil Exploration Company to a viewing. Two charming Italian gentlemen and spouses enjoyed our hospitality and Mowgli (from the *Jungle Book*). After the film the good wing commander asked me to join him in chatting to the Italians who, as well as being charming had, I now realise with the benefit of hindsight, clearly worked out how to achieve a specific aim. It transpired that they had an exploration drilling rig on a platform in the Mozambique Straits off Majunga; it needed refurbishment. They had planned to fly refurbishment equipment and materiel using, they said, a Britannia into Tananarive. This was about 12-18 hours trucking time from Majunga, with serious question marks over the ability of some bridges to take the weight. Ingratiating wing commander, 'I think we might be able to help you there'. Naïve flying officer, 'We should be able to help, but we would need an indemnity signed in case of accidents, and a significant contribution to the airmen's amenities fund'. The response in Italian-accented English came at the speed of light: 'Issa no problem'.

"On the day, we watched a Brit appear on a very, very long finals approach with three engines smoking and one prop feathered. As it taxied in, we could see it was a UK-registered Transmeridian CL-44. For those who have not come across them (I hadn't), this Britannia-based type had a swing tail unit which could open through 90 degrees allowing access from the rear to the freight/passenger hold.

"Off came three or four aircrew. One was recognised, by a detachment Shackleton pilot, as having been thrown off his Cranwell course for some misdemeanour a few years previously. They were accompanied by half a dozen black ladies who were introduced as stewardesses on familiarisation training. It later transpired these ladies had been embarked at Nairobi on the way in, and I heard that they certainly knew how to be familiar – in exchange for a consideration!

"The aircraft was abandoned to our tender mercies. The Britannia freight lift platform (BFLP) just fitted into the space when the swing rear door was open – and my heart sank. The hold was full, front to back and top to bottom with huge pieces of steel bits to refurbish the oil rig. Some were small if heavy, but could be relatively easily manhandled. Others were very large and very heavy. They were sitting on the aircraft floor, without any load spreading or rollers underneath, so it was extremely difficult to prize them off the floor to get anything underneath in order to shift them. But the biggest and most immediate challenge was a piece of perforated steel decking. It was about 15 inches deep, about 25 feet long and so wide that it just fitted within the shape of the curved aircraft ceiling. It was lying on top of everything else at a height of about five feet, and was also extremely heavy. It had clearly been put in last using a powerful fork-lift truck – not something we had at our disposal. It had to come out first before we could move the stuff under it, but how?

"We tied lashing tape around the outermost end and looped that around the big cast knuckle which locked the swing tail in place when closed. With several taking the strain with the tape to pull the decking upwards a little, and others pulling it, all whilst standing on the BFLP with others pushing at the innermost end we shifted it outwards a few inches. Reposition the tape through another perforation and move it again. This was repeated several times with masses of pulling, shoving and sweating in the tropical temperature until we had it very near the point of balance sitting on the rearmost edge of the stuff below it. Conscious that another inch or two would tip the outer end down, and the inner end up into the aircraft ceiling only inches above, we decided to get as many as possible on the BFLP to keep the bloody thing level with some again holding the tape around the knuckle as a precaution. Precaution against what I am now not sure.

"But then disaster struck. It was just too heavy for our combined strength, the outer end dipped, the inner end rose and it slid down and out until the bottom crashed on the ground. The top was lying at an angle against the platform of the BFLP 15 feet or so in the air. I heard a shout of pain behind me on the BFLP and looked round to see Sgt Cameron, the motor transport fitter, lying with the frame apparently on his leg. But the God of naïve movers was on one of my shoulders. He was accompanied on the other shoulder by the God of movers who can hack it! The inner end had indeed risen but had only just touched the ceiling, scratching it but doing no damage as it slid out. Sgt Cameron's leg was bruised, but thankfully not broken.

"We eventually got the rest off, shut the aircraft and went off to replace, with appropriate liquid, the gallons of sweat we had lost over four or five hours grappling with this monstrous load. Interestingly the officer commanding detachment was nowhere to be seen during the effort, although I did receive moral support from the presence of the adjutant/interpreter. Next morning the aircraft took off on three smoky engines, all crew of all 'trades' were accounted for and on board.

"We were the toast of the detachment as several thousand Francs Malgaches found their way into the amenities fund. Thankfully the ladies with the CL-44 had indeed left by then, so did not feature as part of the amenities. Naïve – yes, stupid – yes, rewarding – yes to be loyally supported by a team of excellent guys, rewarding – yes again; the proceeds funded an outboard motor for water-skiing, character forming – yes, good for morale and the esteem in which the supply and movements team were held – yes, to be repeated – absolutely no bloody way!

ECONOMICAL WITH THE TRUTH

"France was always suspicious that Britain had designs on the country, and allegedly applied pressure on the recently independent Madagascar to deny Perfidious Albion any opportunity to become a fixture. One implication was that anything imported from the UK into Madagascar had to be defined as aircraft spares – despite the fact that of course all sorts of things were carried in. These ranged from motor transport spares to soft furnishings, catering and medical supplies, to uniforms and office supplies – in short everything required by a 120 or so strong detachment living in, and operating from, this temporary base. Relationships with the Malgache customs officer, who inspected every incoming flight, had to be especially nurtured. In particular, the team in the supply squadron at St Mawgan, who parented the detachment, knew that all manifests had to be written as Shackleton spares – regardless of the true contents of the cartons – which had to be sealed so as not to arouse suspicion.

"One day I received a signal from Lyneham stating that on the next Hercules flight there would be a consignment of 50,000 cigarettes. These had been seized from returning squaddies by my Malgache customs man's professional brothers-in-arms at Lyneham. They were issued to us under the strict constraints that they were for senior non-commissioned officers and airmen only, were to be issued free of charge, and were not to be re-sold.

"In came the Herc. I escorted the customs man as we clambered over miscellaneous bona fide Shackleton bits and cartons, some of which were a bit less bona fide. Eventually we got to the ramp where, lashed down next to the Elsan, was a consignment labelled as 'valuable and attractive'. Yes, those bloody cigarettes which, originating at Lyneham, had escaped the St Mawgan cover-up and stood out like the proverbial whatsits on a navvy's whippet. 'C'est quoi ça?' from the customs man. 'Ce sont des pièces de rechange pour Shackleton,' I answered, with crossed-fingers, remembering the sage advice from my predecessor, Tom Mitcham, to call everything Shackleton bits. The customs man smiled and moved on. Later, I discreetly presented him with a carton of 200 'Shackleton spares', and all was well.

"These fags, sitting in the airmen's club, turned out to be even less popular than the daily anti-malarial pills sitting alongside them on the bar. They were all obscure brands of poor-quality tobacco and were being consumed very slowly by the 80 senior non-commissioned officers and airmen. Even if all of the 80 personnel had been smokers, which of course they were not, I leave you to do the calculation on daily smoke rate to get through this lot.

"A month later, I received another signal alerting us they had loaded another consignment of 50,000 fags on the Herc, too late for us to protest. Why were they so keen? In came the Herc. I was busy and the wing commander boss said 'I'll show the customs man over the aircraft'. Conscious of the fags I tried to protest that I could do it, but he insisted he should do it and his insistence outranked mine. Half an hour later I saw the boss. 'How did it go?' 'Ah, the customs man asked what was in the carton on the ramp labelled 'valuable and attractive'. I said they were cigarettes and tried to explain the rules and conditions, but he was having none of it'. So they stayed on the aircraft and returned to Lyneham. Strangely, once word got round, not a soul complained about losing out on more free cigarettes. Maybe the boss was wilier than I had given him credit for?

THE WHEEL THAT WAS TO TURN FULL CIRCLE

"Supply support for the detachment, of never more than two Shackletons flying the Beira patrol, was mounted from many places; usually the parent units of the Shackletons in the Middle East. By my time, 1971, aircraft were initially from Ballykelly, and then Honington, but supply support was provided from St Mawgan. Loads of spares and the other paraphernalia to keep the detachment going were consolidated at either Brize Norton for Britannia schedules, or Lyneham for Hercules schedules, both of which were fortnightly. A logistics recipe for disaster, as readers will imagine.

"Demands from our supply and movements flight were prepared in a standard signal format. Like all signals emanating from the detachment they were passed to the communications centre (tent), who transmitted the contents to a Royal Navy base in Mauritius in Morse code. Then, some Royal Navy ratings took each signal and re-transmitted the contents, using Morse code, to somewhere in the UK – possibly Rudloe Manor. They then used the Morse information to input demands onto the supply control centre system, which was managed centrally by Hendon. St Mawgan now gained visibility of the information relating to Majunga's demands, and became responsible for ensuring they were met and items despatched to Brize or Lyneham. To use a hackneyed phrase – you couldn't make it up – but somebody did! In fairness, the detachment was only supposed to exist for a few months – but it dragged on for six years.

"My small team (one corporal mover and one SAC supplier) had received a demand from the engineer team for quantity six bolts in the 26 SH range, we'll say it was 26SH12345678. A demand was launched into the ether via the matelots at Mauritius. Several weeks and re-supply flights went by, and no sign of the demand being met. Not a high priority demand, and no-one was much excited about it.

"Then late one afternoon a Hercules came into long finals, after 14 hours from Muharraq, and disgorged its load of white-kneed passengers. We set to, like good little movers, to unload the incoming freight and re-load the aircraft, whilst sorting out the trim sheet. This was always a trial with no calculators and a max fuel load for a 14-hour leg back to Muharraq. And we always had to be quick about it as the aircraft had to take off in the cool of the early morning. The movements corporal, Dave Stevens, press-ganged his chums into acting as movers, so we had motor transport fitters, caterers, anyone who could not avoid his persuasive charm. When I had time to take a quick look at the incoming freight I saw there were six pristine, bright yellow Shackleton towing arms sitting on the tarmac.

"Observant readers will observe that I mentioned earlier two Shackletons. A quick check of the accompanying paperwork indicated the demand number we had raised for SH12345678, but these towing arms were two numbers out. We kept two of them, reloading four onto the Herc along with two knackered ones for good measure. I should here explain that the memorandum of understanding, between the Ministry of Defence and its Malgache equivalent, stipulated the detachment was to leave nothing behind – everything had to be airlifted out.

"The subsequent checks revealed that as there were no stocks anywhere of towing arms, the relevant supply management branch at Ministry of Defence Harrogate had tasked 7 MU Quedgeley to manufacture the items. It was not realised that the section reference was for anything other than bolts! No-one at 7 MU had queried the demand, and they had manufactured and despatched the six towing arms – hence the long wait. Investigations failed to identify where the error had been introduced. We never heard anything more.

EPILOGUE: OPERATION SEDBERGH

DAVID FORSYTH CONTINUES

"Fairly early in my stay the detachment commanding officer pilot told me to review, and update, the secret Operation Sedbergh order for the withdrawal from Majunga. The initial deployments from the Middle East had been done on a shoe-string. However over the intervening years, as the detachment became more of a fixture, the engineering support facility and its equipment, like the supply stores and the assorted vehicles and accommodation facilities had grown and grown, as these things do. This presented a particular problem. Under that memorandum of understanding, when the RAF withdrew, it had to remove all of its equipment – leaving nothing behind. No doubt in 1966 that had seemed easy to achieve but five years later it was a different kettle of fish.

"The operation order detailed every bit of kit, together with weight and dimensions, which would have to be shipped out by air. It also included associated draft trim sheets for X number of Britannia flights, and Y number of Hercules flights to recover all the personnel and all the kit to Muharraq. I spent many long hours deleting kit no longer there, and adding kit which was now there. I came up against a conundrum: the last two flights had to be a Britannia for the last tranche of personnel who were needed to keep the detachment viable until the end, and a Hercules for the last lot of kit.

"A Hercules was able to start engines unaided, but a Brit needed external power. I had to envisage, so that both aircraft could get under way: starting the Brit using a Houchin external power source, then using the remaining Land Rover to pull the Houchin to the ramp of the Hercules and getting it on-board a very full aircraft. The Hercules, fully fuelled, had just enough space and trim lee-way to accommodate the volume and weight of the Houchin – but not the Land Rover needed to get it on board. Remember, we were not allowed to leave anything behind. With no obvious need to activate the operations order in mid-1971, I unilaterally decided that the pragmatic solution would be to drive the last Land Rover off a nearby cliff into the sea, with the driver running back half a mile to board the waiting Hercules.

"In the spring of 1972 the president, Philibert Tsiranana, was very ill and began to lose political control. He had been well-disposed to France, the former colonial power who was still heavily involved in Madagascar. Many French nationals were instructed to leave pretty much overnight, and the detachment was suddenly brought to an end – Operation Sedbergh was dusted off and activated.

"By then I was long gone. I understand from my successor that lots of kit was sold off or donated locally, and the airlift, sensibly, was considerably reduced from the 50 or 60 flights defined in the operations order. This was doubly-sensible since all the vehicles were Far East or Middle East surpluses which had found their way to Majunga and were worthless. Knowing the fantastic Malgache capability to make, mend and recycle, I would happily wager that somewhere around Majunga there are still some RAF blue vehicles with roundels doing sterling work, almost 60 years later. A legacy of the RAF's time in Madagascar of which relatively few will be aware."

F J BALDWIN – AIR MOVEMENTS

"I was often based in transport command as an air movements officer in the 1950s, both at home and in overseas posts. My story was staged at Fayid in the Canal Zone of Egypt in 1954. By a strange twist of fate, transport command was unconsciously responsible for the introduction of rock and roll into Egypt.

"At Fayid we 'dined in' once a week. This was a very formal affair with white uniforms, gold braid, and brass bands. It was a setting that would do justice to any movie depicting the typical British Empire. The barracks at Fayid were picturesque, being set in a square with balconies, and a grassed centre. After the usual toasts following an excellent dinner, we usually sat outside the mess whilst the local army band or some celebrity entertained us.

"I had been on duty on the evening in question, and had received a transport command Hastings, with crew and passengers bound for Egypt and Kenya. The pilot was a very popular figure, Flt Lt Winterbottom, who for obvious reasons was known as 'Frosty'. He had a reputation as a cartoonist, his style and humour were equal to those of the fabulous 'Giles' of the *Daily Express*, but on this occasion we found that Frosty had other talents to offer.

"Following dinner, we sat beneath the balconies and were entertained by an army cornet player. During a break in the official entertainment, we suddenly heard this strange sound, and out into the grass came 'Frosty' Winterbottom who danced and jived like an African native to the strains of this extraordinary music. We later discovered that his accompaniment was the original rock record of Bill Haley's 'Rock Around the Clock'. Now, so many years later, whenever I hear that tune I never fail to visualise that remarkable scene, performed by this transport command pilot on the shores of the Suez Canal."

DAVID LANGLEY – METEOROLOGIST

"The postings notice was put on the dartboard, and a handful of arrows was picked up – the one marked Langley stuck in the space called RAF Nicosia. In those days there were more overseas jobs than volunteers, meteorology was slowly withdrawing from home and empire, and there were lots of stick-in-the-muds who had never left Lincolnshire or HQ for their entire career. Neither my wife nor I knew where Cyprus was, I thought it was off the coast of East Africa.

"The postings people sorted our passports, jabs and a flight in no time at all, so a green rookie junior forecaster and his 20-year-old beautiful wife arrived at Hendon on 1 April 1961, severing all contact with home except by letter – my parents had no phone. Joyce and I, and a very young army officer, were ushered into one room, whilst everyone else were ushered into a larger one. A smart RAF officer thrust a bag at me, saying I was the senior officer on board the RAF Britannia, so 'take care of this and hand it in when you arrive'. Me guv'nor? Apparently a Ministry of Defence met assistant experimental officer outranked a second-lieutenant by a whisker. However I successfully sloped shoulders and passed it on. The flight was my first ever and as with all RAF flights, the seat configuration was backwards – it took forever.

"Nicosia at 06:00 in April was magical, the smell of pine and spices is with me still. We were 'shagged-out', so the senior met officer kindly took us for a round-the-island car tour for a couple of hours. I was the first forecaster not to be armed with a pistol, the EOKA threat having been downgraded. We were expected to wear officer-cut Khaki Drill (KD) with badges, and to join the mess. While waiting for a married quarter on station, we had a hiring in Ayios Dhometios and a new VW Beetle. I had no driving licence, so my wife, now pregnant, took me to work and back home for about a year.

"The job was airfield met looking after resident Hastings and visiting Javelins, and as Nicosia was joint-user, all civil flights. The station commander was Harold 'Micky' Martin of Dambuster fame, and most mornings he did a round of met ops and ATC, all close neighbours. At each he would pat his pockets, search unsuccessfully for a cigarette, accept a freebie, beg a light, exchange pleasantries, and move on. Pat, fag,

Our hiring in Ayios Dhometios, awaiting a married quarter, 1961. [David Langley]

light, move. He was said to be the best low-level bomber pilot of the war, and at Nicosia he used to fly a Hastings through the Kyrenia Pass.

"If it reached the airfield, the sea-breeze was our big weather problem. It came late morning, if at all, and brought a wicked wind-reversal. I wangled several flights in Army Air Corps choppers to fly instruments into the breeze to get some sort of science into forecasting, with modest success.

"The set-up for met was absurd. The airfield forecaster staff, who were very young and junior, covered 24/7, and were responsible for airfield warnings and nine-hour TAFs (take-off/landing significant weather). They also provided the local area forecast up to 50 miles radius. We did all the face-to-face briefings and issued all flight paperwork. Meanwhile a mile up the road (and also within the wire) was main met NEAF. This was staffed by senior forecasters and responsible for coded route forecasts (ROFORs) for the Mediterranean. This absurd arrangement whereby the most junior, and therefore notionally least expert, did all the safety-critical work, whilst the elderly war-time staff managed to make not a lot of not very accurate work seem important.

"This anomaly was brought home to me during Exercise Solinus II in 1963, when 16 Parachute Brigade Group was dropped by augmented 38 Group in about 30 assorted Beverleys, Hastings and Argosies on to the Morphou DZ. It was a shockingly irresponsible decision to task airfield met with the entire exercise weather cover. Our training had not touched the very tricky subject of winds, gusts, low-level jets and weather as applied to parachutes and cargo drops. And yes, I, Langley was the duty met to cover the drop briefing, the drop forecast and the following days' resupply flights.

"With the arrogance of youth, I found *Meteorology for Parachuting 1943* in the cupboard and became an instant expert. The mass briefing was easily the biggest I ever saw, attended by multitudes of brigadiers and the station commander's boss. Fortunately I could brief rather better than minima weather, and the assembled brass were easily pleased. Several hours later I stood on the ATC balcony to watch the take-offs. The Beverleys were a magnificent sight as they lumbered away, clam-shell doors removed and internal lights on. Deep breath, fingers crossed. A few legs were broken; a few pallet loads were wrecked – but the drop was deemed successful. In later years, remembering the risks taken when a very inexperienced Langley was lumbered, and I had climbed the greasy pole, I made a point of supervising forecasts that were mission critical. These included special weapon return flights from RAF Germany to UK, and the major Arnhem 50th anniversary drop in 1994.

"Banking was difficult, although the pay was good if one could get at it. Withdrawing cash from the Nicosia bank was a laborious process of queueing, passing scrutiny, and having the ledgers checked to confirm a positive balance. Almost all shops, especially in Ledra Street, practised man-to-man marking if the prospective customer wandered around. We became accustomed to Cypriot measures; Cypriot piastres, pics, okes and kartos. One pic was equal to two feet (cloth for our KD officer quality, and Girl Guide captain, was sold by the pic). Three KD shirts, three shorts and four shirts were made up in three days! The shirts lasted 30 years. One oke weight or liquid was equal to 2.8 lbs, and a kartos equalled four okes, 1.6 Cyprus litres, or 1.12gallons. These units were still in semi-official use well after 1964.

"One jolly, which was highly prized, was the run to and from Aden by Hastings. Provided a forecaster signed a blood chit (document requesting safe passage if captured), and demonstrated the financial wherewithal to get back one way or another, he could hoover up various duty frees. This abruptly came to an end when one of our number, briefed to be honest with customs maximum efforts on return, attempted to conceal Bolex cine camera, camera and watch. The station commander was exceeding wrath! I was exceeding wrath also, as I had been nominated as the next beneficiary.

"In those days all junior forecasters were also trained as observers, and the tradition was to allow the duty observer an hour's sack time 00:01 to 01:00 Zulu when observations from all sources were staggering in. The forecaster did both jobs. We all had RAF airfield passes on lanyards, and habitually took them off once inside the office. Even at Nicosia there was sometimes low stratus so the height of the cloud base needed to be measured by cloud searchlight. One dark night I made my way to the sighting alidade (a device for measuring angles). This was on a little roundabout, disguised by shrubs and with the mandatory white kerbstones. After noting the degrees, I was taken a bit short, so decided the bushes were as good as anywhere. A dog's hot breath interrupted my flow. With button flies agape, no ID, and only a stupid tale to tell I was escorted to the met office where there was nobody awake to vouch for me. The 'snowdrop' (RAF Police) saw the funny side of it, and whilst we had a coffee, the dog drank a saucer of milk. The sting was that I had forgotten the angle, so had to repeat the more conventional part of the exercise.

"On more serious notes, and almost unbelievably, I cannot recall any flap, any awareness even, of the Cuban Missile Crisis of October 1962. No unusual movements, no tightened security – zilch! The news of the assassination of President Kennedy was broken at a party in officers' married quarters on Comet Crescent – the party ended in tears.

"For most of the time we had the last of the National Service airmen. They were excellent, and several were graduates or otherwise highly qualified or well-connected. They included the nephews of a Cunard commodore and the 'Mad' Major Draper, a World War I flying ace with a penchant for flying under bridges. Everyone ran a 'chuff chart' calendar, marking days done versus days to go. Being young men, they lusted after female company, and mixing with Cypriot girls was extremely difficult; the daughters of regular RAF NCOs and officers were almost in purdah regarding a mere conscript SAC. One lad decided to save for an encounter in the red-light district (I knew not where it was, nor how large). He hitched and walked about six miles into town and was apprehended by an RAF Police patrol who kindly lectured him and drove him back to the billet. Nothing daunted he repeated the exercise, only to be picked up by 'redcaps' (army police) virtually on the brothel doorstep. They read him the riot act and took him back home, at which point he gave up.

"Around Christmas 1963, Greek v Turk communal violence broke out in Nicosia and spread rapidly, disturbing RAF Nicosia like an anthill poked with a stick. Surprisingly little history is to be found of the consequences and actions regarding the British neutrals caught up in matters. I can only record what I saw and heard. We were boat-happy, and only four months from tourex. Only two other forecasters, the chief met officer and his deputy, lived on camp inside the wire, but they were not current in their duties.

"Within hours all met personnel off base were told to stay indoors, and not a few forecasters had bullet holes in walls and broken windows. They were sustained over the next few weeks by armed convoys carrying huge Union Flags and provisions. The RAF Regiment emplaced a Vickers .303 at the bottom of my garden in Comet Crescent, and a Bofors next door but two. Thus we stocked up with NAAFI tea, coffee, sugar, milk and Jammy Dodgers and adopted 'our' gunners. The chief met officer, a Scotsman's Scotsman, was unwisely outside the wire one day and was stopped at a Greek roadblock, shoved against a wall and frisked. 'Ah, English, is OK, you can go!' To his shame he confessed to being English!

"Workwise the three remaining met men kept the airfield and the airbridge supplied with forecasts. Substantial numbers of our military were trooped in, and families near tourex were compulsorily sent home after some very cursory march-outs from their married quarters. These included my little family, (a daughter and son had been born) – this was when my daughter learned to swear like a sailor. I went to live in a mess bungalow (two to a room) and the Turkish orderly kindly offered me one of his very clean daughters, because I must be in need of solace. We worked eight hours on and 16 off for what seemed like a long, long time. I flew out exactly three years after arrival on April Fool's Day, and have no idea what arrangements were made after. In those circumstances one doesn't look back.

"I arrived home with a Cypriot driving licence, not valid in the UK. That was understandable; such licences were only gained by the driving instructor bribing the examiner with my NAAFI whisky. The instructor then bribed the professional queuer (yes, truly, they occupied half the long queue) at the licence office, with yet more whisky plus cash. I also came home with a new car, a big deposit for a £2,800 three-bed semi and two genuine Rolexes. I still have the watches, but cannot afford maintenance – my £140 Seiko keeps better time."

DEAN PRINGUER

Off-duty time has already been touched on, and Dean made good use of his position in 233 Squadron to fly home to Kenya when he could.

"Valettas of 233 Squadron flew to Nairobi at least once a week, and so I was able to get 'home' frequently. My parents lived in Nairobi where I did all my schooling, and I joined the RAF from there. All scheduled flights to RAF Eastleigh, or sometimes Embakasi airport, involved a night stop at home. All my annual leave was taken there and on one occasion, whilst on leave, I took my Lambretta scooter on board the Valetta to Nairobi. After a week's holiday, I once rode it 300 miles along the unsurfaced road to Mombasa and back again in a day. Looking back on it, I was a bit foolhardy with wild animals around, and the lack of back-up in the bush.

"Khormaksar was my first posting (1962-64). I arrived there before the troubles started in Aden and so it was easy to travel around the area exploring the place. I never experienced any animosity from the locals to my presence and I used to photograph them up close. I enjoyed the Aden work day, 07:00 to 13:00, which left the afternoon free to enjoy Tarshyne beach with its female attractions. It was the start of a three-year romance which petered out when my sun tan faded; RAF life in the UK took its inevitable toll on our relationship. However the companionship provided a welcome distraction for both of us and softened the impact of the harsh climate. I used to do a lot of surfing in the hot season (relatively). The waves could reach two metres, and we used to wait for the waves about 100 yards from the shore working on the theory (probably an old wives' tale) that sharks do not enter the surf – we had no frights.

"The first six months were in the main mess accommodation, and then into an air-conditioned room. What bliss such a contrast in temperature – I can still feel it

Ma'alla school buses with guard. [Jock Manson]

today. I remember the horribly tasting fruit squash (lime or raspberry) made from powder, and the salt tablets on the dining tables. Every evening dressing for dinner in Red Sea mess kit – white shirt, black cummerbund and I think No.1 SD trouser, and after that changing into comfortable clothes and going out."

> *Finally, thought must of course be given to the airmen's families for whom suddenly finding themselves in Aden would have been quite a shock to the system.*

DAVID RICHMOND – AIR SIGNALLER

"Domestic life for the families was not straightforward. Those who qualified for an on-base married quarter were relatively well provided for, with spacious airy rooms and outside space where children could play. It was a different matter for those families who only qualified for a hiring. Most of the hirings were in six-storey apartment blocks situated on the Pass Road in Ma'alla; this was the main thoroughfare into Crater town which was the commercial and administrative centre of the colony. To the front was the busy road and to the rear was the steep barren rock face formed by the rim of the long-defunct volcano; this left little accessible outdoor space for young children to play. To escape the heat, noise and boredom of domestic life, many of the families hired an 'ayah', or local nursemaid, usually Somali, to care for the infants and perform domestic duties. The wife could then spend the morning socialising with friends at the Tarshyne Officers' Club, taking her older pre-school children with her. Their husbands could either meet up with them at the club for lunch, or the family would re-assemble at the flat for lunch. Because of this arrangement, where the youngest child spent long periods in the care of the ayah, some infants learnt to speak Arabic, with the ayah in parallel speaking English with their parents and siblings. The extreme heat and limited space or opportunity discouraged families from keeping domestic pets, although some did keep cage birds in their hirings as company."

ALEC AUDLEY – AIR RADIO

Alec trained as an air radio mechanic in 1958. Having then served on 81 (Meteor) Squadron in Singapore, he found himself entering the Shackleton world at Kinloss when he returned to the UK in 1961.

"Around April 1966 I was summoned to admin at Kinloss and told I was posted to 131 MU at Khormaksar in August. This was not welcome news. Claire, our first daughter, had been born ten months earlier and Aden was in turmoil. This was due to the activities of the Nasser-backed rebels, the National Liberation Front (NLF) and the Front for the Liberation of South Yemen (FLOSY), who both wanted the British out of Aden and South Arabia. Still as the saying goes, 'If you can't take a joke, you shouldn't have joined up.'

"When my year's tour in the desert sun was coming to an end I was looking forward to returning to my wife Helen and my young family. Kathryn, our second daughter, had been born in February 1967 whilst I was away."

CHRIS DANCE – ENGINES

"When 37 Squadron closed in September 1967 I was in charge of bringing back the four Shackletons to the UK. As we flew out of Aden at about midnight, I looked out and thought I was glad not to be coming back there. My wife had been out there, and we'd been living in Ma'alla. She was uncomfortably close to a grenade attack, resulting in the families being returned to the UK; I was on my own a lot of the time. On top of this we had to do guards when we were at home in Ma'alla, so that was extra guard duty."

Challenging though things were for the wives, for at least one accompanying child Aden was an excitement-filled playground.

MICHAEL MCRITCHIE – SCHOOLBOY

Michael's father Sgt Stanley McRitchie served from 1936-1962 as an airframe fitter II(A). In 1959 he was posted from 9 Squadron at Binbrook, to 8 Squadron in Khormaksar.

A MEDICAL ISSUE

"Khormaksar is a wonderful place for a precocious 10-year-old with lots of exciting things to discover, not least in the medical officer's surgery which I am visiting for an ear infection. On the wall is a huge poster bearing the interesting legend: GUARD AGAINST VD. 'Mum, what's VD?' I pipe up. 'Just be thankful you haven't got it son, you'll find out soon enough,' she replies. 'Yes, but how can I guard against it if I don't know what it is?' Mother looks imploringly at the medical officer, Flt Lt Powell, who has bowed his head and is shuffling papers on his desk. 'That's right, you don't have to worry about it. It's something that only affects grown-ups.' 'How do you catch it, sir?' I persist. 'Is it something like the flu? Do you get it at home, or just out here in Aden?' 'Well, it's not quite like flu, but you honestly don't need to worry, only grown-ups catch it.' 'Have you had it, sir?' I ask.

"Then I notice that the medical officer is in some distress. His face has turned red, his eyes are watering and he has his hand over his mouth the way my little sister does when she's going to throw up. 'That's enough', says mum, 'show the doctor your sore ear.' 'No swimming for another fortnight,' he says, exchanging glances with my mother. I think there's something going on here, but there's no further discussion and, despite the heat that hits us like a wave as we emerge from the cool sick quarters, I am marched schoolwards at the double.

"Our house is on the corner, overlooking the school and only 50 yards away. This can be a mixed blessing, as my best friend David Brindley and I found last week when re-enacting 'She Wore a Yellow Ribbon' after its showing in the Astra Cinema. We galloped into our living room ahead of the Seventh Cavalry to find Miss Buckle, our teacher, having tea with my parents. Miss Buckle was taller than my parents and really ancient, I overheard Mum tell Dad she was about 38. Like a cobra, she reacted instantly to any sudden movement by small boys and impaled us with her basilisk stare, before she remembered where she was and bared her teeth in a terrifying smile instead. It gave me quite a fright while David was so shaken he didn't come near our house for a week.

"Mum leaves me at the classroom door, I slip into my seat and tell Miss Buckle that I won't be able to swim in the school contest. 'That's a pity Michael, is your ear still sore?' 'Yes miss, but mum says I should be thankful I haven't got VD.' 'She said WHAT?' I wilt under Miss Buckle's terrifying glare, and fear I've said something wrong. 'Please miss, it says about VD on the medical officer's wall and when I asked him what it was, he said it's a grown-up problem and I'm not to worry because children can't catch it.'

"Miss Buckle's face turns red, her mouth twitches, she lifts her desk lid and rummages around inside it, head down. What's wrong, I wonder? Miss Buckle is not well, maybe she has caught ... an awful possibility crosses my mind. I also hope that Graham Suitor hasn't caught another locust and placed it in her desk so it flies out with a mighty whirr when the desk is opened, because Miss Buckle gets very excited when this happens and while it's most entertaining to watch we are clearly in an unstable situation here. Robert Dawkins pokes me in the back with a ruler and asks what it's all about, while David is muttering something from across the aisle. We don't notice Miss Buckle racing down the classroom until the crack of ruler on close-cropped head and a yelp of pain brings further discussion to an end.

"When school ends at lunchtime we agree that Robert Dawkins should ask his father about VD, and report back when we meet at the pool where we spend our afternoons – but Robert fails to appear. Next day he tells us that his father gave him a clip round the ear and sent him to his room until teatime. Strange.

"We turn to Sgt Trinnick, the genial pharmacist from station sick quarters who always helps his neighbours' kids. Besides, the others fancy his lovely daughter Marcia with her dazzling smile, though I think she's getting a bit past it – she must be 17 if she's a day. Mrs Trinnick invites us in and splits an ice-cool Coca-Cola between the three of us, an expensive treat at 50c a bottle, about 4p in today's money. 'Please Mr Trinnick, what's VD?' Both parties watch us warily as we explain what has happened, then Mr Trinnick beckons us closer. 'I can't tell you, it's a state secret', he says. We plead for just a teeny inkling. 'Well, only if you promise never never never to mention it again. You know about the Russians?' Even we had heard about the Cold War and the conflict in Korea. Wide-eyed, we nod agreement. 'And you've heard about things that come from space?' Again we nod, for a film about such creatures had shown in the Astra Cinema only last month, with an H certificate to protect the under-16s like us. 'The Russians want to give us something like that, but we're guarding against it. We don't want them to know we know, and that's why you mustn't breathe another word about it. Now I require all of you to sign the Official Secrets Act.' The Act, which happens to be printed on an envelope cunningly concealed in the wastebasket, is duly signed in shaky hand and we leave, carefully checking the street for Russian spies. I glance back to see Mrs. Trinnick displaying all too familiar symptoms. Her face is red, her eyes are streaming, and she is making funny choking noises. Oh well, I think, Mr. Trinnick can get tablets to treat all sorts of infections.

"My father had been posted to Aden from Binbrook. Like all service families our journey began 12 weeks ahead with the inoculation parade. The queue of National Servicemen stretched all the way round station sick quarters. We were waiting for the jabs for yellow fever, smallpox, tetanus and the dreaded TABC; a cocktail against typhoid and typhus which laid out both mother and myself with flu-like symptoms which lasted a week. Meanwhile our belongings were crated up for storage or for Aden, marked 'not wanted on voyage' as you could take only a suitcase to the cabins. With Father posted ahead, as usual, Mum had to do the packing and take the three of us to Southampton to board the *Dunera* headed for Aden.

"Khormaksar had yet to undergo the massive development of the 1960s, so new arrivals were housed in bungalows. Long before the days of TV, the family would sit happily under the security light watching the lizards feeding on the insects it attracted. Around us the land crabs formed a companionable circle, their eyes on little stalks like periscopes following us if we moved from chair to chair. Each evening my parents listened to the news on crackly shortwave, with 'Lillibulero' playing in Radio Newsreel on Saturday nights and Family Favourites one Sunday a month. Most people wrote home weekly for there were no phones in airmen's quarters.

"We were delighted to find that school began at 8 a.m. and ended at 1 p.m., leaving adults to sleep and ourselves to head for the seawater pool alongside Khormaksar beach which was across the isthmus at the far end of the runway. Once a week Mum would stump up 50 cents for the gharry, or three-ton Bedford lorry, which daily left the Families Club for Steamer Point lido. The road ran through Ma'alla, in those days still a very poor fishing village with simple homes on one side and dhows hauled up on the other. The smells of rotting fish and open drains made a fearsome combination which became a family joke. Years afterwards anyone who forgot to open the bathroom window could expect an angry yell of 'MA'ALLA!' from sensitive souls below.

"Everyone loved the lido. There was a spacious cafe for the adults, a beach of rough sand, a big swimming pool and a sea swimming area inside shark-proof netting. Each ship was followed 20 minutes later by its wash, three-foot waves rolling in to bring us basic surfing though the modern sport had yet to be invented. Those days of endless sunshine and swimming blended into happy memories.

"Khormaksar must have been a grim posting for adults, the tiny RAF community having nowhere to go except Steamer Point and perhaps Crater. But we youngsters loved it, perhaps because life was disciplined by our environment and we had clear boundaries, both physical and mental. The young National Servicemen hated the place. Most treated us like little brothers and spoiled us rotten.

"My bed was a charpoy, the Indian word for bed, and comprised a wooden frame with rattan ropes tied across it in grid pattern. It was very comfortable once you got used to it, for a mattress would have been unbearable in that heat. While our native bearers Mo and Saleh did the housework, Mum did the cooking on two Primus stoves and a paraffin oven which often gave a unique aroma to the food. Kitchen temperatures often topped 40 degrees, but she never faltered. We soon became used to taking salt tablets every day, and the sherbet-flavoured lemon or orange drink made from tinned powder. We all preferred Coca-Cola, but at 50 cents per wasp-waisted bottle we were lucky to share one a month. The other drink was the one-third of a pint of milk given to every British child each morning. It arrived from the RAF dairy farm at Steamer Point in crates which were already smelling of sour milk, something which turned my stomach.

"The headmaster was Laurence Acheson, son of my mother's family dentist at home in Belfast. They had known each other since childhood and on my second day this kind-hearted man did his best to make me feel at home. 'Drink up your milk Michael, it's good for you,' he said. 'Please sir, it makes me sick, I'd rather not have it.' Reluctantly I took a gulp before spraying it, and my breakfast, all over sir's spotless white shorts. This feat gained me considerable peer respect, and nobody offered me milk again. But my class teacher Miss Buckle soon had me taped. Her first report stated that 'Michael works extremely well at any subject which interests him, otherwise he does the minimum'.

SCHOOLWORK AND AEROPLANES

"I was obsessed with aircraft (and still am) and when Miss Buckle at school asked each pupil to recite something from memory a couple of pupils recited poems, someone else gave a few lines of prose, and I contributed the take-off checklist for the Avro Lancaster. She shook her head sadly, but a couple of days later gave me a sheet of handwritten problems. The Avro Lancaster carries 2,000 gallons of petrol, its four engines each consume 50 gallons an hour, and it cruises at 200 mph. How far can you fly before the tanks run dry? Your Lancaster cruises at 200 mph, it is 1,400 miles from Khormaksar to Khartoum. How much fuel will you need? This was great I thought. Totally absorbed, it was the only time I did not lead the rush home at lunchtime. A faintly smiling Miss Buckle checked my flight plans. 'Oh dear, I don't know much about flying Michael, but on these figures you're going to come down in the Red Sea. And what do we have in the Red Sea?' 'Sharks, Miss Buckle'. 'Exactly. Now I'd like you to take this home and re-calculate your flights for tomorrow.' I fell for it hook, line and sinker. More flying problems followed, and by the end of the next term we had explored every mathematical possibility of Lancaster operation, and I had at last learned some arithmetic.

"My next report noted a considerable improvement. In my final report she noted that Michael always showed a keen interest 'but aircraft and flying will always come first'. Long afterwards my father told me that Miss Buckle had been waiting at Flying Wing one morning when it opened at 07:00. There she had asked questions about the Lancaster and the basics of navigation so that she could set my problems. She told my father that she feared his child was obsessed, but she would teach him maths if it was the last thing she did. Two decades later I would have both pilot's and engineering licences, as well as my own aircraft! At least some part of these achievements is down to dear dedicated Miss Buckle, who has long ago gone to the great rollcall. I owe her a lot.

THE KHORMAKSAR LAND CRAB DERBY

"This has up to a dozen runners along furrows which we dig in the sand. Saleh, our chico servant, has caught me a magnificent six-inch crab in the native compound. I have named him Ahmed, and he's been in training for a week. Saleh suggests a cockroach diet, and sure enough Ahmed scoffs a medium-sized roach with relish – it sounds like Graham eating potato crisps. There's a loud scream from the bathroom where Mum is bathing Christine. The shoebox stable is under my bed, but Ahmed is not, for he has eaten a hole in the side. I find him in the bathroom doorway, claws pattering on the tiles, little eyes sparkling on their half-inch stalks, pincers waving hopefully in the hope of a tasty cockroach. 'Get that damn thing out of here!' yells Mum. I try to point out the benefits of a trained cockroach-killer but Dad grabs Ahmed and throws him out onto the sand. He scuttles into the dark, and I'm out of the big race. But Robert's mother has also ejected his crab, while Henry, Barry's champion racer, has been savaged by the neighbour's cat. Disheartened, the Khormaksar racing industry goes into terminal decline.

CAMEL TROUBLE

"Dave and I are crossing the Sheik Othman Road on our way to the pool, with Graham and Robert a short distance behind. Along comes a camel cart, its driver asleep on top of his load. Dad says the Arabs have a special chewing gum that makes them sleepy. The carters pull their dishdasha over their heads, and leave the camel to plod the 18 miles from Crater to Sheik Othman or vice versa. Dodgy things camels, they will bite, kick or spit from both ends, so we're careful as we walk alongside and gently pull on the rein. This one is quite amenable and is soon padding back towards Crater, but Graham turns it around again. This upsets the beast's autopilot, for as we wait to turn it back it swings to the left, then right, then hard left and now is heading towards the gate.

"Abdullah the chowkidar (gatekeeper) guards the families' gate from his little sentry box, leaving one section open for pedestrians and opening the other only for the gharri (horse-drawn cart). Everyone likes Abdullah, who spent many years in India, so we converse in a mixture of Arabic, Hindi and English. We watch in horror as the camel plods wearily through the pedestrian gate. One wheel of the cart brings down the closed section of gate, the other topples Abdullah's box which acts as a chock and brings it to a halt! A furious driver slides down from its side and begins to shout in Arabic; an equally angry Abdullah emerges from his wrecked box. We flee to the swimming pool and forget all about it.

"On our return, the good fairy had repaired both gate and sentry box, or so we thought. The shouting had awakened nearby households, who told our parents. They had to leave their afternoon naps, and carry tools and timber, half a mile from the hangars to repair the damage during the hottest part of the day. This is explained to us in a prolonged and very painful interview.

"Ten days' detention later and I'm woken by a terrible racket from below. It's very late, about 9:30 p.m., and I peep down from the top of the stairs to see David's parents with Mum and Dad. The air is thick with cigarette smoke, and they have a bottle of special grown-up cola that I'm not allowed, not that I'd want it anyway. I tried a sip of Dad's once when he was in the bathroom and it's foul, it's nearly as bad as milk. Mum is all giggly, the way she is at Christmas. The two fathers are roaring with laughter over a big green folder which they pass to David's mum, who reads it, turns bright red and collapses onto the sofa making a gasping noise. I recognise the symptoms. I'm about to go down and tell Mrs Brindley I'm sorry she has caught VD and I hope she gets better soon when, just in time, I remember the Official Secrets Act. I tiptoe back to bed and go out like a light.

"I wake to the bugle calls from the Aden Protectorate Levy lines half a mile away. My parents are still sound asleep, and I consider flinging their doors open shouting, 'wakey wakey, rise and shine' the way Dad does with mine – but some sixth sense warns that this might not be the wisest course today. From the veranda, I see Dave mooching towards our house, his parents are still asleep too. On the table beside the overflowing ashtray is the green folder they had last night. Inside we find a single typed sheet: 'Station Routine Orders, RAF Khormaksar. Addendum ref. 234/52. It has been brought to the notice of the station commander that personnel have been interfering with camels on the Sheik Othman Road. This practice will cease forthwith. Signed: officer commanding.'

"'What's funny about that? Last week they give us a whacking for turning the camel, now they laugh about it,' says Dave. We commiserate on the problems of having grown-ups.

Mum comes downstairs and we assure her that we are not hungry, we don't mind having no breakfast. She looks guilty and says Dave can stay for breakfast, after which he can ask his parents if he can go to the lido, and here's a shilling for the gharri. We can't believe our luck.

"As we pass Abdullah, he says, 'naughty boys, naughty boys,' but his eyes are smiling. I lean from the gharri, put my hands together in Indian greeting, and say, 'Salaam, Abdullah sahib'. 'Salaam, chota sahib,' he replies, points at his gate and breaks into a roar of laughter. We wave to each other until the gharri goes out of sight. We're friends again, the sun shines and all's well in our happy little world.

CHRISTMAS AND HOME TIME

"It's December 1952 and everyone has a part in the Khormaksar pantomime. Warrant Officer Haden brings the house down as Baron Hangover, LAC John Elliott tap-dances brilliantly as Buttons, and Marcia Trinnick steals the show as Cinderella in a dress of white parachute silk. It's like a huge meringue, with an alarming amount of creamy Marcia topping yards of layered silk. The thunderous roar from the appreciative airmen can be heard inside Dad's hangar half a mile away.

"All too soon it's time to go back to England, and for the first time on a posting I don't want to go. I look down from the departing Hastings at the little square of houses that once was home. That little speck is our school, inside are my friends at their desks and dear Miss Buckle... my last glimpse of Khormaksar is blurred by the tears which stream down my cheeks. To the engines' throb I find myself singing the Aden Song from the pantomime finale:

All the little phones go brrr brr brrr
HQ staff want you ...
Bound to be a panic, flap brr flap,
Last thing on a Saturday, too!
The Vampires go wheeeeeee, the Brigands crash,
Main gate guards shout 'Aintcher gotcher pass'?
Watching all the troopers, sailing out to sea,
Here we are in Aden, happy as can be!

> *The family left Khormaksar in early 1953 when Stanley was posted to Leuchars, followed by his final posting to 202 Met Squadron at Aldergrove. Michael attended 11 different schools during the family wanderings, and he says, "some would say this explains a lot". One of very few licensed aircraft engineers in Ireland at that time, he also flew his own aircraft for many years, including as a member of the 'Barnstormers' display team. He pursued a career in journalism which ultimately led to the launch of a highly successful construction equipment magazine.*

AND IN THE END

PETER KENDALL – SHACKLETON NAVIGATOR

"In May 1966 a 'one-off' sortie was a combined operation to the north-east of Khormaksar involving 78 Squadron Wessex helicopters, 8 Squadron Hunters, a forward air controller and ourselves armed with anti-personnel bombs. The rebels were spotted, but because of the possibility of there being women and children amongst them acting as human shields, the air controller had no option but to call off the attack. We had to ditch our weapons in the sea and we heard later that two helicopters had been damaged by small-arms fire, one hit in the fuel tank and one in the gearbox, resulting in two federal soldiers on board being killed.

"In December 1966 we were called out on SAR to locate a downed army Sioux helicopter in the Radfan area to the north of Aden. The wreck was located and a recovery team dispatched. Unfortunately, the deceased pilot had been through Arab rebel hands reinforcing to us the need to take great care of our 'goolie chits'!

A Hastings to go home. [Michael McRitchie]

"We were issued with a Smith and Wesson 8-mm pistol, and did evening security around our multi-story flats throughout each night, on a well organised rota basis. This was essentially to deter booby trap bombs being planted under our private cars. We also patrolled around our respective messes on 'film nights', when most members' attentions were concentrated on watching the films. One evening during a film we heard the scream of mortars heading toward the mess – everyone ducked as they hit the deck. The mortars had been intended to hit the station power station near the camp entrance but had overshot, exploding harmlessly on the station sports field adjacent to the mess. The story goes that when everyone ducked not a drink was spilt!

"The security situation began to deteriorate rapidly during early 1967, our children were taken to their schools in armed convoys and in May that year all families were evacuated back to the UK. My last sortie before leaving Aden was on 22 August 1967. Sqn Ldr James was the pilot captain when we flew a night illumination sortie dropping sticks of 4.5 recce flares. The area was north-west of Aden along the then Yemen border. We were passed ranges and bearings from an upward beamed light which was set up in the mountains at a pre-determined position. The system worked well and we carried out a number of runs during the eight-hour sortie, being able to clearly see the rebels caught in the lit-up sky, and suffering very accurate tracer machine-gun fire from the federal army units below us. We knew where to expect any AA fire so gave those areas a wide berth.

"All in all, a fascinating, albeit challenging, tour. The esprit de corps was very good too despite the difficult, extremely hot and humid (not to mention noisy), working conditions. The groundcrews, many on unaccompanied tours lasting up to a year, did a remarkable job ensuring we had a serviceable aircraft, armed up and fuelled at all times." [1]

The political situation in Aden from 1966 onwards became increasingly difficult. As described by Chris Mead in chapter five the last fixed-wing RAF aircraft to leave Khormaksar, just before 14:00 hours on 29 November 1967 were: a single Argosy flown by Wg Cdr E C Rigg, OC 105 Squadron, and a pair of Hercules C.1s. The first Hercules carried the final freight plus Visiting Aircraft Servicing Flight (VASF) groundcrew and the crash crew, while the second (XV203) carried staff of HQ Aden Brigade / Joint HQ and C Company 1 Kings Own Royal Border Regt. Following those the last military departures from 15:00 hours were 42 Commando (who had been keeping the perimeter secure) to HMS Albion *by Wessex HU.5s of 848 Naval Air Squadron. Wessex HC.2s of 78 Squadron were also in action until quite late delivering people to HMS* Intrepid.

There is a nice quote from an anonymous RAF man who said: "I was key orderly on the final day and once my duties were complete, I had to rush to board the aircraft and kick the steps away at the last moment before take-off."

With the final withdrawal from Aden HQ Air Forces Gulf came into being at Muharraq in September 1967. It disbanded on 15 December 1971, leaving only Masirah to continue a 'permanent' RAF presence in the Middle East until it shut down for good in March 1977. Since then, RAF forces have returned in times of tension, most notably during Gulf War 1 in 1990-1991 (Operation Granby) and Gulf War 2 in 2003 (Operation Telic).

[1] *Shackleton Boys 2* by Steve Bond

AFTERWORD

THE AIRFIELDS IN 2026

EASTLEIGH

When the RAF vacated Eastleigh, it was taken over by the newly formed Kenya air force as its headquarters and renamed Moi Air Base. It is also the home of the East African School of Aviation run by the Kenya Civil Aviation Authority.

HABILAYN, YEMEN

Habilayn was abandoned in 1967, with no discernible trace remaining.

KAMARAN ISLAND, YEMEN

The airfield survives to serve Kamaran village, but is described as having a "poorly defined north–south runway with a reported length of 1,800 metres (5,906 ft). The runway is not easily seen, but does have markings."

KHORMAKSAR, YEMEN

Khormaksar is now known simply as Aden International Airport. Since the RAF left the west end of Khormaksar has been abandoned, with the hangars and other buildings becoming completely derelict.

MASIRAH, OMAN

When Masirah was closed as an RAF station in 1977, it was handed over to the Sultan of Oman's Air Force (SOAF). However, it continued to be used by transiting RAF aircraft. For example, in November 1986 Exercise Saif Sareea saw 229 OCU

Khormaksar west end, former RAF hangars and pan, in 1998. [Dean Pringuer]

Tornados detached here. In 1990 SOAF was renamed the Royal Air Force of Oman (RAFO), and Masirah most recently has been home for their Pilatus PC.9, Hawk and Super Lynx fleets.

MUHARRAQ, BAHRAIN

The RAF was a lodger at Muharraq airport until it left following Bahrain independence in December 1971. What is now Bahrain International Airport has been developed and expanded to the extent that there remains little, if any, evidence of the RAF's presence.

SALALAH, OMAN

Salalah opened as a civilian airfield in 1977. In 2015 it was replaced as Oman's secondary international airport by a new airport immediately north of what was RAF Salalah. The old airport continues in use with resident RAFO units flying NH.90 and Bell 429 helicopters and C295M transports.

SHARJAH, UNITED ARAB EMIRATES

Opened in 1932 and vacated by the RAF on 14 December 1971, Sharjah too has become an international airport. The most notable traces of its former use are the original control tower and adjacent buildings, now home to the Al Mahatta aviation museum.

GLOSSARY

AC	Air Commodore
ADC	Aide-de-Camp
AEO	Air Electronics Operator
AFC	Air Force Cross
AFME	Air Forces Middle East
ALM	Air Loadmaster
ALO	Air Liaison Officer
AM	Air Marshal
AOC	Air Officer Commanding
AQM	Air Quartermaster
ATAF	Allied Tactical Air Force
ATC	Air Traffic Control
AVM	Air Vice-Marshal
AVGAS	Aviation Gasoline
AVPIN	Aviation Isopropyl Nitrate
BFPO	British Forces Posted Overseas
BOAC	British Overseas Airways Corporation
Cat	Category of Damage
CFS	Central Flying School
CMC	Chairman of the Mess Committee
CO	Commanding Officer
CofG	Centre of Gravity
Col	Colonel
Cpl	Corporal
DFC	Distinguished Flying Cross

DFM	Distinguished Flying Medal
DME	Distance Measuring Equipment
DSO	Distinguished Service Order
DZ	Drop Zone
EFTS	Elementary Flying Training School
ENSA	Entertainments National Service Association
EOKA	National Organisation of Cypriot Fighters
ETA	Estimated Time of Arrival
FB	Fighter Bomber
F/E	Flight Engineer
FEAF	Far East Air Force
FGA	Fighter Ground Attack
Fg Off	Flying Officer
FL	Flight Level
FLOSY	Front for the Liberation of South Yemen
Flt Cdr	Flight Commander
Flt Lt	Flight Lieutenant
Flt Sgt	Flight Sergeant
FR	Fighter Reconnaissance
FSA	Federation of South Arabia
FTS	Flying Training School
GGS	Gyro Gun Sight
Gp Capt	Group Captain
HCU	Heavy Conversion Unit
HE	High Explosive
HMG	His/Her Majesty's Government
HMT	His/Her Majesty's Troopship
IAS	Indicated Airspeed
I/C	In Charge
IP	Initial Point
IRE	Instrument Rating Examiner
Jebel	Mountain, hill, or range of hills
JPT	Jet Pipe Temperature
J/T	Junor Technician
KD	Khaki Drill
LAC	Leading Aircraftman

LOA	Living Out Allowance
Lt Col	Lieutenant Colonel
MARDET	Maritime Detachment
MASB	Master Armament Safety Break
MEAF	Middle East Air Force
MEC	Middle East Command
MFPU	Mobile Field Photography Unit
MoD	Ministry of Defence
MP	Member of Parliament
MR	Maritime Reconnaissance
MT	Motor Transport
MU	Maintenance Unit
NAAFI	Navy Army and Air Force Institute
NCO	Non-Commissioned Officer
NDB	Non-Directional Beacon
NEAF	Near East Air Force
NF	Night Fighter
NLF	National Liberation Front
OBE	Order of the British Empire
OC	Officer Commanding
OCU	Operational Conversion Unit
OMQ	Officers' Married Quarters
ORB	Operations Record Book
OTU	Operational Training Unit
PI	Photographic Interpreter
Plt Off	Pilot Officer
POW	Prisoner of War
PR	Photo Reconnaissance
QFI	Qualified Flying Instructor
RATG	Rhodesian Air Training Group
RFC	Royal Flying Corps
RN	Royal Navy
RSU	Repair and Salvage Unit
R/T	Radio Telephony
SAC	Senior Aircraftman
SAR	Search and Rescue

SAS	Special Air Service
SD	Service Dress
SFTS	Service Flying Training School
SHQ	Station Headquarters
Sgt	Sergeant
SNCO	Senior Non-Commissioned Officer
SNEB	Societé Nouvelle des Etablissements Edgar Brandt
SOAF	Sultan of Oman's Air Force
SOP	Standard Operating Procedure
Sqn	Squadron
Sqn Ldr	Squadron Leader
STOL	Short Take-Off and Landing
SWO	Station Warrant Officer
TOC	Top of Climb
TOS	Trucial Oman Scouts
UDI	Unilateral Declaration of Independence
UHF	Ultra-High Frequency
VASF	Visiting Aircraft Servicing Flight
VHF	Very High Frequency
Wadi	Valley or ravine
Wg Cdr	Wing Commander
WO	Warrant Officer
WOp	Wireless Operator
WRAF	Women's Royal Air Force
W/T	Wireless Telegraphy

SELECT BIBLIOGRAPHY

Bowman, Martin, *Bombers Fly East,* Pen & Sword, 2017

Deacon, Ray, *Hunter over Arabia,* Pen & Sword, 2019

Deacon, Ray, *Tales from the Frontline – Middle East,* Pen & Sword, 2020

Fairbairn, Tony, *Action Stations Overseas*, Patrick Stephens, 1991

Flintham, Vic, *Truculent Tribes Turbulent Skies*, Air Britain, 2015

Jefford, C G, *RAF Squadrons*, Airlife, 2001

Lee, David, *Flight from the Middle East: A History of the Royal Air Force in the Arabian Peninsula and Adjacent Territories,* HMSO, 1981

Philpott, Ian, *The Royal Air Force an encyclopedia of the inter-war years*, Pen & Sword, 2005

Pook, Jerry, *Flying Freestyle,* Pen & Sword, 2009

Shores, Christopher, *Dust Clouds in the Middle East*, Grub Street,1996

INDEX

Abadan, Iran, 65, 128
Abu Sueir, Egypt, 25, 39, 100
Adamson, AC2 Kenneth, 29
Aden, 9-10, 12, 25, 39, 48, 78-80, 82-91, 93, 95-97, 100, 104, 108, 112-113, 115-116, 118-120, 124-125, 129, 132-133, 137-139, 142, 144-147, 151, 153-154, 156-160, 167-168, 174, 176, 182, 190, 197, 200-204, 227, 229-232, 234, 238-242
AFME, 10
Akrotiri, Cyprus, 68, 72-73, 75-76, 86, 100, 142, 148, 160-163, 165-166, 168, 170, 174
Allen, Flt Sgt Derek, 128-129
Ali, Raschid, 29
Amman, Jordan, 77
Anderson, Andy, 151
Andrus, Flt Lt, 139
Aqir, Palestine, 39
Armstrong, John, 174
Arrandale, Sgt Ray, 127-129
Ashley, Wg Cdr Brian, 68
Ashton, Fg Off Basil, 128
Aspinall, Bill, 154
Ataq, Aden, 132, 140, 147, 202
Audley, Alec, 231

Bachelor, Fg Off Brian, 84
Baghdad, Iraq, 14, 16-18, 29, 32, 45, 144, 148
Bahrain, 12, 73, 89, 91, 94-95, 100, 108, 117, 124, 131, 134, 136, 141, 144, 146, 148-149, 152, 155-158, 167, 178-181, 183, 188-191, 195, 199, 243
Baldwin, F J, 224
Barfoot, WO Eric, 31
Barton, Dick, 149
Bartram, Wg Cdr, 58
Basra, Iraq, 21, 41, 65
Battrick, Driver Charles, 128
Baugh, Dave, 197
Beard, Sgt John, 128
Beere, Ken, 72-74, 77
Bender Qassim, 125
Beihan, 84, 97, 141, 150, 202
Beira, Mozambique, 48, 69, 210, 212, 221
Bell, Gertrude, 198
Belvedere, Rhodesia, 36
Benson, Cpl Reginald, 33
Berrill, AC2 Thomas, 29
Bilbeis, Egypt, 33, 53
Blake, Vic, 150
Blythe, Joe, 88
Bolt, Capt, 29
Bottom, Fg Off Sid, 96, 99, 110
Bowie, Roy, 110
Bradley, Eric, 43, 46
Bruton, Cpl Frederick, 128
Butler, Sqn Ldr Colin, 80, 164

Cairo, Egypt, 11, 17, 19, 25, 31-33, 54-55, 58
Carran, Ray, 203
Checkley, Bill, 204
Chichester, Flt Lt P G, 10
Chisholm, Fg Off, 20, 28-29
Church, Fg Off John, 154

Churchill, Winston, 12, 15
Clayton, Len, 124-126, 132, 135, 139, 169, 208
Cogill, Sqn Ldr John, 61-62
Colonial Police Service, 12
Cook, Wg Cdr Doug, 217
Cooper, John SAS, 131
Copsey, Flt Lt Ernest, 33
Cranborne, Rhodesia, 36
Cross, Nav III Peter, 80
Cuckney, AVM Ernest, 48, 50

Deacon, Ray, 90, 96, 98, 153
Dennard, Caroline, 22
Dennis, Harry, 33
Dhala, British Aden Protectorate, 83, 126, 131, 135, 147, 200-202
Didwell, Cpl Norman, 57-58, 77
Djibouti, 70, 142, 174
Docherty, Sgt, 127
Drinkwater, David, 139
Dubai, UAE, 170-172, 181, 188, 193
Dymond, Jim, 100-102, 104

Eastleigh, Kenya, 89, 91, 108, 124, 130, 132, 135, 142, 164, 167, 176, 205, 208, 229, 242
Ein Shemer, 39
El Adem, Libya, 64-65, 73, 127, 156, 166, 168, 198
El Ballah, Egypt, 39, 42, 54-55
Elliott, Bryan, 76
Evans, Ray, 69
Evans, Flt Lt Ronald, 138

Farouk, King, 63
Fayid, Egypt, 39-40, 125, 127-128, 224
Fensome, Flt Sgt Roy, 54-57
Firq, Oman, 130, 137
Ford, Harry, 174
Forsyth, David, 210, 222
Foster, Alan, 156
Foster, Flt Lt David, 83
Front for the Liberation of South Yemen (FLOSY), 231

Gianaclis, Egypt, 39
Gibbons, Guy, 160
Gibson, Flt Lt John, 35-36
Golds, Chris, 104
Goodwin, Peter, 83, 86-87, 89
Grant, Cpl Gerald, 33, 58
Graziani, Marshal, 29
Guinea Fowl, Rhodesia, 36-38

Habbaniyah, Iraq, 21, 25-26, 29, 31-32, 57, 64-65, 85, 125, 127
Habilayn, Yemen, 126,131-132, 139, 242
Haifa, Palestine, 22-23
Halkiew, Joe, 60
Hall, Driver Nicholas, 128
Hall, Flt Sgt Ron, 42, 47, 79
Hall, LAC Stephen, 19, 25, 31
Harper, Fg Off Roy, 33
Hawkes, Plt Off Corliss, 33
Hayes, Sig II Lionel, 80
Heliopolis, Egypt, 14-15, 18-19, 21, 25, 29, 33-34, 39
Helwan, Egypt, 25, 54
Henderson, Robert A, 162
Henthorn, LAC James, 138
Hinaidi, Iraq, 16-19, 21
Hinds, Tony, 198
Hubert, Willie, 35-36

Ibn Saud, 11
Idris, Libya, 156, 166, 168
Induna, Rhodesia, 36
Ingle, Wg Cdr Hubert, 51
Iraqi Levies 18
Irwin, WO Vern, 33
Ismailia, Egypt, 14, 18, 21-22, 32, 39, 60

Jackson, Pete, 125, 127
James, John, 123, 129-130, 143, 149, 156
James, Sqn Ldr, 240
Jebel Akhdar, Oman, 84, 118
Jeddah, Saudi Arabia, 127, 149
Jenkins, LAC Cyril, 29
Jennings, Wg Cdr John, 99-100, 107
Jerusalem, 23
John, SAC 'Taff', 96
Johnson, Flt Lt Martin, 99

Kabrit, Egypt, 27, 59, 62, 66-68, 125, 127
Kamaran Island, Yemen, 130, 202-204, 242

Kemp, Pat, 142
Kendall, Peter, 239
Kennedy, Titch, 86
Keyes, Lt Col, 31
Khartoum, Sudan, 19-20, 29, 39, 52-53, 125, 127-128, 156, 236
Khormaksar, Aden, 42, 68, 78-81, 84, 89-98, 100-101, 103-104, 109, 116-117, 119-121, 123-125, 130-132, 135, 137-128, 140-141, 143-146, 148-149, 152-160, 164-165, 167, 190, 196, 200-205, 208, 229, 231-232, 234-236, 238-239, 241-243
King, Flt Sgt John, 50-52
Kingerban, Iraq, 16-17
Kirkuk, Iraq, 16-17, 65
Koggala, Ceylon, 36
Kumalo, Rhodesia, 36
Kuwait, 48, 65, 91, 128, 142, 148, 179

Langley, David, 224-226
Lawrence of Arabia, 14, 77, 198
League of Nations, 11, 18
Leckie-Thompson, Sqn Ldr, 86
Lennard, Flt Sgt John, 202
Lennon, Sqn Ldr, 32
Lewis, Flt Lt Peter, 99-101
Livermore, Fg Off Dickie, 136
Locke, Flt Lt, 205
Lowe, Gp Capt
Lusaka, Zambia, 73-75, 77, 143, 149
Lynn, Vera, 41

Macmillan, Ian, 143, 145, 190
Maidment, Flt Sgt Roy 'Mick', 40
Majunga, Madagascar, 69-70, 210-211, 213, 216, 218, 222-223
Mandera, Kenya, 142
Manson, Jock, 147, 154, 230
Maritime Detachment (MARDET), 197
Martin, AM Sir Harold 'Micky', 225
Masirah, Oman, 12, 84, 89, 108, 117, 126, 142, 144, 157, 168-176, 191, 241-243
Mastin, AC2 Dennis, 80
Matsapha, Swaziland, 143, 146, 153
Mau Mau, 48, 176
Maxwell, Sgt Kenneth, 42
Maynard, Ken, 198
McBryde, Sgt George, 33
McCandless, Flt Lt Dave, 69-70, 79, 117, 121, 210
McCue, Flt Sgt Pete, 29
McHarg, Sgt John, 129
McRitchie, Michael, 232, 240
Mead, Chris, 140, 157, 241
Mersa Matruh, 14, 21, 26, 34
Mesopotamia, 11, 14
Middle East Air Force (MEAF), 9, 144, 146, 165, 167-168, 200, 205
Mills, Sgt Arthur, 33
Mitchell, Lt Col Colin, 146, 157
Moascar, Egypt, 14
Moffat, Rhodesia, 36
Mombasa, Kenya, 34, 36, 39, 70, 108, 142, 145, 229
Morris, Johnny, 100-102, 104, 108-109, 114
Mount Hampden, Rhodesia, 36
Muharraq, Bahrain, 10, 12, 73, 89, 124, 129, 133, 142-144, 146, 157-158, 164, 178-179, 181, 185-186, 192-194, 211, 213, 217, 222-223, 241, 243
Mukeiras, Yemen, 141-142, 147, 202, 208
Murphy, Sgt Richard, 129
Murrells, Sgt Alan, 60

Nairobi, Kenya, 70, 73, 107-108, 116, 119, 125, 127, 135, 140-141, 143, 145, 149, 154, 174, 176-177, 218, 229
Nakuru, Kenya, 39
Nasser, Gamal, 63-64, 86, 231
National Liberation Front (NLF), 231
Ndola, Zambia, 72-76, 142
Near East Air Force Command (NEAF), 10, 165, 226
Nicholls, Cpl John, 128
Nichols, Flt Lt, 119
Nicosia, Cyprus, 9, 39, 65, 68, 81, 95, 118, 127-128, 138, 156, 160-161, 168, 224-228
Niven, Flt Lt David, 57
Norton, Rhodesia, 36

Operation
- Bronze, 118, 199
- Granby, 241
- Lopen, 146

Mizar, 69
Musketeer, 68
Ranji, 105, 107
Sedbergh, 222-223
Telic, 241
Turquoise, 199
Ottoman Empire, 11, 14

Palestine, 9, 11-12, 15, 19-20, 22-23, 30, 33, 42, 45, 51
Palmer, Ted, 46
Pemba, Tanzania, 141
Penrose, Desmond, 122
Perim, Yemen, 80, 142, 152, 202-203
Persian Gulf, 12, 17, 167, 178, 186, 199
Perry, Sqn Ldr K H, 137
Pike, Fg Off Michael, 138
Piper, Sqn Ldr A H, 127
Plant, WO Walter, 33
Plumley, Jonathan, 162, 169, 171, 194
Pook, Jerry, 178-179, 183,187, 192-193
Port Sudan, 44
Preston, Joe, 63
Pringuer, Dean, 158, 176, 201-203, 205-207, 209, 229, 243
Proctor, WO Peter 'Percy', 36, 39
Prouch, Ted, 58
Pryde, Fg Off Andy, 136

Qastina, Palestine, 42, 51, 53-54
Qatar, 145, 180-181

Radfan, Yemen, 105, 111, 114-115, 118, 139, 239
RAF Squadrons and units
2 ATAF, 84
4 FTS, 25-26
6, 22-24, 60, 68, 174-175, 192
6 FTS, 168
7 MU, 222
8, 24-25, 42, 68, 78-83, 85-91, 95-96, 98, 100-101, 110, 125, 176, 178, 184, 189, 192-194, 196, 198, 205, 232, 239
9, 232
11, 39
13, 68, 91, 95, 166, 176, 189
13 Air Gunnery School, 42, 54-55
14, 14-15, 24
17, 15
21, 124, 130-132
22 SFTS, 38
24, 123, 156
26, 124, 159-160
26 EFTS, 37
27 MU, 75
29, 72-74, 76-77, 142
30, 14-15, 24, 124, 132-133
32, 87
37, 68, 116-121, 138, 196-197, 231
39, 59, 62, 65, 68
40, 51
40 Staging Post, 57
42, 85, 117, 197
43, 91, 95, 98, 100, 104, 141, 192
44 Staging Post, 57, 192
45, 16, 18, 24, 32, 176
46, 169-171, 194
46 Staging Post, 55
47, 24, 54
51, 50
53 RSU, 45-46
54, 95
55, 24-25
56, 76
57, 42, 47
59, 51
60, 25
66, 160
67, 15
70, 16-18, 24-25, 31, 68, 125, 138, 156
71 MU, 73
73 OTU, 40
77 OUT, 42
78, 124-125, 127, 130, 132, 164, 178, 192-193, 198, 202, 239, 241
84, 24, 68, 123-125, 132-133, 137, 139-143, 149, 157-164, 192-193
99, 57-58, 170
103 MU, 75
105, 123-124, 143-146, 148, 150, 152, 154, 190, 241

114, 68, 78, 124-125, 143
117, 29
131 MU, 231
142, 62
192, 62
203, 21, 24, 78, 85
204, 125, 127, 203
205, 85
208, 25, 68, 81, 89, 91, 95, 100, 108, 122, 176, 178-179, 186-187, 189-190, 192-194, 205
209, 34-35
210, 70, 193-194, 197
216, 18-19, 24-25, 27, 29, 31, 54, 58, 125, 171
216 Group Comms Flight, 54
219, 62, 67
224, 33
228, 196
228 OCU, 42
233, 124-126, 152, 158, 191, 202, 205, 207-208, 229
233 OCU, 80
240 OCU, 125
242 OCU, 142, 156
249, 68, 192
267, 31, 33
296, 51
317 MU, 58
511, 170
541, 68
621, 78
644, 50-52, 54
683, 124
1333 Transport Support Training Unit, 125
1417 Flight, 98, 100-101, 103-105, 107, 110-112, 115
1665 HCU, 50
Aden Protectorate Communication and Support Flight, 124, 159
Communications Flight PAI, 32
Gulf Communications Flight, 124
Mediterranean and Middle East Comms Sqn, 49, 55
Middle East Comms Flight/Sqn, 124, 156
Rhodesian Air Training Group (RATG), 36
Ramleh, Palestine, 22-23, 42
Ras Karma, Yemen, 205, 207
Rawandiz, Kurdistan, 16, 65
Reynolds, Flt Sgt, 42
Rhodesia, 12, 38, 40, 69, 72, 76, 146, 148-149
Richmond, David, 133, 230
Rigg, Wg Cdr Eddie, 146, 241
Rimmer, Tony, 100
Rogers, Kenny, 148
Rongai, Kenya, 39
Ross, Sgt Ian, 128
Royal Navy Sqns
826, 30
848, 241
Rutbah, 18-19
Riyan, Yemen, 105, 142-144, 191, 205, 207

Salalah, Oman, 117, 129, 142, 144, 147-149, 151-152, 157, 170-171, 190-191, 194, 208, 243
Salisbury, Rhodesia, 36
Salmond, AM Sir John, 15
Salonika, Greece, 15
Sandys, Rt Hon Duncan, 83, 89
Saunders, Sqn Ldr Charles, 22-23
Scott, Fg Off Terence, 79-80
Shadbolt, Brian, 165-167, 208
Shaibah, Iraq, 55-57, 65
Shallufa, Egypt, 42
Sharjah, Trucial States, 10, 25, 57, 81-85, 89, 91-92, 117-118, 131, 133-134, 136, 143, 147, 164, 166-167, 174-175, 178, 181, 191-199, 243
Smith, Ian, 69
Smith, Flt Sgt John, 138
Smyth, Wg Cdr John, 33
South Arabia, Federation of, 78, 90, 200, 231
Speake, Mick, 194
Steamer Point, Aden, 9, 90, 94, 234-235
Stevens, Cpl Dave, 222
Stirling, David SAS, 31
Stone, WO Percival, 36
Suez, 33, 40, 48, 67-68, 81, 85-86, 88, 127, 165, 224
Syme, Sqn Ldr Tam, 96
Syria, 11, 23

Taif, Saudi Arabia, 127
Taimur, Sultan Said ibn, 129
Ta Kali, Malta, 68
Taylor, Pete, 41
Tehran, Iran, 148
Thesiger, Wilfred, 198
Thomerson, Plt Off, 36
Thornhill, Rhodesia, 36, 38
Thumier, Yemen, 139
Timms, Geoff, 100-102
Trucial Oman Scouts, 118, 134, 167, 193, 196, 200
Trans-Jordan, 9, 11, 20, 23, 28
Trench, Plt Off John, 33
Trenchard, Sir Hugh, 11-12
Tsiranana, Philibert, 223
Turkey, 11, 14-15, 161, 167
Turner, Plt Off Jeffrey, 29
Tyack, Bill, 117, 197

United Arab Emirates, 12, 181, 191, 197, 199, 243

Verney, Sgt Peter, 59, 61-62, 66
Von Berg, Nick, 85

Wade, Jack, 34, 48-49
Wadi Gazouza, Sudan, 39
Wadi Halfa, Sudan, 19, 44, 53-54, 125, 127-128
Walker, Plt Off David, 33
Walter, SAC Eric, 138
Wavell, Field Marshal, 57-58
Webber, Paddy, 174
Weet, Fg Off Anthony, 138
Whelan, Paddy, 144
Whiskey, 'Soda', 32
Williams, Chief Tech, 215
Williams, Flt Lt Crispin, 174, 177, 196
Williams, Flt Sgt Royston, 36
Wilson Rt Hon Harold, 69, 196
Wilson, Norman, 34
Winslade, AC1 Ronald, 29
Winterbottom, Flt Lt, 224
Withers, Wg Cdr Harold, 57-58
Wreford, SAC Keith, 138
Wright, Flt Lt Ron, 158
Wynne-Eyton, Wg Cdr Charles, 33

Yandell, Flt Lt Raymond, 128
Yemen, 48, 78, 83, 94-95, 114, 122, 132, 138, 141, 167, 199, 203, 205, 207, 231, 240, 242
Yeomans, Fg Off Eric, 36